T0301599

Intellectual Property, Agriculture and Global Food Security

Intellectual Property, Agriculture and Global Food Security

The Privatization of Crop Diversity

Claudio Chiarolla

Institut du développement durable et des relations internationales (Iddri) and Sciences Po. Paris, France

Edward Elgar
Cheltenham, UK • Northampton, MA, USA

Published by
Edward Elgar Publishing Limited
The Lypiatts
15 Lansdown Road
Cheltenham
Glos GL50 2JA
UK

Edward Elgar Publishing, Inc.
William Pratt House
9 Dewey Court
Northampton
Massachusetts 01060
USA

A catalogue record for this book is available from the British Library

Library of Congress Control Number: 2011924308

ISBN 978 1 84980 733 3

Typeset by Columns Design XML Ltd, Reading
Printed and bound by MPG Books Group, UK

Contents

Acknowledgements

My most sincere thanks are due to my PhD supervisors, Duncan Matthews and Graham Dutfield, for their unfailing support, encouragement, inspiration and fairness throughout the entire course of my doctoral studies. I am also grateful to Niels P. Louwaars and Philippe Cullet for their feedback, constructive criticisms and comments on earlier versions of this manuscript and for examining my PhD thesis.

Between 2004 and 2006, the research project that led up to this book was funded by a grant from the University of Milan (*Università Statale*), Italy. In particular, I am indebted to Antonio Gambaro and Nerina Boschiero for inspiring me to pursue an active involvement in international law-making as well as in legal research. I am also obliged to the Herchel Smith bequest for funding my research at Queen Mary, University of London between 2006 and 2008, and to the Centre for Commercial Law Studies for allowing me to attend numerous conferences. The help provided by Malcolm Langley, Queen Mary Intellectual Property Archive, has been invaluable.

In connection with the research undertaken on the FAO International Treaty between 2005 and 2006, I have benefited from working closely with Daniele Manzella, Marta Pardo, Stafano Burchi, Clive Stannard, Martin Eric Smith, Dan Leskien, Irene Hoffman, Gerald Moore and many others at the FAO Legal Office. I am particularly thankful to Luis Bombín, former FAO Legal Advisor, for allowing me to assist his work during the Second Meeting of the Contact Group for the Drafting of the Standard Material Transfer Agreement (April 2006) and the First Session of the Governing Body of the FAO International Treaty (June 2006).

In October 2006, I was delighted to accept a Fellowship at the United Nations University—Institute of Advanced Study (Yokohama, Japan). This experience influenced the development of this book by helping me to bridge the gap between legal and policy research, and broadened my knowledge on issues of access to genetic resources and benefits sharing, traditional knowledge and capacity-building for national implementation of biodiversity-related treaties. My research has benefited from many interesting conversations with Balakrishna Pisupati, Sam Johnston, Brendan Tobin and all the staff and fellows of the UNU–IAS, whom I thank for their comments and considerable inspiration.

As regards the country study of Viet Nam, I would like to express my gratitude, *inter alia*, to Michael Halewood for inviting me to participate in a workshop on promoting Farmers' Rights (Hanoi, Viet Nam, October 2006), to Andrew Speedy (FAO Representative in Viet Nam), to Patricia Moore and Laura Cunial (IUCN), and to several officials, researchers and staff of the Ministries of Agriculture and Rural Development and of Natural Resources and the Environment of Viet Nam.

The Reporting Service of the International Institute for Sustainable Development has allowed me to participate in relevant international negotiations between 2007 and 2010. I learned a great deal from this experience as a member of the *Earth Negotiations Bulletin* team. I am thankful to my friends and colleagues at IISD with whom I have shared the pleasure and the burden of long nights and remote travels at all times. Besides, I would like to thank François Meienberg and Bell Batta Torheim for their inputs and feedback throughout the preparation of a background study paper on *Outstanding Issues on Access and Benefit Sharing under the FAO Multilateral System* (2011), and to Stefan Jungcurt, who co-authored the above study. In relation to this book, the background study paper is important because it has provided the opportunity to fine tune some of its most important findings and conclusions.

Finally, I am grateful to my colleagues at the *Institut du développement durable et des relations internationals*, especially to the Biodiversity Programme team, for their supportiveness, friendship and critical perspectives on the many challenges ahead.

This book is dedicated to Aziza, Anna and Mario for being the most important part of all my journeys.

Paris, 17 March 2011

Abbreviations

ABS	Access to genetic resources and benefit sharing
AgGDP	Agricultural gross domestic product
AnGRs	Animal genetic resources for food and agriculture
ASEAN	Association of Southeast Asian Nations
ASSINSEL	International Association of Plant Breeders
BIOS	Biological Innovation for Open Society
BITs	Bilateral investment treaties
BMZ	Bundesministerium Für Wirtschaftliche Zusammenarbeit (German Federal Ministry for Economic Development Cooperation)
CAMBIA	Centre for the Application for Molecular Biology to International Agriculture
CAS-IP	CGIAR Central Advisory Service on Intellectual Property
CBD	Convention of Biological Diversity
CIEL	Center for International Environmental Law
CIP	Centro Internacional de la Papa (International Potato Center)
CGIAR	Consultative Group on International Agricultural Research
CGRFA	Commission on Genetic Resources for Food and Agriculture
COP	Conference of the Parties
CPC	Community Patent Convention
CPVO	Community Plant Variety Office
CPVR	Community plant variety right
DBL	Draft Biodiversity Law
DUS	Distinctness, uniformity and stability test
EC	European Commission
ECAP II	EC-ASEAN Intellectual Property Rights Cooperation Programme
FAO	Food and Agriculture Organization of the United Nations

FTAs	Free trade agreements
FTAA	Free Trade Area of Americas
GMOs	Genetically modified organisms
GRAIN	Genetic Resources Action International
GSP	Generalised System of Preferences
GTZ	Deutsche Gesellschaft für Technische Zusammenarbeit GmbH (German Society for Technical Cooperation)
IARCs	International agricultural research centres
ICIS	International Crop Information System
ICSID	International Centre for the Settlement of Investment Disputes
ICTSD	International Centre for Trade and Sustainable Development
IFPRI	International Food Policy Research Institute
IGC	Intergovernmental Committee on Intellectual Property, Genetic Resources, Traditional Knowledge and Folklore
IISD	International Institute for Sustainable Development
IPGRI	International Plant Genetic Resources Institute (now Bioversity International)
ISF	International Seed Federation
IUCN	International Union for the Conservation of Nature
IUPGR	International Undertaking on Plant Genetic Resources
ITPGRFA	International Treaty on Plant Genetic Resources for Food and Agriculture
IPRs	Intellectual property rights
LDCs	Least developed countries
LIFDCs	Low-Income Food-Deficit Countries
MARD	Ministry of Agriculture and Rural Development
MAS	Marker assisted selection
MAT	Mutually agreed terms
MDGs	Millennium Development Goals
MFN	Most favoured nation
MiGRs	Microbial Genetic Resources
MLS	Multilateral System of Access and Benefit Sharing
MoNRE	Ministry of Natural Resources and the Environment

MTA	Material transfer agreement
NA	National Assembly
NARIs	National agricultural research institutes
OECD	Organisation for Economic Co-operation and Development
PBRs	Plant breeders' rights
PGR	Plant genetic resources
PGRFA	Plant genetic resources for food and agriculture
PIC	Prior informed consent
PIPRA	Public Sector Intellectual Property Resource for Agriculture
PRSP	Poverty Reduction Strategy Paper
PVP	Plant variety protection
PVPO	Plant Variety Protection Office
R&D	Research and development
SGRP	System-wide Genetic Resources Programme
SMEs	Small and medium enterprises
SMTA	Standard Material Transfer Agreement
SPLT	Substantive Patent Law Treaty
S&T	Science and technology
TA	Technical assistance
TK	Traditional knowledge
TNCs	Trans-national corporations
TRIPs	Trade-Related Aspects of Intellectual Property Rights
UN	United Nations
UNCITRAL	United Nations Commission on International Trade Law
UNCTAD	United Nations Conference on Trade and Development
UNDP	United Nations Development Programme
UNESCAP	United Nations Economic and Social Commission for Asia and the Pacific
UNIDROIT	International Institute for the Unification of Private Law
UPOV	Union Internationale pour la Protection des Obtentions Végétales (Union for the Protection of New Varieties of Plants)
US	United States
USD	United States Dollar

USDA	United States Department of Agriculture
USPTO	United States Patent and Trademark Office
USTR	United States Trade Representative
VND	Vietnamese Dong
WSSD	World Summit on Sustainable Development
WTO	World Trade Organization

Treaties, international, national and non-national legal instruments

Cases

Canada

Monsanto Canada Inc. v Schmeiser, [2004] 1 SCR 902; (2004), 239 DLR (4th) 271; 31 CPR (4th) 161; 320 NR 201; 2004 SCC 34 **87**

European Patent Office

Plant Cells/Plant Genetic Systems, T 356/93, OJ EPO 1995, 545 **92**
Novartis AG, T 1054/96, OJ EPO, 1998, 511 **92**
Transgenic Plant/NOVARTIS II, G 0001/98, OJ 2000,111 **92**

International Court Of Justice

Case Concerning the Continental Shelf (Tunisia/Libyan Arab Jamahiriya), ICJ Reports (1982) 18 at 60, para. 71 **13**

United States

Clarke Blade & Razor Co. v Gillette Safety Razor Co., 187 F 149, 149 (CCDNJ 1911), aff'd, 194 F 421 (3d Cir. 1912) **46**
Diamond v Chakrabarty, 447 US 303, 206 USPQ 193 (1980) **90**
Ex parte Hibberd, 227 USPQ 443 (Bd. Pat. App. & Int., 1985) **90**
Graver Tank & Mfg. Co., Inc. v Linde Air Prods, Co., 339 US 605, 609 (1950) **47**

Imazio Nursery v Dania Greenhouses, 69 F. 3d 1560, 36 USPQ 2d 1673 (CAFC 1995) **88**
J.E.M. Ag Supply Inc. v Pioneer Hi-Bred International, 534 US 124 (2001) **94**
Madey v Duke University, 64 USPQ2d 1737 (Fed. Cir. 2002) **94**
Monsanto Co. v McFarling, 302 F.3d 1291, 1299, 64 USPQ 2d 1161, 1166 (Fed. Cir. 2002) **96**
Monsanto Co. v Scruggs, et al, 459 F.3d 1328 (Fed. Cir. 2006) **97**
SRI Int'l v Matsushita Elec. Corp. of America, 591 F. Supp. 464, 468, 224 USPQ (BNA) 70, 73 (ND Cal. 1984), rev'd, 775 F.2d 1107, 227 USPQ (BNA) 577 (Fed. Cir. 1985) (en banc 47) **47**
The Incandescent Patent Lamp, 159 US 465 (1895) **46**

World Trade Organization

Canada – Patent Protection of Pharmaceutical Products, WT/DS114/R, WTO (17 March 2000), available at: http://www.wto.org/english/ tratop_e/dispu_e/ 7428d.pdf **105**

1. Introduction and overview

1.1 GENERAL AND SPECIFIC OBJECTIVES

This book considers the proposition that global institutional reforms that govern the present and future allocation of rights on, and wealth from, crop diversity are insufficient—and in some respects inappropriate—to achieve international equity in terms of the way plant genetic resources are transferred, how agricultural research is conducted, and its benefits are shared. Its focus on ownership regulation derives from the paramount importance that both the design and allocation of rights in plant genetic resources might have for global food security due to their implications in terms of wealth and resource allocation within the agriculture sector. Thus, the subject matter under consideration is the study of normative aspects of global institutional reforms that concern agricultural innovation systems and the commodification of crop diversity.

The commodification of crop diversity can be defined as the adoption, harmonization and implementation of laws and international law instruments, which determine the allocation of legal entitlements to manage and control plant genetic resources, their derivatives and the benefits thereof. On the other hand, 'the concept of 'innovation' refers to the search for, development, adaptation, imitation and adoption of technologies that are new to a specific context'.[1] Within the above subject matter, this book has three specific objectives:

1) to analyse the limitations and systemic weaknesses of global institutional reforms that concern agricultural innovation systems and the commodification of crop diversity;
2) to assess the developmental implications of changes in the legal status of plant genetic resources for food and agriculture (PGRFA),

---

[1] 'The "system of innovation" approach and its relevance to developing countries' (2005), SciDevNet available at: www.scidev.net/en/policy-briefs/the-system-of-innovation-approach-and-its-relevanc.html (accessed October 2006). Definition based on G. Dosi (1988), 'The Nature of the Innovative Process', in L. Soete (ed.), *Technical Change and Economic Theory*, London, UK: Pinter Publishers, p. 222.

taking into account the need to secure a more equitable distribution of wealth among affected stakeholders, including those who operate in the informal seed sector and their development needs; and

3)   to elaborate available options to facilitate access to PGRFA, agricultural knowledge, and science and technology for sustainable agricultural development through enabling legal instruments and mechanisms, including the full implementation of the Multilateral System of access and benefit sharing under the International Treaty on PGRFA and its Standard Material Transfer Agreement.

The innovation system perspective is useful to place the appropriate emphasis on institutions, because it postulates that social and economic development 'is driven by the institutional context in which technological change occurs', rather than by such change *per se*.[2] Therefore, in order to meet the first specific objective, which focuses on limitations and systemic weaknesses, this book addresses the question of how global institutional reforms regarding plant genetic resources are changing the balance of rights on which access to, and reward of, agricultural innovation depends.

In order to meet the second specific objective, the book frames the policy debate on the developmental implications of international agreements concerning crop diversity in terms of transition between property regimes. However, this approach does not intend to prove the validity of a particular theory in the chosen context. Rather, it uses the lessons learned from various theoretical insights and conceptual tools (that are useful to explain such a transition) to supplement the legal analysis of relevant agreements and negotiating processes, and to assess the prospects for improvements in the law towards international equity in agriculture.

This approach leads one to wonder what the implications of the transition between property regimes (and of the consequent rebalancing of rights) are, taking into account the need to secure a more equitable distribution of wealth among affected stakeholders, including those who operate in the informal seed sector, and their development needs.[3]

---

[2]   D.J. Spielman (2006), 'A Critique of Innovation Systems Perspectives on Agricultural Research in Developing Countries', *Innovation Strategy Today*, 2/1, 41–54, at p. 50.

[3]   On the importance of informal or farmers' seed systems, Louwaars highlights that:

Farmers' seed systems are by far the most important suppliers of seed, and are particularly important for resource-poor farmers. Formal seed systems, on the other hand, provide tested seed to farmers through an organised and often

In order to meet the third specific objective—i.e. to elaborate available options to facilitate access to PGRFA, agricultural knowledge, and science and technology for sustainable agricultural development—this book needs to discuss the question of whether exclusion rights promote more efficient outcomes than an open access regime, in particular by supporting research and domestic innovation capabilities of agricultural innovation systems in developing countries. The analysis of the literature on law, economics, and intellectual property is helpful to assess the validity of the frequent assumption that the creation and allocation of exclusion rights in biological materials is more efficient than a regime of less cumbersome access rules, such as a common pool regime.[4]

At the outset, this book establishes the factual and theoretical background that is necessary to understand relevant global regulatory instruments in the areas of plant intellectual property and access and benefit sharing (ABS), in other words, the interrelated law-making processes and agreements that concern agricultural innovation systems and the commodification of crop diversity.

---

regulated chain that includes genebanks, breeders, seed producers and seed marketing and distribution organisations. In practice, these different systems operate side by side to serve the needs of different types of farmers for different types of crops.

N.P. Louwaars (2007), 'Seeds of Confusion: The Impact of Policies on Seed Systems' (Wageningen University) at pp. 5 and 29. See below section 2.2.5. Today, the decades-long neglect of developing countries' agricultural research priorities and needs is having an apparent, outstanding impact on the current food crisis, especially in the African region:

> The large increases in food prices in recent years have led to a global food crisis of which low-income food-deficit countries (LIFDCs) are the greatest victims. The fact that most LIFDCs are in Africa has raised serious questions about the performance of the agricultural sector in the aftermath of trade liberalization. … while trade liberalization addressed policy-induced barriers to trade, it was not integrated with sectoral policies that could have addressed supply-side response issues. The sharp decline in aid to agriculture since the early 1990s reflects not only the limited success of aid to agriculture, but also a shift towards adjustment lending with a greater focus on economic liberalization.

See UNCTAD (2008), 'Economic Development in Africa 2008—Export Performance Following Trade Liberalization: Some Patterns and Policy Perspectives', New York and Geneva, at pp. 39–42.

[4] As Boyle suggests, 'our conceptions of efficiency (and thus of innovation) themselves already contain strong and frequently unannounced or justified distributional assumptions'. J. Boyle (2003), 'Enclosing the Genome: What the Squabbles over Genetic Patents Could Teach Us', *Advances in Genetics*, available at: www.law.duke.edu/boylesite/low/genome.pdf (accessed 10 November 2006).

1.2 BACKGROUND AND SIGNIFICANCE

In agriculture, the achievement of equity outcomes for small-scale farmers is crucial for innovation policy reforms towards poverty and hunger eradication.[5] PGRFA, in their dual aspect of environmental and informational resources, may be considered as fundamental components of the 'technological infrastructure' that underpins agricultural research.[6] As such, one may argue that they should be managed in an openly accessible manner, because such *non-traditional infrastructural resources* may generate higher social value and positive externalities if they are managed as commons.[7]

However, legal or contractual obligations which restrict the exchange and use of PGRFA have emerged regardless of whether the social benefits of establishing (and strengthening) such exclusion rights exceed their social costs. Legislative models that may apply to crop diversity, such as patent and ABS systems, were initially developed for other industry sectors such as the chemical and pharmaceutical sectors. This raises concerns as to the future availability of PGRFA as international public goods and calls into question the contribution that the paradigm of a privatized science can make to meet the target of reducing by half the

---

[5] The 1960s saw the first Green Revolution. This was based on the so-called 'package of inputs' approach, which included the use of *improved* seeds, irrigation, chemical fertilisers and pesticides. In Asia, this approach increased yields and average farm incomes. However, it was 'far from a complete solution to poverty and hunger', as the gap between the rich and the poor increased. This is an important lesson 'to keep in mind as it highlights the dangers of focusing only on increasing crop agricultural yields while ignoring the social and environmental implications of new technologies'. K. Lobe (2007), 'A Green Revolution for Africa: Hope for Hungry Farmers?' Canadian Foodgrains Bank Working Paper. Compare with the views of N. Ngongi, President of the Alliance for a Green Revolution in Africa, who argues that:

> Because they have been selected for low-input agriculture, the seeds saved by African smallholder farmers do not have the potential to respond to improvement in soil fertility. ... Continuous cultivation in the absence of nutrient replenishment from organic and inorganic fertilizers has resulted in serious soil nutrient depletion ... With good agronomic practices and wise use of fertilizers and irrigation, the large-scale adoption of improved varieties should double or triple current yields.

N. Ngongi (2008), 'Policy Implications of High Food Prices for Africa', Responding to the Global Food Crisis: Three Perspectives, IFPRI, at pp. 22–4.

[6] M.B. Frischmann (2005), 'An Economic Theory of Infrastructure and Commons Management', *Minnesota Law Review*, 89, 917–1030, at p. 927.

[7] See below section 2.3.6

proportion of people who suffer from hunger by 2015 in accordance with goal 1 of the Millennium Development Goals (MDGs).[8]

In April 2008, UN Secretary General Ban Ki-moon set up a task force to tackle the global food crisis.[9] This crisis not only threatens economic growth and social progress, but has also generated political instability and social unrest in at least twelve countries.[10] In a few months, high food prices pushed 100 million people back into poverty and thwarted seven years of development efforts towards poverty reduction.[11] This crisis is not a natural disaster; it is rather a man-made disaster, which reflects a trend that was evident several years ago.[12]

---

[8]   J. Esquinas-Alcazar, former Secretary of the Commission on Genetic Resources for Food and Agriculture, who has been instrumental for the adoption of the FAO International Treaty, argues that 'access to genetic resources and related biotechnologies is increasingly threatened by the proliferation of intellectual property rights (IPRs) and the expansion of their scope, as well as by the increasing number of national laws that restrict access to and use of PGRFA'. J. Esquinas-Alcazar (2005), 'Protecting Crop Genetic Diversity for Food Security: Political, Ethical and Technical Challenges', *Nature,* 6/12, 946–53.

[9]   United Nations, *The Secretary-General's High-Level Task Force on the Global Food Security Crisis,* available at: www.un.org/en/globalissues/food/index.shtml (accessed on 10 June 2008).

[10]   These countries include, *inter alia*: Burkina Faso, Cameroon, Egypt, Guinea, Haiti, Mauritania, Mexico, Morocco, Nepal, Senegal, Uzbekistan and Yemen. FAO (2008), 'Soaring Food Prices: The Need for International Action', High-Level Conference on World Food Security: the Challenges of Climate Change and Bioenergy, HLC/08/INF/1-Abstract (3–5 June 2008), at para. 4; UN News Service (2008), *Task Force on Global Food Crisis to Move at 'Full Speed'* (5 May 2008).

[11]   UN News Service (2008), *Global Food Crisis 'Silent Tsunami' threatening over 100 Million People, warns UN* (22 April 2008).

[12]   FAO (2006), *High and Volatile Food Prices in the Months to Come,* FAO Newsroom (8 June 2006). The 2007 FAO Food Outlook highlights that seed stocks are being kept at low levels and 'no longer play their traditional role as a buffer against fluctuations in production and demand. This change has come about because of reduced government interventions associated with a general policy shift towards liberalizing agricultural commodity markets.' FAO (2007), 'Food Outlook—Global Market Analysis', Rome, at p. 49; N. Ngongi (2008), above note 5, at p. 20. The author argues that:

Although the price crises appeared to arise suddenly, it has been building in Africa for at least three decades. ... Structural adjustment programs led to the dismantling of many institutions and programs inherited or established after independence. ... instead of improving the functioning of [parastatal corporations, food security reserves, extension services and cooperatives], donors and, in turn, African countries pursued market solutions that decimated these institutions.

Part of the problem is that in the developing world appropriate inputs such as seeds and fertilisers that can increase agricultural production are unavailable or too expensive for most small-scale farmers. Historically, both at the national and international levels, IPRs and ABS laws and policies have never received the attention given to other global environmental issues that impinge on food security, such as climate change and the production of biofuels.[13] Nonetheless, such laws and policies have a decisive long-term structural impact on the conditions under which crop diversity and, in particular, seeds can be made available.

Other factors, such as insufficient investments and limited human, technical and institutional capacity, also constrain the application of agricultural knowledge, science and technology to agricultural production in poor countries.[14] Against this backdrop, the implementation of relevant multilateral trade and environmental agreements that regulate the use of PGR in a way that is appropriate to domestic needs is a major challenge for the majority of developing countries. In particular, both plant intellectual property and ABS requirements do shape the rules of the game for private and public actors, including countries, corporations, individual researchers and plant breeders down to farmers and consumers.[15] This is because the availability of both seeds and the upstream results of agricultural research—including the research that is undertaken in public universities—depend to a remarkable extent on these rules.

---

[13]   Experts have recently considered some of the most important causes of the present critical situation, including: adverse weather and climate change; increased biofuel production and distorting subsidies; high oil prices, which impinge upon the costs of chemical fertilisers and transport; the raising demand for food products from the fast-growing economies of some developing countries, such as China, India and Brazil; and the unintended consequences of measures taken to counter the emergency, such as export bans that will increase prices in low-income food-deficit countries. FAO (2008), above note 10.

[14]   This has severe implications for agricultural production, environmental management, food security and poverty reduction. 'The imminent threat of increased hunger would have been lessened if recent decades had not been marked by a lack of investment in agricultural and rural development in developing countries.' UN (2008), 'The Millennium Development Goals Report', at p. 3, Foreword.

[15]   G. Tansey and T. Rajotte (eds) (2007), *The Future Control of Food. A Guide to International Negotiations and Rules on Intellectual Property, Biodiversity and Food Security*, London, UK: Earthscan.

1.3 DEFINITION OF KEY CONCEPTUAL ISSUES

The main conceptual issues that inform the development of this book are defined in the following subsections.[16]

1.3.1 General legal and policy framework within which the ITPGRFA arises

A crucial issue for food security is the conservation of genetic resources both *in situ*[17] and *ex situ* in national and international genebank collections.[18] In 1983, given the global interdependency of all states in terms of crop diversity, the international community endorsed the creation of the FAO Global System for the Conservation and Utilization of PGRFA. In particular, three components of the Global System have shaped the international regulation of access to plant genetic resources and associated traditional knowledge (TK), benefit sharing and IPR-related matters. They are: the Commission on Genetic Resources for Food and Agriculture (CGRFA),[19] the International Undertaking on Plant Genetic Resources (IUPGR), and the International Network of *Ex Situ* Collections under the Auspices of FAO.

---

[16] These concepts and the presentation of relevant instruments and agreements as well as their interpretation will be further discussed in Chapter 4 of this book.

[17] Article 2 of the ITPGRFA states: '*In situ* conservation is the conservation of ecosystems and natural habitats and the maintenance and recovery of viable populations of species in their natural surroundings and, in the case of cultivated species, in the surroundings where they have developed their distinctive properties.'

[18] '*Ex situ* conservation is the conservation of components of biological diversity outside their natural habitats.' Ibid.

[19] The CGRFA 'is a permanent forum where governments discuss and negotiate matters relevant to genetic resource for food and agriculture' including their conservation and sustainable utilization, as well as the sharing of the benefits arising from agricultural biodiversity. In the context of this book, the CGRFA has a particular relevance because it has hosted the negotiations of the ITPGRFA. When it was established in 1983, its competence was limited to plant genetic resources. See: FAO Conference Resolution 9/83. However, this mandate was broadened in 1995 to include all biodiversity components relevant to food and agriculture. FAO Conference Resolution 3/95. See also: FAO, 'About the Commission on Genetic Resources for Food and Agriculture', available at: www.fao.org/nr/cgrfa/cgrfa-about/cgrfa-history/en/ (accessed 7 March 2011).

1.3.1.1   The principle of common heritage of humankind and farmers' rights under the International Undertaking

During the 'Green Revolution' two factors contributed in a decisive way to the partial success of the campaign to increase crop yields to feed a growing population. On the one hand, national and international agricultural research institutes could freely disseminate technological and scientific advancements relevant for crop improvement. As a consequence, private and public plant breeders could use, improve, develop, and commercialize these techniques and materials without having to worry about the infringement of third parties' IPRs. This was because at that time IPRs in agriculture were receiving only a limited recognition.[20] On the other hand, public agricultural research institutions were free to collect and distribute plant materials from most countries without the need to obey particular legal requirements, because the problems of sovereignty associated with such resources were also perceived as secondary issues.

The IUPGR is a non-legally binding instrument with the specific aim of promoting international action on conservation, sustainable use and availability of plant genetic resources (PGR). When it was adopted in 1983, the principle that PGR should be treated as a common heritage of humankind was enshrined in it. Even though the IUPGR does not mention TK at all, until the end of the 1980s, most agricultural TK associated with PGR (collected during scientific expeditions) was also documented and transferred without following particular formalities under the principle of common heritage of humankind.[21]

In this period, numerous collecting missions were carried out by international agricultural research institutes, which at a later time joined

---

[20]   M. Blakeney (2003), 'TRIPS Agreement and Agriculture', paper given at ADB Intensive Course on the WTO TRIPS Agreement, Bangkok, 24–28 November 2003, at p. 18.

[21]   The principle of common heritage of humankind plays an important role in explaining the international relations of plant intellectual property and associated environmental issues in the political context of the adoption of the IUPGR. In international law, the principle of common heritage of mankind arises at the end of the 1960s. Its application is confined to non-living resources, which are found in areas beyond national jurisdiction, such as the ocean floor, the space, the moon and Antarctica. I. Mgbeoji (2003), 'Beyond Rhetoric: State Sovereignty, Common Concern, and the Inapplicability of the Common Heritage Concept to Plant Genetic Resources', *Leiden Journal of International Law*, 16/04, 821–37, at p. 826. In the 1979 Moon Treaty and the 1982 UN Convention on the Law of the Sea, such principle entails that 'the resources of these areas cannot be appropriated to the exclusive sovereignty of states but must be conserved and exploited for the

to form the International Network of *Ex Situ* Collections under the Auspices of FAO— also known as the CGIAR. The above activities included the transfer of PGRFA from the countries where such resources where found—i.e. often in the South—to storage facilities, whose 85 per cent was located in the North.[22] These transfers resulted in the South losing direct control over access to a remarkable part of its plant genetic resources.

In the CGRFA, most developing countries initially supported the view that agricultural scientific research and the transfer of *all* PGR should take place in accordance with the principle of common heritage of mankind.[23] However, as soon as the IUPGR recognized the principle of unrestricted access to plant genetic resources, the legal and political environment that had underpinned the Green Revolution underwent a series of deep and—quite possibly—irreversible changes.

In the 1980s, the implementation of plant patents and breeders' rights in industrialized countries was perceived as a matter of importance for the private seed industry and the enfant biotechnology sector. Besides, the pressure to adopt higher international IPR standards was also mounting on developing countries, including through the Union for the Protection of New Plant Varieties (UPOV) and the inclusion of IPR on the trade-related agenda of the Uruguay Round of the General Agreement on Tariffs and Trade that eventually led to the WTO. While the US, Canada, Australia and Switzerland refused to sign the International Undertaking, developing countries saw plant breeders' rights in conflict with the farmers' traditional practices to freely exchange seeds. Developing countries' concerns were not so much related to a limitation of the farmers' practices to reuse and exchange saved seeds, which were generally

---

benefits of all, without discrimination'. P. Birnie and A. Boyle (2002), *International Law and the Environment*, 2nd edn, Oxford, UK: Oxford University Press, p. 143.

[22] C. Fowler (1994), 'Unnatural Selection. Technology, Politics and Plant Evolution', in *International Studies in Global Change*, Vol. 6, Yverdon, Switzerland: Gordon and Breach Science Publishers, p. 184; and R. Andersen (2007), *Governing Agrobiodiversity: Plant Genetics and Developing Countries*, Aldershot, UK: Ashgate, pp. 88–91.

[23] In particular, Article 1 of the IUPGR states that: 'this Undertaking is based on the universally accepted principle that plant genetic resources are a heritage of mankind and consequently should be available without restriction'. As I. Mgbeoji (2003) notes, above note 21, 'in the movement for a new international economic order, the common heritage concept was ... primarily designed to deny the technologically advanced group of states of the North the legal right to exploit and lay claims ... of ownership over the last frontiers of the world ...', including those opened by plant genetic research and biotechnology.

accepted under the 1978 UPOV Act. At that time, they were primarily protesting the alleged violation of the so-called principle of 'reciprocity'. Such principle can be regarded as an application of the principle of equity and entails the moral obligation to give back what is received in equal measure or under equal terms.[24]

Together with the impasse on the limited acceptance of the common heritage principle, the ensuing international controversy on farmers' rights played a pivotal role in leading to the revision of the International Undertaking. Between the late 1980s and the early 1990s the FAO Conference adopted several resolutions with a view to achieving a balance between conflicting interests of developed and developing countries.

In the FAO Conference of 1989, the concept of farmers' rights was conceived by developing countries as a counterbalance to plant breeders' rights under the 1978 Act of the UPOV Convention. FAO Resolution 5/89 endorsed the concept of Farmers' Rights defined as rights 'arising from the past, present and future contributions of farmers in conserving, improving, and making available plant genetic resources, particularly those in the centres of origin/diversity'.[25] In exchange for the moral recognition of farmers' rights, their supporters accepted FAO Resolution 4/89, which recognized that plant breeders' rights were not inconsistent with the IUPGR. The adoption of this agreed interpretation of the International Undertaking marked a turning point after which the principle of common heritage of mankind had lost its momentum.

As the controversy over the application of IPRs to crop diversity continued, with the proponents' positions gaining on the common heritage principle of unrestricted access to *all* PGR, the developing countries asserted that the principle of permanent sovereignty over natural resources should take precedence over the former, as eventually agreed in FAO Resolution 3/91. Finally, in the negotiations of the UN

---

[24] On the principle of reciprocity see: CBD (2009), 'Submission by the International Institute for Environment and Development (IIED) *et al.*— Information and views in preparation for the meeting of the Expert Group on traditional knowledge associated with genetic resources', Answers to the questions posed to the Expert Group on TK associated with GR as specified in COP decision IX/12, Hyderabad, India (16–19 June 2009), at pp. 4–5.

[25] Two years later, in FAO Resolution 3/91, countries expressed their moral and political commitment to implement farmers' rights through the establishment of the International Fund for Plant Genetic Resources. However, this Fund did not receive much support as voluntary contributions fell short of expectations and it was never implemented. R. Andersen (2005), 'The History of Farmers' Rights—A Guide to Central Documents and Literature', The Farmers' Project—Background Study 1, The Fridtjof Nansens Institute, Lysaker, Norway.

Convention on Biological Diversity (CBD), they called for the explicit recognition that access to genetic resources be subject to national authority.

1.3.1.2 *From common heritage to permanent sovereignty and the principle of common concern of humankind*

During the negotiations of the CBD, countries firmly rejected the proposition that biological diversity should be treated as a common heritage of mankind.[26] The reaffirmation of the principle of national sovereignty over natural resources, and the related idea that they shall be exploited in accordance with domestic environmental policies, contributed to the emergence of the principle of 'common concern' as the new paradigm of international environmental law after Rio. The application of the principle of common concern of humankind lays the foundation for defining states' collective responsibilities to protect biodiversity by: conferring on them an *erga omnes* character; differentiating the degree of responsibility of developed and developing countries in accordance with their respective capabilities and their historical contribution to biodiversity loss; and requiring the use of the precautionary approach in carrying out potentially harmful activities.[27]

The preamble of the CBD affirms that 'the conservation of biological diversity is a common concern of humankind'. In the wake of the CBD, the preamble of the ITPGRFA also includes a lexicon, which conceives PGRFA as 'a common concern of all countries, in that all countries depend very largely on PGRFA that originated elsewhere'. The principle of common concern 'gives the international community of states … a legitimate interest in resources of global significance'[28] and it balances national sovereignty with the duties and responsibilities that derive from its exercise, pursuant to the global importance that is recognized to biodiversity and PGRFA.

---

[26] The Convention on Biological Diversity was adopted on 5 June 1992 and came into effect on 29 December 1993.

[27] The principle of common concern of humankind globalizes international environmental obligations in the sense that for the first time it overcomes the paradigm, which conceived the latter as a system of norms that merely concern transboundary relations among states. P. Birnie and A. Boyle (2002), above note 21, p. 99.

[28] Ibid.

1.3.1.3   The revision of the IUPGR and the adoption of the ITPGRFA

With the political controversy surrounding the realization of farmers'
rights firmly standing to catalyze the North–South divide over IPRs at the
FAO and the whole set of principles regarding control over access to PGR
shaken by the agreed interpretations of the International Undertaking,
the time was finally ripe for the revision of this instrument.

In 1992, the Conference for the Adoption of the Agreed Text of the
Convention on Biological Diversity had recognized that the regime
developed under the CBD was not well suited to PGRFA and handed this
issue over to the FAO.[29] In November 1994, as a consequence of such a
request from the CBD, the CGRFA started negotiations to bring the
IUPGR into conformity with the CBD and, in particular, its benefit-
sharing provisions. The mandate, which was established by FAO
Conference Resolution 7/93, included: 1) the adaptation of the IUPGR in
harmony with the CBD; 2) consideration of the issue of access on
mutually agreed terms to plant genetic resources, including *ex-situ*
collections not addressed by the CBD; and 3) the realization of farmers'
rights.

In 2001, this revision eventually came to an end. After seven years of
negotiations, the FAO International Treaty on Plant Genetic Resources
for Food and Agriculture was adopted by the FAO Conference on
3 November 2001.[30] The latter is a legally binding international treaty,
whose provisions fully reflect the compromise that was needed to preserve
some elements of an open access regime in our times of private science
through its multilateral benefit-sharing mechanism. The ITPGRFA
provides an internationally agreed framework for the conservation and
sustainable use of crop diversity and the fair and equitable sharing of
benefits, in accordance with the CBD.[31] This Treaty was specifically
created to suit the needs of agriculture and plant breeding. In particular, it
does not require *ad hoc* negotiations between providers and recipients of
PGRFA and by doing that it reduces transaction costs. Thus, the Treaty
facilitates access to PGRFA through the MLS and sets out specific ABS
rules in the Standard Material Transfer Agreement (SMTA) that

---

[29]   Resolution No. 3 of the Nairobi Final Act of the Conference for the
Adoption of the Agreed Text of the Convention on Biological Diversity, UNEP
Headquarters, Nairobi, 22 May 1992.

[30]   The Treaty entered into force on 29 June 2004 and it has 119 contracting
parties as of March 2009.

[31]   G. Moore and W. Tymowski (2005), *Explanatory Guide to the International
Treaty on Plant Genetic Resources for Food and Agriculture*, IUCN Environmental
Policy and Law Paper No. 57, Gland, Switzerland and Cambridge, UK: IUCN.

implements it. This mechanism ensures that some benefits flow back to the Multilateral System when a product based on MLS materials is commercialized on the market.

1.3.1.4 *Differential treatment, international equity and North–South aspects of ABS*

In most international environmental treaties, the elaboration of the principle of 'common but differentiated responsibility' contributes to address North–South divides through the normative recognition of their uneven degrees of responsibility in causing environmental problems and their different capacity to address them.[32]

The concept of benefit sharing under both the CBD and the ITPGRFA provides the basis for a normative differentiation between the obligations of developed and developing countries under these treaties. Their benefit-sharing objectives are a clear emanation of the principle of international equity in international environmental law. The concept of equity 'is a direct emanation of the idea of justice', which could be distinguished as a general principle of law from any other principle recognized by national or supranational legal systems.[33] International equity has been further

---

[32]   P. Birnie and A. Boyle (2002), above note 21, p. 81. In particular, Principle 7 of the Rio Declaration formulates the concept of 'common but differentiated responsibilities' as follows:

> States shall cooperate in a spirit of global partnership to conserve, protect and restore the health and integrity of the Earth's ecosystem. In view of the different contributions to global environmental degradation, States have common but differentiated responsibilities. The developed countries acknowledge the responsibility that they bear in the international pursuit of sustainable development in view of the pressures their societies place on the global environment and of the technologies and financial resources they command.

See: UN (1992), 'Declaration on Environment and Development', A/CONF. 151/26/Rev. 1, Report of the UN Conference on Environment and Development.
[33]   *Case Concerning the Continental Shelf (Tunisia/Libyan Arab Jamahiriya)*, ICJ Reports (1982) 18 at 60, para. 71. Equity principles are an integral part of international law and can be applied regardless of the will of the parties in accordance with Article 38, para. 1 (c) of the Statute of the International Court of Justice, which provides that the ICJ decides the cases submitted to its jurisdiction in accordance with international law, comprising 'the general principles of law' recognized by civilised nations. On the one hand, Article 38, para. 2, states that that ICJ can decide 'a case *ex aequo et bono* if the parties agree thereto'. The application of this provision has emphasized the use of non-legal principles of justice, morality, usefulness or common sense, which may not be related at all with

articulated into the concepts of 'inter-generational equity' and 'intra-generational equity'.[34] Under the CBD and the ITPGRFA, the concept of 'intra-generational equity addresses inequity within the existing economic system'[35] by promoting the establishment of legal mechanisms under which developing countries are entitled to receive a 'fair and equitable' share of the benefits arising from the use of their genetic resources and associated TK.

---

judicial considerations. For instance, this concept may be defined as 'the compendium of concepts supporting, promoting and implementing those entitlements, benefits and satisfactions which are validated by society's contemporary sense of justice and fairness'. Such concepts operate 'to temper the rigors of positive international law's application to those specific situations where generalizations would produce anomalies, inequities, or injustice ...' L.F.E. Goldie (1987), 'Equity and the International Management of Transboundary Resources', in A. Utton and L. Teclaff (eds), *Transboundary Resource Law*, London/Boulder: Westview Press, at p. 107. Thus, the decisions based on this provision are the result of a compromise reached in a procedure that is more akin to conciliation, rather than the arbitral or judicial settlement of a dispute based on equity as a general principle of international law.

[34] For instance, the concept of inter-generational equity is enshrined in Principle 3 of the Rio Declaration, which states that: 'the right to development must be fulfilled so as to equitably meet developmental and environmental needs of present and future generations'. While the rhetoric of 'inter-generational equity' has come a long way 'from Stockholm to Rio de Janeiro to Johannesburg', it does not seem to have promoted a great deal of international binding obligations and its practical implementation remains outstanding. At paras 3 and 4, the Johannesburg Declaration on Sustainable Development states:

> ... the children of the world spoke to us [the representatives of the peoples of the world] in a simple yet clear voice that the future belongs to them, and accordingly challenged all of us to ensure that through our actions they will inherit a world free of the indignity and indecency occasioned by poverty, environmental degradation and patterns of unsustainable development. As part of our response to these children, who represent our collective future, all of us, coming from every corner of the world, informed by different life experiences, are united and moved by a deeply felt sense that we urgently need to create a new and brighter world of hope.

UN (2002), 'Johannesburg Declaration on Sustainable Development', A/CONF.199/20, Report of the World Summit on Sustainable Development, Johannesburg, South Africa, 26 August–4 September 2002. Despite the difficulties to create enforceable rights for future indeterminate generations, this important moral obligation reminds us of our collective responsibility to sustainably use natural resources, in a way that does not compromise their quality and availability for the future, which is central to the idea of sustainable development.

[35] See P. Birnie and A. Boyle (2002), above note 21, at p. 91. For instance, the Johannesburg Declaration on Sustainable Development states that 'poverty eradication, changing consumption and production patterns and protecting and

The rational for benefit sharing (as an international obligation that entails various forms of fair and equitable *compensation*, including through the provision of technology under most favourable or concessional terms) is the principle of international equity as a general principle of law recognized by civilized nations. For instance, the provisions on technology transfer of the CBD and the ITPGRFA state that 'access to and transfer of technology' to developing countries 'shall be provided and/or facilitated under fair and most favourable terms, including on concessional and preferential terms where mutually agreed'.[36]

1.3.2 The relationship between the CBD and the ITPGRFA with particular regard to the legal principles underlying control over biological resources/PGR

The essence of the relationship between the CBD and the ITPGRFA can be understood by looking at the mandate for the negotiation of the latter. While the CBD embraces within its scope all the biological resources on earth, including PGRFA, it is essentially an environmental treaty. On the other hand the ITPGRFA provides an internationally agreed framework for the conservation and sustainable use of crop diversity and the fair and equitable sharing of the benefits arising from the use of such resources, in accordance with the CBD.[37] Thus, the ITPGRFA has been specifically designed to suit the needs of agriculture and plant breeding. Within biological diversity, it defines a subset of resources of particular importance for agriculture and food security—i.e. PGRFA—and it limits the scope of application of its norms to them. In this respect, the ITPGRFA could be considered as a *lex specialis* for the agriculture sector, whereas the CBD provides the general enviromental framework for the protection of biodiversity, whose principles have guided the development of the former.

---

managing the natural resource base for economic and social development are overarching objectives of and essential requirements for sustainable development'. The Political Declaration continues by reaffirming the commitments 'to speedily increase access to such basic requirements as clean water, sanitation, adequate shelter, energy, health care, *food security and the protection of biodiversity*' and to '... work together to help one another gain access to financial resources, benefit from the opening of markets, ensure capacity-building, use modern technology to bring about development and make sure that there is technology transfer, human resource development, education and training to banish underdevelopment forever'. UN (2002), above note 34, at paras 1 and 18.

[36] Article 16.2 of the CBD and Article 13.2(b)(i) of the ITPGRFA.
[37] G. Moore and W. Tymowski (2005), above note 31.

The fundamental principle contained in Article 3 of the CBD clarifies that the obligations and commitments of contracting parties shall not be interpreted in a way that impinges upon their rights to exploit their biological resources pursuant to national policies, including the regulation of access to genetic resources and benefit sharing.[38] In accordance with the above principle, Article 10 of the ITPGRFA states that 'the Contracting Parties recognize the sovereign rights of States over their own [PGRFA], including that the authority to determine access to those resources rests with national governments and is subject to national legislation'. However, it also specifies that

> in the exercise of their sovereign rights, the Contracting Parties agree to establish a multilateral system, which is efficient, effective, and transparent, both to facilitate access to [PGRFA], and to share, in a fair and equitable way, the benefits arising from the utilization of these resources, on a complementary and mutually reinforcing basis.

The practical modalities for the implementation of the principles that underlie control over genetic resources and PGRFA under these two treaties—and in particular, access to genetic resources and benefit sharing—are central to understanding their complementarity. In sum, the bilateral approach to ABS that characterizes the CBD is complemented by the multilateral approach of the ITPGRFA, which applies to the PGRFA that are listed in Annex I of that Treaty.

1.3.3   The concept of access to genetic resources/PGRFA as developed in the CBD and the ITPGRFA, including the principle of Prior Informed Consent

Under 'Access to Genetic Resources', Article 15.1 of the CBD specifies that 'the authority to determine access to genetic resources rests with the national governments and is subject to national legislation'. This provision entails that national legislation identify those who might be

---

[38]   Article 3 of the CBD provides that:

States have, in accordance with the Charter of the United Nations and the principles of international law, the sovereign right to exploit their own resources pursuant to their own environmental policies, and the responsibility to ensure that activities within their jurisdiction or control do not cause damage to the environment of other States or of areas beyond the limits of national jurisdiction.

granted a right to share in the benefits arising from the use of genetic resources and from whom prior informed consent (PIC) needs to be obtained prior to their collection.[39]

While reaffirming the sovereign rights of states to their natural resources, Article 15 of the CBD regulates access to genetic resources by: stipulating that parties shall endeavour to facilitate access to genetic resources; providing that access shall be subject to PIC and granted on mutually agreed terms (MAT); and requesting parties to take measures to share benefits from the utilization of genetic resources on MAT.[40]

Article 15.4 of the CBD further provides that 'access, where granted, shall be on mutually agreed terms ...'. Therefore, the conclusion of an access agreement, including the MAT, envisages bilateral negotiations between the recipient of genetic resources and the providing party. Such negotiations are facilitated if an ABS focal point has been established in such country. Besides, the ABS focal point can be identified as the competent authority for granting PIC in accordance with Article 15.5 of the CBD, which states that: 'access to genetic resources shall be subject to prior informed consent of the Contracting Party providing such resources, unless otherwise determined by that Party'.[41]

---

[39] Unfortunately, the CBD does not give guidance on how to address the problem of the allocation of property interests/rights on the genetic resources that are under national sovereignty of contacting parties. Therefore, this matter has been regulated in different ways by different countries within a spectrum that goes from the complete inalienability of genetic resources, which may belong to the state under a regime of public property, to the allocation of private property rights or other interests to different stakeholders, who may control the intangible/informational contents of GRs, the tangible material and/or the area where the specimen is found. M.J. Cabrera and L.C. Silva (2007), *Addressing the Problems of Access: Protecting Sources, While Giving Users Certainty*, IUCN Environmental Policy and Law Paper No. 67/1, Gland, Switzerland: IUCN, at pp. 40–46.

[40] Besides, the CBD Conference of the Parties (COP), at its sixth meeting, adopted the Bonn Guidelines on Access to Genetic Resources and the Fair and Equitable Sharing of the Benefits Arising from their Utilization (the Bonn Guidelines), a non-legally binding instrument that is 'meant to assist Parties, Governments and other stakeholders when establishing legislative, administrative or policy measures on ABS and/or when negotiating contractual arrangements for access and benefit-sharing'. CBD COP Decision VI/24, April 2002, The Hague, the Netherlands and CBD Website, available at: www.cbd.int/doc/publications/cbd-bonn-gdls-en.pdf (accessed 7 March 2011).

[41] As regards the establishment of a system of PIC, the Bonn Guidelines include provisions on: basic principles; key elements; competent authority/ies; timing and deadlines; specification of use; and procedures. An important aspect of PIC is the specification of use, since PIC

As highlighted above, the CBD promotes the development of a regime of contractual rules for the exchange of genetic resources that is based on bilateral contracts.[42] However, the contractual approach of the CBD is inappropriate for genetic resources that have been widely shared across national borders, such as PGRFA. In such a case, it might be very difficult—if not impossible—to identify their country/ies of origin. Besides, the possibility of acquiring these materials from intermediaries or other sources without obtaining PIC means that potential users may in practice avoid undertaking to share the benefits arising from the use of such resources. In the case of crop diversity research, the transaction costs associated with bilateral ABS negotiations may be sufficient to discourage most plant-breeding efforts, as a high number of breeding materials from different sources are necessary to breed new plant varieties. Besides, while no country can be said to be self-sufficient in terms of plant genetic diversity, most countries—if not all—are enormously interdependent.

Part IV of the ITPGRFA establishes a Multilateral System that facilitates access to 64 important crops and forages to ensure worldwide food security.[43] These pooled resources are available under the facilitated access mechanism of the MLS only if access is requested for the purpose of utilization and conservation for research, breeding and training for food and agriculture.[44]

Under the Treaty, access to PGRFA included into the MLS does not require *ad hoc* negotiations between providers and recipients of PGRFA. Thus, this mechanism will reduce transaction costs in accordance with

---

... should be based on the specific uses for which consent has been granted. While [PIC] may be granted initially for specific use(s), any change of use including transfer to third parties may require a new application for prior informed consent. Permitted uses should be clearly stipulated and further prior informed consent for changes or unforeseen uses should be required.

Ibid. para. 34 of the Bonn Guidelines. Other types of use restrictions for which PIC may be required are the restrictions on the users' ability to obtain (or file applications for) IPRs over the genetic resources, associated TK and their derivatives, as well as commitments on the exclusivity of the access granted to a particular user. M.J. Cabrera and L.C. Silva (2007), above note 39, at pp. 12–13.

[42]   The conventional access agreements thus developed are called material transfer agreements (MTAs). Queen Mary Intellectual Property Research Institute *et al.* (2000), 'Study on the Relationship between the Agreement on TRIPs and Biodiversity Related Issues', Final Report, at pp. 54–74.

[43]   The species of included crops are listed in Annex I of the ITPGRFA.

[44]   This means that national ABS laws that are consonant with the CBD may apply if recipients intend to make use of PGRFA for other purposes, 'such as chemical, pharmaceutical and/or other non-food/feed uses'. Article 12.3(a) of the ITPGRFA.

Article 12.3(b), which states that: 'access shall be accorded expeditiously, without the need to track individual accessions and free of charge, or, when a fee is charged, it shall not exceed the minimal cost involved'. In particular, the tracking requirement of this provision needs to be interpreted in conjunction with Article 12.4, which envisages the use of standard material transfer agreements for any transfer of PGRFA within the MLS.[45]

These provisions indicate that the ITPGRFA does not require a burdensome mechanism to track individual accessions, as providers of PGRFA do not have the obligation to keep track of all subsequent transfers of the material. However, the conclusion of SMTAs will be automatically recorded to ensure that some benefits flow back to the Multilateral System when a product based on MLS materials is commercialized on the market.[46] Therefore, the SMTA is an important legal instrument, which may enable to follow the chain of transfers between individual providers and recipients of PGRFA.

1.3.4 The concept of benefit sharing under the CBD and the ITPGRFA

Under the CBD, the implementation of legal mechanisms to control access to generic resources and their subsequent use is inextricably linked with benefit sharing, as access restrictions usually provide the most powerful motivation to potential users for engaging in the negotiations of the MAT, including the form, amount and modalities for benefit sharing. In particular, Article 15.7 of the CBD states that

> each Contracting Party shall take legislative, administrative or policy measures, as appropriate, ... with the aim of sharing in a fair and equitable way the results

---

[45]   Article 12.4 of the ITPGRFA states that:

facilitated access ... shall be provided pursuant to a standard material transfer agreement, which shall ... contain the ... the benefit-sharing provisions set forth in Article 13.2(d)(ii) and other relevant provisions of this Treaty, and the provision that the recipient of the [PGRFA] shall require that the conditions of the MTA shall apply to the transfer of [PGRFA] to another person or entity, as well as to any subsequent transfers of those [PGRFA].

[46]   Besides, in the case of non-compliance by recipients with the SMTA, the latter provides for binding international arbitration and confers upon the FAO so-called third party beneficiary's rights to represent the interests of the Multilateral System. All the relevant ABS features of the ITPGRFA are explained in Chapter 4.

of research and development and the benefits arising from the commercial and other utilization of genetic resources with the Contracting Party providing such resources.

This provision further specifies that 'such sharing shall be upon mutually agreed terms', which 'could cover the conditions, obligations, procedures, types, timing, distribution and mechanisms of benefits to be shared'.[47]

The benefit-sharing mechanism of the ITPGRFA differs from the CBD since benefits are shared on a multilateral basis in the MLS. Article 13.1 of the Treaty provides that facilitated access to PGRFA that are included in the Multilateral System constitutes itself a major benefit of the MLS. This Article also envisages four different tools through which benefits can be shared, namely: the exchange of information; access to and transfer of technology; capacity building; and the sharing of monetary and other benefits from commercialization. Besides, the Benefit-sharing Fund of the Treaty provides funding for the operationalization of the above tools to implement activities, 'plans and programmes *for farmers* in developing countries, especially in least developed countries and in countries with economies in transitions, *who conserve and sustainably utilize PGRFA*'.[48]

In June 2006, with the adoption of the SMTA, the Governing Body of the ITPGRFA established the level, form and manner of mandatory payments to be made by users of PGRFA to the Benefit-sharing Fund of the Treaty.[49] If certain legal requirements are met, compulsory benefit sharing of 1.1 per cent of incomes, which derive from the sale of seeds, must be paid by recipients to the Multilateral System.[50] The first

---

[47]   See paras 44 and 45 of the Bonn Guidelines. The Bonn Guidelines also specify an indicative list of typical MAT, which may comprise *inter alia*: type and quantity of genetic resources, and the geographical/ecological area of activity; limitations of use; capacity-building measures; renegotiations of terms under specified circumstances; third party transfers; references to TK aspects associated with the genetic resources; confidential information; and 'provisions regarding the sharing of benefits arising from the commercial and other utilization of genetic resources and their derivatives and products'.

[48]   Article 18.5 of the ITPGRFA. *Emphasis added.*

[49]   Under the SMTA, recipients are free to transfer received materials to third parties without the need to seek the providers' PIC. However, they must ensure that subsequent recipients are bound by the same benefit-sharing conditions. Thus, a chain of SMTAs ensures that benefit-sharing obligations are passed onto any 'other person or entity' that receives materials (e.g. seeds) derived from the Multilateral System.

[50]   See Article 6.7 of the SMTA and C. Chiarolla (2008), 'Plant Patenting, Benefit Sharing and the Law Applicable to the FAO Standard Material Transfer Agreement', *The Journal of World Intellectual Property*, 11 (1), 1–28.

requirement is that the commercialized 'Product' must incorporate 'the Material' received from the Multilateral System.[51] The second requirement is that payments are due only if the 'Product' (i.e. seeds) is not freely available for further research and breeding.[52] Thus, Article 6.7 of the SMTA not only seems to legitimize the patenting of seeds that incorporate materials accessed from the MLS, but also creates a strong link between benefit sharing and the patenting of biotechnological products and processes.[53] To conclude, it seems that under the ITPGRFA and the CBD the existence of IPRs, which restrict access to a product based on genetic resources/PGRFA, is a precondition for the sharing of the monetary benefits arising from the commercialization of such a product.

Given that the development of a new plant variety may take more than ten years, during this period recipients are not normally required to make payments. Therefore, the SMTA also envisages an alternative payment scheme, which may provide an immediate flow of financial resources to the Benefit-sharing Fund. This is because it derogates to both requirements of Article 6.7 of the SMTA. In sum, the alternative payment scheme provides that recipients may voluntarily choose to make crop-based payments at the discounted rate of 0.5 per cent of the overall sales of seeds pertaining to the same crop species obtained from the MLS by the recipient.[54]

[51] The definition of 'Product' which is given in Article 2 of the SMTA excludes products other than PGRFA and other products used for food, feed and processing. Hence, the commercialization of bulk goods that are 'sold or traded as commodities' shall not be considered.

[52] In essence, this requirement entails the existence of a patented product (legal restrictions) or restrictions deriving from particular technologies, such as Genetic Use Restriction Technologies (GURTs), or certain licensing practices.

[53] Article 5(d) of the SMTA provides that intellectual and other property rights must be respected. However, interpretative problems may arise because the SMTA prohibits recipients to claim 'any intellectual or other property rights that limit the facilitated access to the Material ... or its genetic parts or components, in the form received from the Multilateral System'. Thus, it is questionable whether patent claims to the 'material', its 'progeny' and 'unmodified derivatives' should be allowed. This is because such claims can restrict access to germplasm, genome sequences and their functional characterizations, which 'may be deemed to be international public goods'. R. Fears (2007), 'Genomics and Genetic Resources for Food and Agriculture', Background Study Paper No. 34, FAO, Rome, Italy.

[54] Article 6.11 of the SMTA.

1.3.5 Farmers' rights under the ITPGRFA

It is important to introduce the concept of Farmers' Rights as they interact with most issues analysed in this book. While there is no agreed definition for farmers' rights in international law, the Farmers' Rights Project by the Fridtjof Nansen Institute has elaborated the following working definition:

> Farmers' Rights consist of customary rights that farmers have had as stewards of agrobiodiversity since the dawn of agriculture to save, grow, share, develop and maintain plant varieties, of their legitimate right to be rewarded and supported for their contribution to the global pool of genetic resources as well as to the development of commercial varieties of plants, and to participate in decision making on issues that affect these rights.[55]

This definition is based on Article 9 of the ITPGRFA, which recognises:

> ... the enormous contribution that the local and indigenous communities and farmers of all regions of the world, particularly those in the centres of origin and crop diversity, have made and will continue to make for the conservation and development of [PGR] which constitute the basis of food and agriculture production throughout the world.

Article 9 provides that 'the responsibility for realizing Farmers' Rights, as they relate to PGRFA, rests with national governments' and specifies three possible elements of these rights, namely: the protection of traditional knowledge relevant to PGRFA; the right to equitably participate in sharing benefits arising from the utilization of such resources; and the right to participate in making decisions on matters related to the conservation and sustainable use of PGRFA. Finally, it states that 'nothing in this Article shall be interpreted to limit any rights that farmers have to save, use, exchange and sell farm-saved seed/ propagating material'. Thus, all the above elements constitute a bundle of rights, which states can confer upon the farmers to preserve and promote their traditional practices, knowledge and innovation that help conserving and developing crop diversity.

---

[55] 'The Farmers' Rights Project', the Fridtjof Nansen Institute, available at: www.farmersrights.org/ (accessed 10 April 2009).

1.4 THE COMMODIFICATION OF CROP DIVERSITY

Three global trends are shaping a new complex institutional environment within the paradigm of a privatized science, which has remarkable implications for agricultural research and plant breeding.[56] First, in 1994, the successful conclusion of the Uruguay Round of trade negotiations led to the integration of world markets into the World Trade Organization (WTO) framework, developing countries included. Second, the strengthening of uniform market conditions for trade and investment fostered the emergence of a highly concentrated private sector as a major player in creating and commercializing biotechnological inventions and proprietary research tools. Third, over the last 30 years radical changes have occurred in the legal framework that applies to the exchange and use of genetic resources.[57]

Since the adoption of the Brundtland Report by the World Commission on Environment and Development in 1987, the idea of sustainable development has conveyed the fundamental lesson that 'the world's environment and its economy are so closely linked that policies in one area that ignore the other are bound to failure'.[58] The concepts of 'inter' and 'intra-generational equity', the principles of 'common but differentiated responsibilities' and 'common concern', as developed in the Rio and Johannesburg Declarations, have became essential elements of sustainable development.

The imperatives of economic growth, including industrial food production, and biodiversity conservation have dramatically influenced PGR laws and policies. Nevertheless, sustainability principles have been

---

[56] J. Cohen (1999), 'Managing Intellectual Property—Challenges and Responses for Agricultural Research Institutes', in Agricultural Biotechnology and the Poor: Proceedings from an International Conference, 21–22 October 1999, at pp. 209–17.

[57] 'In recent years the CGIAR's activities have been increasingly conditioned by a rapidly changing intellectual property rights environment and the issue of Farmers' Rights.' See the 'Guiding Principles for the Consultative Group on International Agricultural Research Centres on Intellectual Property and Genetic Resources', Washington DC 1996, in SGRP (2003), *Booklet of the CGIAR Centre Policy Instruments, Guidelines and Statements on Genetic Resources, Biotechnology and Intellectual Property Rights*, Version II.

[58] D. Runnalls (2008), 'Why Aren't We There Yet? Twenty Years of Sustainable Development', 2007–2008 IISD Annual Report—Sustaining Excellence, Winnipeg, Manitoba; and World Commission on Environment and Development (1987), *Our Common Future*, Oxford, UK: Oxford University Press.

largely ignored as the commodification of crop diversity has prevailed over the need to promote diversified seed systems to preserve diversity in agriculture and in people's diet.[59]

However, there seems to be an increasing awareness of the potential problems arising from the commodification of crop diversity. The UN Special Rapporteur on the Right to Food has recently expressed concerns about

> corporate marketing practices and corporate lobbying that are contributing directly both to forms of malnutrition and forms of obesity. ... industry lobbying ... has increasingly become stronger in those forums where standards aimed at contributing to the protection of the right to food are discussed and adopted.[60]

In relation to the impact of trade agreements on global food security, the lack of clarity as to the links between intellectual property policy-making, biodiplomacy and sustainable agricultural development is a crucial problem.[61] In the related field of medical biotechnology, the argument that has persuaded policy-makers to enact the first permanent amendment to the WTO Agreement on Trade-Related Aspects of

---

[59]   On the differences between formal and informal systems of seed provision see below section 2.2.5 and N.P. Louwaars (2007), 'Seeds of Confusion: The Impact of Policies on Seed Systems' (Wageningen University), at pp. 7–8. The author argues that:

> Current seed laws and IPRs cater for the needs of a relatively small segment of the total seed supply sector. ... Legislation based on disconnected and inconsistent policies lead to problems with implementation, to confusion, and—in the field of genetic resources and seeds—to juridification and 'hyperownership' when proponents of national, communal or individual rights systems are caught in an increasingly dense thicket of rights.

[60]   UN (2007), 'Report of the Special Rapporteur on the Right to Food', A/62/289, by Jean Ziegler (22 August 2007), at paras 9 and 64(b). In particular, he has recommended that 'all States should ensure that their international political and economic policies, including international trade agreements, do not have a negative impact on the right to food in other countries'.

[61]   G. Winter, for instance, argues that patent law policies should focus on the question of 'the benefits and desirability of scientific and technical progress', including not only the competitiveness of the economy, but also the environmental and social implication of technological change. A regards the agricultural sector, the author adds that risk factors increase when high-yielding varieties 'are employed on the basis of agricultural methods which seeking economies of scale prefer monoculture'. G. Winter (1992), 'Patent Law Policy in Biotechnology', *Journal of Environmental Law*, 4/2, 167–87; See also G. Tansey and T. Rajotte (eds) (2007), above note 15.

Intellectual Property Rights (the TRIPs Agreement)—to allow compulsory licences for exports of generic medicines to countries with no manufacturing capacity—is based on evidence that shows that patent protection may seriously impinge on the effective possibility to have access to life-saving drugs at affordable prices.[62]

By contrast, food security concerns are largely decoupled from issues of access to PGRFA and IPR protection. For instance, while the European Parliament expressed 'concern about the consequences of higher rice prices, particularly for poorer households in rice-importing ASEAN countries', this statement does not have the prescriptive strength of the European commitment on access to medicines, which should prevent the introduction of drugs-related TRIPs-plus standards into the EU-ASEAN FTA.[63]

Notwithstanding the increasing awareness of the potential problems that derive from restrictions on access to PGRFA, including their impact on the provision of international public goods, which contribute to food security and pro-poor agricultural research, countries have not

---

[62] C. Pérez-Casas (2000), 'HIV/AIDS Medicines Pricing Report. Setting Objectives: Is There a Political Will?' Campaign for Access to Essential Medicines and Medecins Sans Frontieres. This report 'compares institutional prices of 10 essential drugs for HIV/AIDS in 8 countries and examines the effect on prices of generic availability and patent status'. See also: WTO (2003), 'Implementation of Paragraph 6 of the Doha Declaration on the TRIPs Agreement and Public Health—Decision of 30 August 2003', WT/L/540, WTO, Geneva; and D. Matthews (2006), 'From the August 30, 2003 WTO Decision to the December 6, 2005 Agreement on an Amendment to TRIPS: Improving Access to Medicines in Developing Countries?', *Intellectual Property Quarterly*, 10, 91–130. To some extent, public health concerns have been reflected in the international legal regulatory framework to preserve access to medicines, including by preventing that IPRs-related flexibilities, which are agreed at the WTO level, are restricted through bilateral or regional agreements. However, this seems to be an exception rather than the general rule. In negotiating a free trade agreement with the ASEAN countries, the European Parliament pointed out 'that nothing in the agreement should create legal or practical obstacles to the maximum use of flexibilities set out in the Declaration amending the ... TRIPs Agreement and access to medicines', and recalled 'the EU commitment to support the Doha Declaration and the use of TRIPs flexibilities in favour of public health and of access to medicines in developing countries'. European Parliament (2008), 'European Parliament resolution of 8 May 2008 on Trade and Economic Relations with the Association of East Asian Nations (ASEAN)', A6–0151/2008/P6_TA-PROV(2008)0195, Brussels (8 May 2008), at paras 13–14.

[63] Ibid. at para. 17.

consistently responded with legislation to address these problems at the multilateral, regional and national levels.[64]

1.5   LEGAL, TEMPORAL AND GEOGRAPHICAL SCOPE AND LIMITATIONS

As mentioned at the outset, the subject matter of this book is the study of legislations and related law-making processes that concern the commodification of crop diversity, in particular, the adoption, harmonization and implementation of laws, including international law instruments, that determine the allocation of legal entitlements to manage and control plant genetic resources, their derivatives and the benefits thereof. The focus on ownership regulation derives from the paramount importance that both the design and allocation of rights in plant genetic resources might have for global food security.

This book considers two specific sets of policies and legal instruments that are not being addressed in mainstream discussions about food security, and it intends to fill this gap. Therefore, its scope is limited to private exclusion rights, such as patents and plant variety rights, as well as state ownership, government regulation and private contracts, which arise primarily from the implementation of the access and benefit-sharing pillar of the UN Convention on Biological Diversity.

This book also discusses the issue of farmers' rights as they relate to crop genetic resources under the ITPGRFA. In particular, attention is devoted to the analysis of the legal provisions and mechanisms concerning the recognition of the rights that indigenous and local communities and farmers have to participate in benefit sharing and

---

[64]   The FAO ITPGRFA is the most remarkable exceptions to this trend. Besides, general efforts are underway in the context of the WIPO Development Agenda to ensure that 'WIPO's norm-setting activities' are 'supportive of the development goals agreed within the UN system, including those contained in the Millennium Declaration'. In particular, under Recommendation No. 22:

> The WIPO Secretariat ... should address in its working documents for norm-setting activities ... issues such as: (a) safeguarding national implementation of intellectual property rules (b) links between intellectual property and competition (c) intellectual property-related transfer of technology (d) potential flexibilities, exceptions and limitations for Member States and (e) the possibility of additional special provisions for developing countries and LDCs.

See WIPO (2007), 'The 45 Adopted Recommendations under the WIPO Development Agenda', Geneva, Switzerland.

decision making, and to provide access to their PGRFA-related traditional knowledge in accordance with PIC and MAT.

The North–South dimension of international law-making processes relevant for the protection of crop diversity will provide a useful background to understand relevant treaties. However, such dimension is not further analysed because this book focuses on positive law and on the discussion of how the law can be improved for international equity and sustainability.

Seed legislation, which plays an important role in the development of seed systems, is not covered by this book, because neither does it regulate the ownership of PGR nor is its implementation at the national level driven by developments at the international level. Similarly biosafety legislation, which regulates the approval and commercialization of transgenic seeds, is outside the scope of this study because it does not influence the assignment of legal entitlements to control PGR. Finally, relevant legal and policy instruments are analysed here as a matter of economic and sustainable development policy rather than from the standpoint of bioethics.[65]

In theory, future negotiating outcomes from World Intellectual Property Organization (WIPO) discussions on genetic resources both in the Intergovernmental Committee (IGC) on Intellectual Property, Genetic Resources, Traditional Knowledge and Folklore and in the context of Substantive Patent Law Treaty (SPLT) negotiations could be relevant for crop diversity.[66] However, such negotiating processes are outside the scope of the book because the above WIPO bodies have not yet adopted binding IP protection standards applicable to member states.

The temporal scope of this study spans from the advent of plant-related IP in the US during the early twentieth century up to the analysis of present-day law-making processes. In terms of geographical scope,

---

[65] However, doctrinal arguments based on bioethical concerns may be considered, if they are necessary to explain specific legal provisions, such as those referring to the morality and *ordre public* exceptions from patentability.

[66] In particular, the WIPO General Assembly explicitly mandates the IGC to address access to genetic resources and benefit sharing, even though the IGC has become embroiled and stalled on protection of traditional knowledge and folklore technicalities. WIPO (2000), 'Matters Concerning Intellectual Property and Genetic Resources, Traditional Knowledge and Folklore', WIPO General Assembly, Twenty-Sixth (12th Extraordinary) Session, Geneva, 25 September–3 October 2000, WO/GA/26/6; and N. Brahy (2008), *The Property Regime of Biodiversity and Traditional Knowledge—Institutions for Conservation and Innovation*. Brussels: Larcier. On the SPLT, see: W.T. Morten (2005), 'How Will a Substantive Patent Law Treaty Affect the Public Domain for Genetic Resources and Biological Material?', *JWIP*, 8/3, 311–44.

particular attention is paid to international law due to the global dimension of food security concerns. However, this study covers developments at various levels, including: national, bilateral, and multilateral instruments. Selected national and regional experiences are analysed. The plant-related IP laws of the European Union and the US are studied because of these countries' influential status as trade partners, technology and technical assistance providers, and for their continuing importance as legislative models for the drafting of international norms.

The case study of Viet Nam receives particular attention in Chapter 5. This is because Viet Nam has undergone a profound modernization of its economic and legal systems, which has remarkable implications for the regulation of crop diversity. Therefore, it exemplifies the potential outcome of the national implementation of international norms through the interaction between public and private actors, including technical assistance providers. In Viet Nam, the study of the transition between property regimes provides the scope to investigate the extent of the capacity deficit that needs to be matched to deliver appropriate assistance in the implementation of global institutional reforms governing the present and future allocation of wealth from crop diversity.

1.6 OUTLINE OF THE BOOK

Following this introduction, Chapter 2, *Patents, Agricultural Innovation and Sustainable Development,* provides a critical analysis of mainstream normative approaches to the privatisation of crop diversity and challenges the assumption that the internalisation of externalities from plant breeding and biotechnology is the panacea to fostering private investments in agricultural research. In particular, it examines the economic theories that have been used to justify the function of the patent system and places the current debate about the optimum scope of IP protection within the broader theoretical discussions concerning the question of how innovation can promote agricultural development.

Since the legal history of the commodification of crop diversity and the scientific history of the life sciences go hand in hand, this chapter also presents the fundamental steps of the transition from traditional plant breeding to modern agricultural biotechnology.[67] Finally, it considers the nature of PGRFA and tests the proposition that they are 'non-traditional infrastructural resources', which form part of the technological infrastructure that underpins agricultural research. Against this backdrop,

---

[67]   On the reasons why technology matters see section 2.3.

it highlights the fact that strong economic arguments exist, which point to the conclusion that PGRFA should be managed in an openly accessible manner, because they can generate high social value and positive externalities in the form of public goods.

Chapters 3 and 4 provide the legal and historical background and describe the evolution of the international legal framework that is applicable to the management of PGRFA. They introduce the relevant international agreements and associated negotiating processes: in particular, those that have taken place within four multilateral institutions. Such institutions are: the World Trade Organization, the Union for the Protection of New Plant Varieties (UPOV); the Conference of the Parties of the Convention on Biological Diversity; and the Food and Agriculture Organization of the United Nations.

The resulting agreements constitute what Raustiala and Victor have termed the *Regime Complex for Plant Genetic Resources*.[68] The history of the progressive expansion of exclusion rights in PGR, including both 'patent-based' and 'sovereign-based systems of ownership', reflects the development of this regime complex.[69]

Thus, the understanding of the applicable international legal framework is a fundamental step, which is necessary to appreciate its cumulative effects on the acquisition and management of science and technology relevant for plant breeding and agriculture, including the use of genetic materials and their 'bio-informational' contents. Such understanding is also important not to disregard crucial equity issues that may be associated with such uses and to assess the effective margin for manoeuvre that governments might have to comply with international obligations and standards, while promoting their national interests in agriculture and crop improvement.[70]

---

[68]   In particular, they argue that all such agreements: contribute to define some elements of the regime; partially overlap in scope, subject matter, and time; and have no clear hierarchical order to solve potential conflicts of norms between them. K. Raustiala and D.G. Victor (2004), 'The Regime Complex for Plant Genetic Resources', *International Organization*, spring 2004.

[69]   S. Safrin (2004), 'Hyperownership in a Time of Biotechnological Promise: The International Conflict to Control the Building Blocks of Life', *American Journal of International Law* 98, 641.

[70]   P. Bronwyn notes that 'It is particularly important to understand how this new (resource) economy (in bio-information) will operate, as it has the capacity to create not only new dynamics of biological-resource exploitation but, more importantly, new geographies of justice and injustice.' P. Bronwyn (2004), *Trading the Genome: Investigating the Commodification of Bio-Information*, New York: Columbia University Press, at p. xx of the preface.

The relevant agreements, which are analysed in this book, may differ markedly in nature, scope and objectives. However, in broad terms, they can be distinguished between IPR-related agreements and biodiversity-related agreements, in accordance with their principal subject matter.

On the one hand, the first category of agreements includes: 1) the WTO Agreement on Trade-Related Aspects of Intellectual Property Rights; 2) the Acts of the Union for the Protection of New Plant Varieties; and 3) bilateral and multilateral free trade and investment agreements, which expressly provide for so-called TRIPs-plus standards.[71] Chapter 3, *Plant Intellectual Property Protection: Patents and Plant Variety Rights*, focuses on the above IPR-related agreements and explains the substantive patent standards relevant for the protection of genetic resources, as well as the possible overlap between biotechnological patents and plant variety rights at the national level.

On the other hand, the UN Convention on Biological Diversity and the FAO International Treaty prominently figure in the second category.[72] In addition, other international instruments pertain to the same group, such as the FAO International Undertaking on Plant Genetic Resources (IUPGR), and the Agreements between FAO and the Centres of the Consultative Group on International Agricultural Research (CGIAR).

Chapter 4, *The International Legal Framework of Access to Plant Genetic Resources and Benefit Sharing*, presents the relevant biodiversity-related instruments and associated negotiating processes. In particular, it focuses on their potential impact on the ownership and use of PGRFA in agricultural research and plant breeding, including relevant aspects concerning the protection of farmers' rights and PGRFA-related traditional knowledge under the ITPGRFA. After having introduced the ITPGRFA and explained the coverage of its Multilateral System, this chapter focuses on the provisions of the Standard Material Transfer Agreement. In particular, it considers the links between its benefit-sharing provisions and the treatment of IPRs, which is important to understand the extent to which the ITPGRFA can make a contribution to international equity through benefit sharing.

---

[71] In theory, future negotiating outcomes from WIPO discussions on genetic resources both in the IGC and in the context of Substantive Patent Law Treaty (SPLT) negotiations on the harmonization of substantive legal standards relevant to biotechnology could also be included in this category of agreements.

[72] CBD, *Joint Web Site of the Biodiversity Related Conventions*, available at: www.cbd.int/cooperation/joint.shtml (accessed on 10 April 2008). Biodiversity-related conventions are a subset of so-called multilateral environmental agreements (MEAs).

Finally, with the recent adoption of the 'Nagoya Protocol on Access to Genetic Resources and the Fair and Equitable Sharing of Benefits Arising from their Utilization' to fulfil the third objective of the Convention on Biological Diversity,[73] Chapter 4 considers the relationship between the former and the ITPGRFA and assesses the extent to which the Protocol 'could be in harmony and mutually supportive of the mandates of and coexist alongside ... the ITPGRFA'.[74]

In the face of concerns regarding food security, genetic erosion, and the need to provide equitable accesses to seeds and strengthen the domestic plant-breeding sector, Chapter 5 presents a case study on *The Regulation of Crop Diversity in Viet Nam*. This case study describes relevant national legislative processes and their outcomes, and analyses the effectiveness and limitations of such reform processes in the area of PGR.[75]

Viet Nam is one of the richest countries in the world in terms of agro-biodiversity and the most important source of income is agriculture, which employs two-thirds of the population. The *do moi* reform process, which began in the mid-1980s, has greatly contributed to a shift from subsistence farming to commercial agriculture. Thus, the country has an economy in transition, which has undergone deep economic and legislative changes to modernize its national innovation and trading system. As part of this process, it has recently acceded to both the WTO and the UPOV Convention.[76]

The Biodiversity Law, which was passed in November 2008, is meant to reorganize all national legal environmental instruments related to biodiversity protection, including access to genetic resources and benefit sharing.[77] With the Law's entry into force in July 2009, its implementing

---

[73] The third objectives of the CBD is '... the fair and equitable sharing of the benefits arising out of the utilization of genetic resources, including by appropriate access to genetic resources and by appropriate transfer of relevant technologies, taking into account all rights over those resources and to technologies, and by appropriate funding'. Article 1 of the CBD.

[74] CBD (2008), 'COP Decision IX/27 on Access and Benefit Sharing', CBD, Bonn (30 May 2008), at para. 13(c).

[75] In particular, it focuses on how national obligations are being implemented at the domestic level to bring national legislation in harmony with international requirements, in particular, Article 27.3(b) of the TRIPs Agreement and Article 15 of the CBD.

[76] Viet Nam's accession to these treaties has a remarkable impact on the privatization of crop diversity, because it entails the obligation to comply with international IP standards, whose implementation has an impact on the future use of PGR and related technologies.

[77] 'Biodiversity Law of Viet Nam', *No. 20/2008/QH12* (XII National Assembly, 2008).

provisions will have an impact on domestic and transnational agricultural research, because these activities will need to comply with national ABS standards and procedures.

Viet Nam is also a member of the FAO Commission on Genetic Resources for Food and Agriculture. While the country has not yet ratified the ITPGRFA, the Government of Viet Nam is currently considering this, and has expressed its interest in becoming a party. Against this backdrop, there is a concern that the Biodiversity Law should possibly provide the scope to implement the ITPGRFA in the future.

Viet Nam has received a great deal of development and trade-related technical assistance. This makes it an interesting laboratory to observe how the interests, priorities and goals of different actors have played out in shaping the outcomes of the described law-reform processes. In sum, the case study of Viet Nam shows that such reform processes neither have recognized the need to afford a special treatment to PGRFA nor have strengthened the important role that informal seed systems still play in the country. Besides, it explains why this course of action has taken place as the result of tensions between IPR and ABS policies, interest group activities, and the interaction between public and private actors, including the role of technical assistance and the negotiation of free trade and investment agreements. Finally, it draws some lessons learnt, conclusions and recommendations.

Chapter 6 concludes that global institutional reforms, that govern the present and future allocation of wealth from crop diversity, disregard the important role of informal seed systems and, therefore, they are insufficient—and in some respects inappropriate—to achieve international equity in terms of the way PGR are transferred, how agricultural research is conducted and its benefits shared. It also suggests ways forward to improve existing legal instruments and benefit-sharing mechanisms to facilitate access to agricultural knowledge, science and technology for sustainable agricultural development, and draws key lessons learnt for the developing countries.

2. Patents, agricultural innovation and sustainable development

2.1 INTRODUCTION

This chapter assesses the theoretical proposition that economic law reforms providing for exclusion rights do not necessarily evolve in the direction of promoting efficient outcomes and benefits for the affected communities, as convincingly asserted by Demsetz in 'Toward a Theory of Property Rights'.[1] On the contrary, the privatization of plant genetic resources may fail to enable effective crop research and domestic innovation that is suitable for developing countries' agriculture.

This chapter analyses the central literature on law and economics including: the elaboration of property rights theories relevant for intellectual property policy-making in the fields of biotechnology and agricultural research;[2] and the literature on sustainable agriculture, food security, crop diversity conservation and development.

The purpose of this review is to set the background that is necessary to analyse relevant international negotiations and agreements, which have different objectives and overlapping developments. Given the paramount importance of the long-term sustainability of technological solutions to current problems, the analytical framework incorporates the concept of sustainable development as the cornerstone against which the efficiency of law reforms, including patent law reforms, must be evaluated. It also takes into account static and dynamic efficiency effects and the distributional consequences of strengthening exclusion rights in biological materials,

---

[1] H. Demsetz (1967), 'Toward a Theory of Property Rights', *The American Economic Review*, 57/2, 347–59.

[2] This review includes references to patent law doctrines and focuses on economic and legal arguments that justify a particular coverage of patent law in terms of subject matter and scope of granted claims.

especially in countries that are unlikely to become innovators in the life
science sector but the receivers of others' proprietary technologies,
including seeds.[3]

Boyle argues that 'our conceptions of efficiency (and thus of
innovation) themselves already contain strong, and frequently
unannounced or justified distributional assumptions'.[4] The consequence
is that choices that concern the promotion of particular technologies or
bodies of knowledge—instead of alternative ones—are not neutral with
respect to development goals and long-term sustainability. Instead, the
social and environmental implications, which are implicit in the preference
towards patent-driven agricultural development policies, are an integral
part of the resulting scientific and technological trajectories.[5] Thus, the
consideration of trade-offs is an important one to assess whether
institutional responses, which are provided in the areas of international

---

[3]   Correa defines static efficiency as the 'optimal use of existing resources at the
lowest possible cost' and dynamic efficiency as the optimal introduction of
new/improved products, production processes and organizational arrangements.
In competitive markets, static or allocative efficiency is achieved when 'the price of
a product is equal to the marginal cost of producing a unit of it. IPRs provide the
opportunity for profits over marginal costs ... to promote R&D'. Thus, the
problem is 'how to reconcile providing short-term benefits to consumers (static
efficiency) with the need to ensure that long-term benefits are obtained as a result
of innovation (dynamic efficiency)'. The author argues that 'patent protection
may be justified when the consumer surplus from new products, albeit limited by
the presence of a monopoly, outweighs the consumer surplus from current
products in the absence of patent protection'. See M.C. Correa (2002), 'Managing
the Provision of Knowledge: The Design of Intellectual Property Laws', in I. Kaul
et al. (eds), *Providing Global Public Goods*, New York: Oxford University Press.
[4]   J. Boyle (2003), 'Enclosing the Genome: What the Squabbles over Genetic
Patents Could Teach Us', *Advances in Genetics*, available at: www.law.duke.edu/
boylesite/low/genome.pdf.
[5]   For instance, there is currently a debate about whether agro-biotechnologies
can help to create crops resilient to biotic and abiotic stresses, while concurring
to other environmental problems, such as agro-biodiversity loss. See, for instance:
FAO (2008), *Summary Document of the FAO E-mail Conference: 'Coping with
Water Scarcity in Developing Countries: What Role for Agricultural
Biotechnologies?'*, Electronic Forum on Biotechnology for Food and Agriculture,
available at: www.fao.org/biotech/conf14.htm (accessed10 January 2008); T.V.
Padma (2008), *Can Crops Be Climate-Proofed?*, Science and Development Network,
available at: www.scidev.net/gateways/index.cfm?fuseaction=readitem&rgwid=
3&item=Features&itemid=671&language=1 (accessed 10 January 2008). Compare
with: A.M. Altieri and P. Rosset (1999), 'The Reasons Why Biotechnology Will Not
Ensure Food Security, Protect the Environment and Reduce Poverty in the Developing World', *AgBioForum*, Vol. 2/Number 3 & 4, 155–62.

technology law and policy, are the most appropriate to address environment and development problems related to agriculture.[6]

2.2 ECONOMIC THEORIES, SUSTAINABILITY PRINCIPLES AND THE PATENT SYSTEM

The contemporary international development discourse at the UN emphasizes the expectation that enabling legal and policy frameworks will improve domestic scientific and technological capacity and promote sustainable growth in the developing world. However, there seems to be no agreement as to how an 'enabling' framework should look. A report by the UN Task Force on Millennium Development Goal 8, which is to 'develop a global partnership for development', highlights an important point.[7] The report states:

> At the global level, greater flexibility in the interpretation of TRIPs to adapt the protection of copyrights, patents and industrial designs to the special needs of countries at different levels of development would contribute to accelerating the diffusion of technology for development, as demonstrated by the experience of developed countries in their early stages of industrialization.

The above statement gives a clear indication of the fact that there is no silver bullet and that laws and institutions, which might be 'enabling' in one country, may not work in others, where development conditions are different.

2.2.1 Factual background: agricultural research investment trends

Historically, the amount of plant-breeding investment by the public sector has been considerably higher than private investment. During the green revolution, the increase in agricultural productivity was based on the distribution of improved plant varieties to farmers and farming communities at minimal or no costs.

---

[6] In particular, Chapter 5 presents a case study on the reform of the Vietnamese IP and Biodiversity Laws and focuses on the ways in which international economic and environmental laws interact with laws, institutions and actors at the domestic level.

[7] UN (2008), 'Millennium Development Goal 8—Delivering on the Global Partnership for Achieving the Millennium Development Goals', MDG Gap Task Force, at p. 52.

Before the rise of the new scientific discipline of genomics, private industries were more focused on the development of farm machineries and agricultural chemicals, and they were unwilling to invest their money in basic biological research. In the absence of IPRs, it was difficult to appropriate returns to agricultural research. Their appropriability, namely the possibility to exclude others from replanting seeds of improved varieties, depended exclusively on the plants' mode of propagation and their potential hybridization.[8]

Starting from the 1970s, public and private investment trends have changed in developed countries. The application of molecular genetics to agricultural research has transformed plant germplasm as a source of appropriable information. The hereditary information, which can be found in the double helix structure of DNA, and the identification of genes' functions, have been used in agriculture to confer desirable traits to plants. The combination of technical means, which allowed the identifying and tracking of the plants' progeny, with the expansion of IP regimes over biological materials, have resulted in an increase in private sector investment towards product development and large-scale commercial agriculture.

In 1999 more than 80 per cent of international biotechnology research was conducted by the private sector.[9] In developed countries, between 1985 and 1996 the level of public sector spending increased only by roughly 1.5 per cent per year, whereas private sector investment grew at 4 per cent annually.[10] Much of the proprietary technology, created or acquired by private companies, may have crucial importance to eliminate hunger in the developing world.

In developing countries, the significant predominance of the public sector in plant-breeding activities is often attributed to the importance of agriculture as a source of incomes. The small potential size of seed markets, which in some cases are made up mainly by traditional and small-scale farmers, is another factor that merits attention. However, the growth rate in private research expenditure is accelerating in both

---

[8]   D. Rangnekar (2000), 'Plant Breeding, Biodiversity Loss and Intellectual Property Rights', Kingston University, Economics Discussion Papers–No. 00/5.

[9]   G.D. Persley (1999), 'Agricultural Biotechnology and the Poor: Promethean Science', *Agricultural Biotechnology and the Poor*, 21–22 October 1999, at pp. 3–21.

[10]   S. Bragdon (2004), 'International Law of Relevance to Plant Genetic Resources: A Practical Review for Scientists and Other Professionals Working with Plant Genetic Resources', IPGRI, Rome (March 2004).

developed and developing countries; in the latter, private investment is increasing rapidly from very low levels.

Between 1985 and 1995, the rate of growth in public sector investment increased by 4.5 per cent in developing countries, whereas it grew at a very slow rate in many industrialized countries. Still in 1995, public research institutions attracted roughly 95 per cent of the total agricultural research expenditure in the developing world. Out of this 95 per cent, two-third was funded by national governments and one-third by bilateral and multilateral development agencies. However, only 0.6 per cent of developing countries' agricultural gross domestic product (AgGDP) was spent in agricultural research, while in the mid-1990s, industrialized countries were spending 5.4 per cent of their AgGDP in crop R&D.[11]

The OECD indicates that agricultural biotechnology is the second most important biotechnology sector in terms of R&D investment. It accounts for approximately 5 per cent of all estimated R&D expenditures, following health with 88 per cent. The number of firms specialized in agro-food applications is approximately 22 per cent of all biotechnology firms, compared with 45 per cent of firms in the health sector.[12]

The commercialization of agriculture is ongoing in developing countries and multinational companies are interested in penetrating new markets, where the privatization of national seed industries can confer them a 'government-blessed monopoly'.[13] Besides, an increasing range of activities are taken over by the private sector, starting from seed production, multiplication and marketing. However, agricultural innovation in most developing countries' agriculture still relies on national and international public sector institutions, which transfer new technologies, including seeds, to local producers free of charge.

2.2.2 Patents and the establishment of global markets for agricultural knowledge, science and technology

The *World Development Report 2008* focuses on the pivotal role of agriculture in development and devotes an entire chapter on innovation through science and technology.[14] It notes that 'with the development of

---

[11] Ibid.; and G.D. Persley (1999), above note 9, at pp. 3–21.

[12] OECD (2007), 'OECD Science, Technology and Industry Scoreboard 2007—Innovation and Performance in the Global Economy'.

[13] R.W. Herdt (1999), 'Enclosing the Plant Genetic Commons', paper given at the China Centre for Economic Research, 24 May 1999.

[14] World Bank (2007), 'World Development Report 2008: Agriculture for Development', see Chapter 7, at p. 158.

markets, innovation becomes less driven by science (supply side) and more by markets (demand side). Demand driven approaches stress the power of users (farmers) in setting the research agenda.' However, other authors are more cautious about the effects of market liberalization by arguing that 'whether the establishment of markets for information and techniques that were previously the domain of public science is a plus or not for society depends also on how well these markets work.'[15]

Winter maintains that 'whether the demand-pull or technology-push hypothesis of innovation is correct or not, inventions and innovations will tend to exist where a demand exists or can be created'.[16] The consequence is that investments in plant breeding and crop research are 'directed more to the greater northern markets than to ... markets that are adapted to marginal areas and are suited for extensive agriculture' in the South. He adds that 'subsuming public research under market imperatives' presents the risk of 'losing the focus on basic research, to investigate negative effects and exchange information and materials freely'.

A World Bank Report[17] has identified three priority areas which raise concerns for policymakers in the developing world, namely: the way in which the implementation of IPRs affects the structure and concentration of the seed industry; the way in which IPRs influence priorities and products of public plant breeding; and the need to better identify options available to smallholders. The report has also found that 'none of the case study countries have particular exemptions in their patent law that bring the patent system in line with the plant variety protection system when the scope of patents includes a plant variety or a group of plant varieties'. However, the study points out that little evidence is found with respect to the implementation and enforcement of biotechnological patents.[18] The

---

[15]   R. Mazzoleni and R. Nelson (1998), 'The Benefits and Costs of Strong Patent Protection: A Contribution to the Current Debate', *Research Policy*, 27/3, 273–84.

[16]   G. Winter (1992), 'Patent Law Policy in Biotechnology', *Journal of Environmental Law*, 4/2, 167–87.

[17]   N.P. Louwaars *et al.* (2005), 'Impacts of Strengthened Intellectual Property Rights Regimes on the Plant Breeding Industry in Developing Countries', World Bank.

[18]   Ibid. at p. 3. China is the only exception. As regards plant variety protection, except Uganda, which has yet to establish a PVP system, and India, which has adopted a *sui generis* system not fully compliant with UPOV standards, all other countries are members of the 1978 UPOV Act. On the 2001 Protection of Plant Varieties and Farmers' Rights Act of India, see: P. Cullet (2005), *Intellectual Property Protection and Sustainable Development*, New Delhi: LexisNexis Butterworths, at pp. 270–84. Cullet explains that the inclusion of provisions concerning the protection of farmers' rights and their extant varieties 'goes

report also alerts policy-makers to the need to curb the concentration in the agro-biotech industry through 'measures that allow more widespread access to tools and processes of biotechnology'.[19]

2.2.3 Economic theories about patents

This section examines the economic theories that have been elaborated to justify the social function and coverage of the patent system. In 'Toward a Theory of Property Rights', Demsetz argues that property rights emerge when their net benefits to society exceed their social costs and describes the phenomenon in terms of internalization of externalities.[20] He contends that 'the emergence of property rights takes place in response to the *desire* of the interacting persons for adjustment to the new cost benefit possibilities'. In other words, 'property rights develop to internalize externalities when the gains of internalization become larger' than its costs. This may result from the development of new technologies and the

---

beyond what a "normal" plant breeders' rights regime would do ...' and because of this the Indian accession to UPOV rests 'in a state of limbo'. Besides, Rangnekar argues that:

> This law is ... significant for charting a relatively unique path in differing from the UPOV template that has dominated the regulatory landscape of plant variety protection. While retaining the UPOV template of DUS, the Indian law differs in requiring varieties to distinguish themselves in at least one essential characteristic [from any other known variety. Besides,] the exemption to use a protected variety as a source of initial variation ... is set out as a researchers' right rather than an exception to the rights conferred on breeders.

D. Rangnekar (2006), 'Assessing the Economic Implications of Different Models for Implementing the Requirement to Protect Plant Varieties: A Case Study of India', produced for the European Commission under the project 'Impacts of the IPR Rules on Sustainable Development (IPDEV)', at pp. 50–51.

[19] N.P. Louwaars *et al.* (2005), above note 17 at p. 133. In 1999 six major industrial groups controlled 'most of the technology which gives the freedom to undertake commercial R&D in the area of GM crops. These are: Agrevo/Plant Genetic Systems, ELM/DNAP/Asgrow/Seminis, Du Pont/Pioneer, Monsanto/ Calgene/Delkalb/Agracetus/PBI/Hybritech/Delta and Pine Lane Co., Novartis, Zeneca/Mogen/Avanta.' QMIPRI (2004), 'The Relationship between Intellectual Property Rights and Food Security'; and Nuffield Council on Bioethics (1999), 'Genetically Modified Crops: The Ethical and Social Issues'.

[20] H. Demsetz (1967), above note 1. He considers a particular effect as an externality (positive or negative, pecuniary or technological) when 'the cost of bringing that effect to bear on the decisions' of the persons that carry out the relevant activities 'is too high to make it worthwhile'. A change in the allocation of property rights may enable the effect to bear on those persons, thus, internalizing externalities.

opening of new markets. In his view, this paradigm has broad implications and is applicable to corporations, including with respect to the emergence of copyrights and patents.

In agriculture, technological change has allowed companies to increase the economic value of improved plant genetic resources, which has resulted in a growing demand for stronger IPRs protection.[21] But can it really be assumed that because patent protection for plant-related inventions is burgeoning in various parts of the developed and developing world, then the strengthening of such protection is desirable?

Winter argues that patent law should be discussed primarily as a matter of economic policy, which 'means to consider whether it furthers or impedes industrial progress'. The granting of a patent, he adds, 'is not a neutral device for enabling societal interaction but an interventionist instrument of the state designed to foster progress. ... it has constantly to prove that it serves its goal'.[22]

Mazzoleni and Nelson review various theories about the social functions served by patents and explore whether the recognition of these functions justify 'the current beliefs about the value of strong broad patents'.[23] They distinguish between four theories.[24] First, the 'invention motivation theory', also known as the 'reward theory', postulates that patents enable inventors to appropriate returns from investments in research and 'provide firms with the requisite incentive to invent'. Thus, the argument that 'improvements that would be external benefits to the community under an open-access regime are fully captured by the owner under a regime of property' underpins the reward theory of patents.[25] A corollary of the perceived 'trade-off between the gains from patent incentives and the output constraints of existing patents' is that a temporary monopoly should be granted only if its social benefits exceed its social costs.[26]

Second, the 'induce commercialization theory' emphasizes the distinction between inventive activities *per se*, which may culminate with the award of a patent on upstream technologies, and 'the follow-on work

---

[21]   K. Raustiala and D.G. Victor (2004), 'The Regime Complex for Plant Genetic Resources', *International Organization*, spring 2004.

[22]   Winter (1992), above note 16.

[23]   R. Mazzoleni and R. Nelson (1998), above note 15.

[24]   R. Mazzoleni and R. Nelson (1998), 'Economic Theories about the Benefit and Costs of Patents', *Journal of Economic Issues*, XXXI, 1031.

[25]   W.T. Merrill (2002), 'Introduction: the Demsetz Thesis and the Evolution of Property Rights', *The Journal of Legal Studies*, XXXI (2), 331–8.

[26]   W.E. Kitch (1977), 'The Nature and Function of the Patent System', *Journal of Law and Economics*, XX/1, 265–90.

that needs to be done to develop and commercialize' a product.[27] In particular, it suggests that patents play an important role especially for small firms. These firms need to attract sufficient capital investments to cover development costs or just to stay on the market, and their patent portfolio, including the licensing and sale of IP assets, may be extremely important for them.[28]

Technical change and specialization are the two factors at the origin of the high productivity of the modern capitalist economy.[29] The most evident example of this phenomenon is the spur of dedicated biotechnology firms in the US. 'DNA patents encourage such diversification of business activity' and may be important for both new entrants that do not have access to complementary production assets or an established product market and organizations outside of any particular industry, such as universities.[30] In the latter case, the 'induce commercialization theory' would justify the need for patent protection where the 'invention motivation theory' would fail, because publicly funded research and the resulting inventions would occur regardless of the granting of a patent.[31]

Third, the 'information disclosure theory' focuses on the role of patents as a mean by which technological information is made available to the public and assumes that 'the inventor cannot exploit all uses of the invention'.[32] Patents 'advertise' the relevant information to interested

---

[27] R. Mazzoleni and R. Nelson (1998), above note 15.
[28] R. Buckman (2007), 'Patent Firm Lays Global Plans', The Wall Street Journal, 12 November 2007, available at: http://online.wsj.com/article/SB119482858758489569.html (accessed 10 February 2009).
[29] H. Demsetz (2002), 'Toward a Theory of Property Rights II: The Competition between Private and Collective Ownership', *The Journal of Legal Studies*, XXXI (2), 653–72.
[30] G. Dutfield notes that four distinct types of businesses have emerged in connection with advancements in modern biotechnology and genomic sciences: 'a) the technology providers, who manufacture the DNA sequencing machines; b) the information providers, who do the actual sequencing; c) the research firms ... [or] dedicated biotechnology firms that generally do the upstream research but not the downstream product development; d) the biopharmaceutical ... and life science corporations'. See G. Dutfield (2003), 'Literature Survey on Intellectual Property Rights and Sustainable Human Development', UNCTAD & ICTSD, at chapter 6.
[31] R. Mazzoleni and R. Nelson (1998), above note 15. In particular, the Bay-Dole Act's philosophy postulates that firms would not have enough incentives to develop and commercialize a product without an exclusive licence in the basic technical knowledge developed by universities, while the latter would not have incentives to transfer such knowledge to private firms.
[32] Ibid.

parties through publication and allow for its widespread diffusion. In contrast with the 'induce commercialization theory', the former emphasizes the importance of liberal licensing practices in the technology diffusion process.

Finally, the 'prospect theory' of patents, which can be considered a variant of the 'induce commercialization theory', postulates that an initial invention may open up an array of different prospects. Kitch defines these prospects as 'the opportunity to develop a technological possibility'.[33] He argues that patents, especially broad patents that are issued in the early stage of technical development of an invention with 'a scope that reaches well beyond what the reward function would require', have the important function of assuring that the inventive process is efficient. Because the development of a particular technological prospect competes with any other prospects, the patent system ensures an efficient allocation of resources between alternative technological possibilities. Moreover, it promotes the coordinated management within each prospects and the transparent transmission of information. In doing so, the patent system would solve the classical 'common pool' problem that arises in relation to innovation processes: the right to innovate is a common right and the principle 'first appropriation controls' generates rent-dissipating races to invent.[34] For Kitch, the 'prospect feature' of the patent system increases the efficiency of post-patent investments in developing the technology by 'awarding an exclusive ownership of a technological prospect shortly after its discovery'.[35]

The idea that patent rights curb rent dissipation associated with the inefficient allocation of scarce resources has been further elaborated. Duffy emphasizes that the role of patents is to coordinate the timing of innovation investments by reducing negative rent-dissipating effects associated with patent races. He criticises the prospect theory by focusing on the role of rivalry within the patent system and describes the following two problems concerning rivalry. The first one is that 'rivalry always exists prior to the grant of a patent.'[36] Thus, prospect patents shift back in time rent-dissipating races to invent but do not eliminate rivalry.[37] The second

[33]   W.E. Kitch (1977), above note 26.
[34]   Y. Barzel (1968), 'Optimal Timing of Innovations', *The Review of Economics and Statistics,* 50/3, 448–55.
[35]   W.E. Kitch (1977), above note 26.
[36]   F.J. Duffy (2004), 'Rethinking the Prospect Theory of Patents', *University of Chicago Law Review*, Vol. 71, 439.
[37]   D.G. McFetridge and D.A. Smith (1980), 'Patents, Prospects, and Economic Surplus: A Comment', *Journal of Law & Economics,* 23/1, 197–203.

problem is that rivalry to invent persists within the patent's claims; therefore, other inventors may search for and patent improvements of the technology, a phenomenon that denotes the emergence of so-called 'blocking patents'.

Duffy's contribution is to argue that the prospect features of the patent system serve a socially useful function, that is to determine how rents are dissipated, rather than to eliminate rivalry. He explains that 'races to invent can dissipate patent rents in three ways'. First, investments on developing the technology may be made before the socially optimal time to make such investments. Premature investments are inefficient and entail social costs. Second, duplicative efforts are wasteful because 'once a certain piece of information has been acquired there is no value to acquiring it again'.[38] Third, races to invent 'diminish the patentee's rent by dedicating the invention to the public sooner'.[39] Thus, commercial embodiments of the invention can be exploited under patent protection for less time. However, the author argues, this is a socially efficient way to dissipate patent rents. In his view, a policy that favours the grant of patents on 'embryonic research results' should be endorsed, because it would curb the first two ways of dissipating rents while promoting the third one. In his demonstration, he develops an analogy between the patent system and natural monopoly regulation. On the one hand, he observes that 'the provision of (knowledge) goods by a single firm is superior to the provision by multiple firms'.[40] This is because the research may be expensive, but the marginal cost of knowledge production is negligible. On the other, he shares a rather unjustified optimism that the rivalry to invent prior to the grant of the patent and within patent claims can 'constrain the behaviour of the monopolist so as to maximize social welfare'.

Other authors completely disagree with the above conclusion and argue that: 'the world economy will not benefit from a general broadening and strengthening of patent protection', because in many technology areas strong patents 'entail major economic costs while generating insufficient additional social benefits'.[41] Among these technology areas prominently figure 'cumulative system technologies' and 'science-based technologies'. The next section will show that the creation of a new plant variety presents elements that may fit both models, because plant breeding

---

[38]   P. Dasgupta (1988), 'The Welfare Economics of Knowledge Production', *Oxford Review of Economic Policy*, 4/4, 1–12.
[39]   F.J. Duffy (2004), above note 36.
[40]   Ibid.
[41]   R. Mazzoleni and R. Nelson (1998), above note 15.

requires both the use of multiple genetic components and the ability to access and manage the complex knowledge of modern agricultural sciences.

2.2.4 Technological advance and agricultural research

Aside from subject-matter, *ordre public* and morality exceptions to patentability that are considered in the next chapter,[42] this section places the current legal debate about the optimum scope of patent protection for biotechnological inventions within the broader theoretical discussion concerning the question of how innovation can promote development. In particular, it considers technological change in agriculture and the nature of such innovation.

Merges and Nelson argue that the impact of broad patents on different industries varies in accordance with the way in which technological advance proceeds.[43] In particular, the authors elaborate four distinct innovation models. In the 'discrete invention model', the invention has clear boundaries defined by the claims. In addition, further research carried out on the invention is unlikely to generate 'wide-ranging technological advances'. In this case, strong patent protection would not restrict research efforts by others and is not a problem. Inventions of this kind may arise, for instance, in the field of mechanical engineering.

Chemical technologies normally fit the discrete invention model; however, some chemical inventions, as well as the processes for their production, may point the way to important follow-up inventions and improvements. An example would be the discovery of 'new and unpredictable uses of a particular chemical structure'.[44]

Agricultural innovation is typically a cumulative process. 'Cumulative technologies' are different from discrete inventions, because further innovation depends on previous inventions and can proceed in parallel on different fronts. A peculiar case is that of multi-component products, in which innovation may suffer if the industry's ownership structure is fragmented and other mechanisms do not allow the exploring of promising prospects without the need to negotiate multiple licences. The creation of novel plant varieties is increasingly facing the challenges that

---

[42] See section 3.4.2 which considers Article 53 of the European Patent Convention (EPC).

[43] P.R. Merges and R. Nelson (1992), 'Market Structure and Technical Advance: The Role of Patent Scope Decisions', in T.M. Jorde and D.J. Teece (eds), *Antitrust, Innovation and Competitiveness*, Oxford, UK: Oxford University Press.

[44] Ibid.

characterize the development of cumulative technologies. Actually, each genetic component may be subject to multiple ownership claims, which may be difficult to track. A potential 'anticommons' situation could lead to under-exploitation of plant genetic resources, whereby too many owners claim property over the same resource and need to authorise its use.[45]

Finally, 'science-based technologies' are driven by developments outside the industry; they are characterized by inventive races and, in general, the first individual to perform the invention makes only a small contribution over the prior art, while the patent may cover a large number of applications that are distant from the initial invention. For inventions that are upstream in the product development cycle, we might expect different inventors to have very different ideas of what the final products should be. They would possibly work on different research projects leading to a variety of products.

Therefore, the assumption that the absence of a broad pioneering patent results in duplicative efforts that dissipate rents is far from being proven. Indeed, the opposite is true, that broad patents 'cut down on the number of inventors who would be induced to work on the prospect ... [since] their ability to work the invention would be constrained by their ability to negotiate a licence'.[46]

---

[45]   D.G. Graff *et al.* (2003), 'The Public-Private Structure of Intellectual Property Ownership in Agricultural Biotechnology', *Nature Biotechnology,* 21/9; M.A. Heller and R. Eisenberg (1998), 'Can Patents Deter Innovation? The Anticommons in Biomedical Research', *Science,* 280/5364, 698–701.

[46]   P.R. Merges and R. Nelson (1990), 'On the Complex Economics of Patent Scope', *Columbia Law Review,* 90/4, 839–916. The authors disagree with Kitch's view that centralized and coordinated development is better than rivalrous for three main reasons. First, even if an action is profitable, it may not be taken because inaction could be the most comfortable situation in the absence of competition. Moreover, in the modern world of TRIPs-compliant patent laws it is not allowed to impose a requirement to work locally the invention: this safeguard, instead, existed in the US mineral claim system described in the famous Kitch's analogy with patents. Second, firms—and the human beings that operate through them—present some limits on their cognitive capacity. Once they have become proficient in a specialized area, it may be difficult for them to consider other valuable R&D activities, which may be outside that area, but included in the coverage of a broad patent. Because of this 'many independent inventors [may] generate a much wider and diverse set of explorations than when the development is under control of one mind or organization'. Third, the main characteristic of a 'prospect' for technological developments is uncertainty. This means that different inventors may pursue different technological opportunities. However, the involvement of third parties through selective licensing is expensive and costs are

Another study by the same authors does not deny that after a point rivalrous inventive efforts may generate inefficiencies. However, they believe that 'multiple and competitive sources of inventions are socially preferable to structures where there is only one or a few sources'.[47] Patent claims should be bounded by prior art and by what the disclosure enables, otherwise broad claims would reduce 'incentives for others to stay in the invention game'.[48] Merges and Nelson conclude that there is no evidence to support that control of subsequent developments by a single firm makes inventive efforts more efficient compared with a context where there are multiple sources of inventions.

The economics of the patent system focuses on how the balance between incentives to innovation and the dissemination of inventions can be affected by the changing patent landscape in the long-term multi-actor context of innovation. In this framework, the reduction in the number of available substitute products (i.e. food crops in the case of plant-related inventions) is seen as the societal cost that derives from greater patent protection. Indeed, the mainstream model of intensive agriculture based on monoculture, which is likely to benefit from such protection, is responsible for narrowing our genetic food base: only 30 plants provide

---

higher for the transfer of major innovations. This would result in the potential sub-optimal exploitation of patented knowledge.

[47]   P.R. Merges and R. Nelson (1992), above note 43.

[48]   The disclosure doctrine in patent law constraints allowed claims to what is enabled in the patent disclosure. Normally, such disclosure must enable a person skilled in the art to perform the invention. However, a range of variants may be covered by the claims provided that the specification makes a sufficient disclosure of the 'central core' of the invention. For instance, in the famous Gillette case the court was of the view that not any device that would be covered by patent claims needs to be disclosed. *Clarke Blade & Razor Co. v Gillette Safety Razor Co.*, 187 F. 149, 149 (CCDNJ 1911), aff'd, 194 F. 421 (3d Cir. 1912). Instead, the disclosure of an inventive principle—i.e. 'an underlying characteristic that supplies a family of devices with an identifiable quality'—would be sufficient to sustain the claims. However, 'if the description be so vague and uncertain that no one can tell, except by independent experiments, how to construct the patented device, the patent is void'. *The Incandescent Patent Lamp*, 159 US 465 (1895). It follows that a remarkable amount of independent experimentation beyond the specification disclosure, which may be necessary to achieve a particular embodiment of the invention, can be a defence against patent infringement. However, courts are reluctant to apply this defence in the case of chemical and biotechnological inventions. Another important point is that the inventor's disclosure must be enabling as of the filing date: 'disclosed information [must] enable the person skilled in the art to perform the invention as it was understood on the filing date', regardless of whether such information would not be enabling in the light of subsequent technological developments.

90–95 per cent of the total nutritional requirements that we derive from plants. In addition, three crops (rice, wheat, maize) contribute to 56 per cent of the total plant-derived energy.[49]

In general, 'wide patent scope that exceeds the enablement of the disclosure makes anyone who attempts to invent in that area beholden to the patent owner'.[50] The reverse equivalence doctrine has precisely the function to exclude from the scope of the claims technologies, which are not enabled by the patentee's disclosure, although they may be literally infringing.[51] Merges and Nelson invoke the extension of the application of the reverse equivalence doctrine to product patents that are granted for biological materials that occur in nature. The authors argue that in most cases the real invention is not the product, but the process to obtain it. Thus, products obtained from 'subsequently invented superior processes' should not be infringing.

In the same vein, Winter considers whether biotechnology ought to be patentable and criticizes that 'something is given to the inventor which had not been created by him or her'.[52] This is because 'when it comes to defining patent claims, natural phenomena, such as the programme of the inserted gene or the reproductive capacity of the microorganism cannot

---

[49] FAO (1998), *The State of the World's Plant Genetic Resources for Food and Agriculture*, Rome: FAO. While intensive agriculture enables 'the feeding of substantial levels of human populations, there is evidence of "direct negative impact on biodiversity loss at all levels: ecosystems, species and genetic; and on both natural and domesticate varieties"...'. V.H. Heywood (ed.) (1995), *Global Biodiversity Assessment*, Cambridge: Cambridge University Press; and D. Rangnekar (2000), 'Plant Breeding, Biodiversity Loss and Intellectual Property Rights', Kingston University, Economics Discussion Papers—No. 00/5.

[50] P.R. Merges and R. Nelson (1992), above note 43. For instance, the doctrine of equivalence is used by courts to 'expand the scope of claims beyond its literal boundaries'. In particular, equivalence is based on the requirements identified by the US Supreme Court in *Graver Tank & Mfg. Co., Inc. v Linde Air Prods*, Co., 339 US 605, 609 (1950): 'if two devices do the same work in substantially the same way and accomplish the same result, they are the same, even though they differ in name, form or shape'. A corollary of this doctrine is that pioneering inventions are 'entitled to a broad range of equivalents.' Thus, new technologies, which were not in existence at the time the patent was issued may be infringing, if they 'do not perform a different function or cause the device to operate in a substantially different way'.

[51] 'The law ... acknowledges that one may only appear to have appropriated the patented contribution, when a product precisely described in a patent claim is in *fact* "so *far* changed in principle" that it performs in a "*substantially* different way" and is not therefore an appropriation.' *SRI Int'l v Matsushita Elec. Corp. of America*, 775 F.2d at 1123, 227 USPQ (BNA) 577 (Fed. Circ. 1985).

[52] G. Winter (1992), above note 16.

be separated from the artificial part of the package and must be included into the claims'.[53] In his view, patent law policy should focus on the question of 'the benefits and desirability of scientific and technical progress', including not only the competitiveness of the economy, but also the environmental and social implication of technological change.

Hopkins *et al.* note that 'the context for patenting DNA has changed markedly since the 1990s'.[54] In the distinct but related field of human genomic research, the amount information, which is made available both in the scientific and patent literature, reduces 'the scope for discovery of novel DNA sequences'.[55] This point may not hold true in relation to plant genomic research, because even research focused on major food crops such as rice and wheat remarkably differs from human genomic research in terms of the related patent activity. For instance, only 0.57 per cent of rice genome's coding sequences are actually claimed in granted US patents, compared to approximately 20 per cent of human genome's coding sequences.[56] By contrast, 74 per cent of the rice genome is claimed in US patent applications as the result of the filing of so-called 'bulk sequence applications, which claim hundreds or thousands of nucleotide sequences'.[57]

However, while in Europe the EPO is arguably still granting broad biotech patents, in the US some authors have contended that there is an 'increasing tendency of patent offices to grant patents ... with narrower scope and more robust claims', which should also help maintaining the majority of the rice genome in the public domain.[58] This does not mean that the applicants' interest for patenting has decreased. Applicants may respond by changing their patent filing strategies and the design of the claims. Because of this, 'the possibility of a corresponding upswing in the number of DNA patents entailing narrower claims could reopen concerns

---

[53]   Ibid.

[54]   The authors note that 'national and international guidelines and developments in case law have raised the bar on patentability. Patent offices have ... raised thresholds that make it much less attractive for applicants to file speculative broad claims in the hope of obtaining what many would view as undue rewards.' M.M. Hopkins *et al.* (2007), 'DNA patenting: the end of an era?', *Nature Biotechnology,* 25/2, 185–7.

[55]   Ibid.

[56]   BIOS–CAMBIA (2008), *Rice Genome Landscape*, Patent Lens, 13 November 2008, available at: www.patentlens.net/daisy/RiceGenome/3648.html (accessed on 22 November 2010).

[57]   Ibid.

[58]   M.M. Hopkins *et al.* (2007), above note 54; OECD (2007), above note 12.

about an anticommons effect'.[59] A related issue is the widespread practice of bulk sequence applications that are filed by large life science companies. From a strategic standpoint, their rise in numbers may indicate that they serve monopolistic purposes, because they can contribute to fence a particular research landscape by creating uncertainty as to legal status of the inventions within it.

In the area of plant transformation research, which allows the creation of transgenic crops through the insertion of foreign genes, a fundamental technique concerns the so-called 'agro bacterium-mediated transformation methods'. Michiels and Koo report that during the period between 1996 and 2004 'the majority of patents (55%) on [such technology] were owned by the private sector, but its share has been rapidly decreasing, from 71% in 1996 to 49% in 2004'.[60] This may reflect a global Bayh-Dole induced trend that is characterized by policies that encourage the universities' propensity to apply for patents and prioritize technology transfer to the private sector and licensing as a source of funding for future research. As a result of these policies, over the study period, the role of university patents increased from 19 per cent to 30 per cent and 'the public sector [which comprises universities and research institutes, including privately operated ones] still accounts for about 45% of all patents in the area of agricultural biotechnology, unlike some other industries, where the private sector dominates the number of patent applications'.[61] However, an important consideration is that above figures do not say anything about the licensing status of technologies owned by the public sector, which may be exclusively licensed to private companies and cannot be easily shared.

In 2006, the global seed market was worth USD 30 billion and 49 per cent of its value was appropriated by the ten major agro-biotech life science companies.[62] These companies have increased their total market share by 6 per cent in two years, and in 2008 they controlled '55% of the commercial seed market and 64% of the patented seed market'.[63] To overcome the problems that derive from blocking patents that restrict

[59] M.M. Hopkins *et al.* (2007), above note 54.
[60] A. Michiels and B. Koo (2008), 'Publish or Patent? Knowledge Dissemination in Agricultural Biotechnology', Discussion Paper No. 00795, IFPRI, Environment and Production Technology Division, at p. 11.
[61] Ibid.
[62] S. Laird and R. Wynberg (2008), 'Access and Benefit-Sharing in practice: Trends in Partnerships Across Sectors', Technical Series No. 38, CBD Secretariat, Montreal, Canada, at p. 15 and Table 3.
[63] Ibid. at p. 15

access to enabling technologies and materials patent holders may cross-license disputed patents. For instance, Bayer, CropScience, Monsanto, and the Max Planck Society agreed to share between them their Agrobacterium-mediated transformation technologies free of charge to settle a 'long-standing patent interference and other proceedings in different countries involving the use of [such technologies] to create transgenic crops'.[64] However, non-club members may find it increasingly difficult to use fundamental research tools to carry out their research without compromising its potential to deliver useful products or running the risk of being sued for infringement.

2.2.5   Sustainable agriculture and food security

The ITPGRFA is the first international legally binding agreement that expressly mentions among its objectives sustainable agriculture and food security. The idea of sustainable agriculture is rooted in the concept of sustainable development, which can be defined as development that takes into account not only economic performance, but also the fundamental respect for human needs and the long-term preservation of the environment.[65]

The 1987 Brundtland Report, which had a pivotal role in contributing to the elaboration of sustainable development theories, states:

> Sustainable development is development that meets the needs of the present without compromising the ability of future generations to meet their own needs. It contains within it two key concepts: the concept of 'needs', in particular the essential needs of the world's poor, to which overriding priority should be given; and the idea of limitations imposed by the state of technology and social organization on the environment's ability to meet present and future needs.[66]

The idea of sustainable development is wider than that of 'economic development', which reflects the calculation of a country's economic performance. Sustainable development is also more comprehensive than

---

[64]   Max Planck Society (2005), 'Patent Dispute Resolved', Press Release, 4 February 2005, available at: www.mpg.de/english/illustrationsDocumentation/documentation/pressReleases/2005/pressRelease20050203/genPDF.pdf   (accessed 10 November 2008).

[65]   G. Dutfield (2006), 'Patents and Development: Exclusions, Industrial Application and Technical Effect', paper given at the WIPO Open Forum on the Draft Substantive Patent Law Treaty, Geneva, 1–3 March 2006.

[66]   World Commission on Environment and Development (1987), *Our Common Future*, Oxford, UK: Oxford University Press, at p. 43.

'human development', which is a framework concept adopted by the United Nations Development Programme (UNDP) in its Human Development Reports. The human development index that is used for such reports incorporates several indicators of countries' performance in terms of life expectancy, literacy, education and gross domestic product. Therefore, it attaches due importance to social welfare in enhancing the length and quality of life of the entire population.[67]

When the international community endorsed the concept of 'sustainable development' at the 1992 Rio Earth Summit, it acknowledged that each process conducive to economic and human development should take into account the fundamental importance of conserving nature and natural resources.[68] This is because both human well-being and its sustainability in the long run depend on the preservation of both natural resources and the environment in which they are found.

Agricultural sustainability 'centers on the need to develop technologies and practices that do not have adverse effects on environmental goods and services, and that lead to improvements in food productivity'.[69] In particular, 'agricultural sustainability ... does not mean ruling out any technology or practice on ideological grounds (e.g. GMO, organic farming), provided they improve productivity for farmers, and do not harm the environment'.[70] However, improved productivity for farmers may not necessarily derive from production that heavily depends on external inputs (mainstream model of industrial agriculture), but from 'integrated techniques that may even lower yields of specific crops, but increase the overall productivity of the land, as well as the diversity and overall soundness and resilience of agriculture sector and rural areas'.[71]

An aspect that is implicit in the concept of sustainable agriculture is its multifunctional role.[72] Farmers traditionally save, exchange, and sell their

---

[67]   A. Sen (1999), *Development as Freedom*, Oxford, UK: Oxford University Press.

[68]   P. Cullet (2005), *Intellectual Property Protection and Sustainable Development*, above note 18, p. 35.

[69]   J.N. Pretty *et al.* (2006), 'Resource-Conserving Agriculture Increases Yields in Developing Countries', *Environmental Science and Technology*, 40/4, 1114–19.

[70]   Ibid. at p. 1114.

[71]   S. Murphy and T. Santarius (2007), 'The World Bank's WDR 2008: Agriculture for Development—Response from a Slow Trade—Sound Farming Perspective', EcoFair Trade Dialogue, Discussion Paper No.10.

[72]   M. Pimbert (1999), 'Agricultural Biodiversity: Conference Background Paper No. 1', paper given at FAO/Netherlands Conference on the Multifunctional Character of Agriculture and Land, Maastricht, The Netherlands, 12–17 September 1999.

seeds informally. These practices are still widespread among poor farmers in developing countries, where farmers' systems of seed supply and crop improvement are by far the most important source of seeds, playing a fundamental role in ensuring household food security. Informal systems of seed provision are important mechanisms by which farmers gain access to the stock of different genes that are necessary to select, improve and conserve traditional varieties that are well adapted to the local environment where they live.

Seed production in farming takes place outside the formal seed system because seed policies and regulatory mechanisms have focused mainly on the commercial aspects of seed production. In formal seed systems, conservation, crop improvement and seed production are carried out by different specialized institutions: respectively, gene banks, plant breeders and seed producers. On the contrary, in informal seed systems, the conservation, development and use of crop diversity and seed production are integrated components of farming systems. Indeed farmers are not just 'growers', but have multiple interactions with the farming system of which they are part. Such interactions include activities as different as the selection, storage, production, diffusion and exchange of seeds.[73]

In these systems, seeds also have a multi-functional role, as opposed to the single function that they perform in industrial agriculture, i.e. as primary inputs that are treated as commercial commodities.[74] Such a multi-functional role depends on the agro-ecological, socio-economic, cultural and spiritual values that are attributed to crop diversity.[75] Because of the inherent resource limitations of small-scale farmers in developing countries, many formal practices are not affordable for them and the legal requirements concerning seed certification and plant variety protection are not applicable in relation to the varieties that they use.

---

[73]   M. Halewood *et al.* (2007), 'Farmers, Landraces and Property Rights: Challenges to Allocating *Sui Generis* Intellectual Property Rights to Communities over their Varieties', in S. Biber-Klemm and T. Cottier (eds), *Rights to Plant Genetic Resources and Traditional Knowledge—Basic Issues and Perspectives.* Wallingford, UK: CABI, at p. 179. 'Farmers' systems of informal exchange are crucial to: (i) their ability to constantly introduce new material into their cropping systems; (ii) maintaining high levels of diversity; (iii) maintaining relatively stable yields.'

[74]   C. Chiarolla (2007), 'FAO International Treaty on Plant Genetic Resources and Farmers' Rights', in *Protection of Plant Varieties with reference to Farmers' and Breeders' Rights.* Hyderabad, India: Institute of Chartered Financial Analysts of India.

[75]   A.D. Posey (ed.) (1999), *Cultural and Spiritual Value of Biodiversity*, Nairobi & London: UNEP & IT Publications.

However, these legal regulatory requirements may *de facto* limit the freedom of farmers to continue some traditional agricultural practices, such as the saving of seeds and tubers from consumption as well as subsequent exchange and use. At the national level, the restriction of the rights that farmers currently enjoy and the lack of initiatives to create appropriate incentives may negatively affect the conservation and development of PGRFA and increase food insecurity.[76]

Article 1 of the 1996 Rome Declaration on World Food Security defines food security as follow: 'Food security exists when all people, at all times, have access to sufficient, safe and nutritious food to meet their dietary needs and food preferences for an active and healthy life.'[77] Pretty *et al.* point out that 'increased food supply is a necessary though not sufficient condition for eliminating hunger and poverty. What is important is who produces food, has access to the technology and knowledge to produce it, and has the purchasing power to acquire it.'[78] As to the current state of world food insecurity, regardless of a remarkable increase in food production that is sufficient to feed today's world population, 'hunger and poverty remain widespread', while 'agriculturally driven environmental damage is prevalent'.[79]

A recent trend points to a rise in international cereal export prices that remain high and volatile.[80] The causes of world food insecurity are complex and result from the interaction of multiple factors. One of these factors is the sustained demand, which is foreseen as a consequence of population growth. Various parts of Africa and Asia are continuing to pay the heaviest burden in terms of poor performance of crops, which is certainly related to climate change, severe drought, soil erosion and contamination, although these global environmental threats impact also

---

[76] M. Halewood *et al.* (2007), above note 73, at p. 174. The authors argue that:

... farmers farm the way they do in order to maximize their food security and to improve their livelihoods. There is a significant risk that the gains that might be realized through the introduction of intellectual property incentives to alter their existing practices would be outweighed by the losses realized as a result of these changes.

[77] FAO (1996), 'Rome Declaration on World Food Security', World Food Summit, FAO, Rome (13–17 November 1996).
[78] J.N. Pretty *et al.* (2006), above note 69, pp. 1114–19.
[79] Ibid.
[80] FAO (2007), 'Crop Prospects and Food Situation', Issue No. 6, FAO, Rome, Italy.

other regions. Poor performance of crops limits the local availability of food and pushes food prices up.[81]

Proprietary technologies have the potential to solve some of the above problems. However, more of the same (intensive agriculture) is likely to increase biodiversity loss and soil contamination, just to mention a few negative externalities.[82] Crucial technological developments are coupled with the radical consolidation of the new bioscience industries at the global scale. Acquisitions and the consequent concentration in the seed industry have become effective means to preserve freedom to operate in agricultural biotechnology.[83] However, the negative impact of these industry strategies may include that:

> ... growing agribusiness concentration may reduce efficiency and poverty reduction impacts. ... Concentration widens the spread between world and domestic prices in commodity markets for wheat, rice, and sugar, which more than doubled from 1974 to 1994. A major reason for the wider spreads is the market power of international trading companies.[84]

2.3 CONCENTRATION, TECHNOLOGICAL CHANGE AND THE GENE REVOLUTION

Since the legal history of commodification of crop diversity and the scientific history of the life sciences go hand in hand, the fundamental

---

[81]   S. Johnson, chief economist at the IMF, argues that apart from biotic stresses, responsible factors are 'the increased demand from emerging economies like India and China' and the sustained demand of corn from the fasts growing bio-fuel industry. A. Brookes (2007), 'Corn's Key Role as Food and Fuel', BBC News, available at: http://news.bbc.co.uk/2/hi/americas/7149079.stm (accessed 17 December 2007).

[82]   S. Murphy and T. Santarius (2007), above note 71.

[83]   G. Toenniessen and D. Delmer (2005), 'The Role of Intermediaries in Maintaining the Public Sector's Essential Role in Crop Varietal Improvement', report prepared at the request of the Science Council of the Consultative Group on International Agricultural Research, The Rockefeller Foundation, New York, US. The authors report that:

> IP is used to protect biotechnology tools and reagents; genes and gene sequences; regulatory sequences; processes of transformation, regeneration and diagnosis; and, the resulting modified plants. It is in part to deal with this thicket of patents, and to gain 'freedom to operate' (FTO), that the private sector is becoming greatly centralized through a large number of mergers, acquisitions and cross licensing agreements.

[84]   World Bank (2007), 'World Development Report 2008: Agriculture for Development', at pp. 135–6.

steps that have enabled the transition from extensive to intensive agriculture will be presented in the following sections. Another important reason why technology matters is that the developing countries' reaction to the perceived 'misappropriation' of genetic resources through new technological means has triggered a whole new range of ABS-related restrictions on access to PGRFA.

The crucial technological developments that have enabled the transition from extensive to intensive agriculture are coupled with a radical consolidation of bioscience industries. Merrill highlights that changes in property institutions, which may follow changes in the value of the resources that are commodified, can be explained by both distributional or interest group theories and consensual social norm theories.[85] This book adopts the former as the most appropriate theoretical approach to explain the transition between property regimes that has taken place in the fourth quarter of the twentieth century regarding the ownership of PGRFA.[86]

2.3.1   The origins of agriculture

The origins of agriculture and the consequent domestication of plant species can be traced back to 8,000–10,000 years ago, following the end of the last ice age. In the early twentieth century, Nikolai Ivanovich Vavilov,

---

[85]   Interest group theories postulate that 'property rights emerge when powerful oligarchs control both the largest share of resources whose value would be maximised by the creation of property and the political system through which such a transition is effectuated'. W.T. Merrill (2002), above note 25, pp. 331–8. Banner argues that 'societies reallocate property rights when some exogenous political realignment enables a powerful group to grab a larger share of the pie'. S. Banner (2002), 'Transitions between Property Regimes', *The Journal of Legal Studies*, XXXI (2), 359–71; and S. Levmore (2002), 'Two Stories about the Evolution of Property Rights', *The Journal of Legal Studies*, XXXI (2), 421–51.

[86]   See below section 2.3.4 on 'Distributional Implications of Crop Germplasm Enclosure'. The key reasons that justify such choice are as follows. The collected evidence points to the conclusion that it would be inaccurate to assume that the widely heterogeneous and dispersed multitude of interests related to PGRFA have all been equally weighed and reflected in such transition process with the result that new property regimes have replaced pre-existing ones by consensus. If any, such consensus often cannot reach beyond the lowest common denominator among the key players' positions. On the other end, the inter-governmental nature of international law-making processes, almost by definition, excludes the wide participatory stakeholder involvement, which would be required to discuss meaningfully the notion of 'social consensuses' in relation to the norms that are analysed here.

a Russian botanist, for the first time developed a theory that identified the centres of origins of cultivated plants. His theory was highly influential for the work of agricultural researchers and geneticists, who have studied the evolutions of cultivated species, such as the American agrobotanist Jack Rodney Harlan and others involved in plant collection expeditions during the twentieth century.[87]

Esquinas-Alcazar notes that since 'the appearance of agriculture ... of more than 300,000 plants that have been described, man is estimated to have used more than 7,000 species to satisfy human needs'.[88] According to Demsetz, 'it was primitive farming that brought the most improvements' in terms of food supply. Thus, agricultural production could be increased 'in such quantities that population growth could continue'.[89] He also observes that, on the one hand, the 'land committed to farming land itself ... to privatisation', and on the other, 'the storability and transportability of grain ... combined with higher farm productivity ... opened pathways to specialization of production'.[90]

The transition from extensive, small-scale and labour-intensive agriculture to large-scale input-intensive agriculture can be described from two distinct viewpoints: specialization and genetic erosion. The magnitude of today's specialization in agriculture can be portrayed as follows: 'before the industrial revolution 90 per cent of the world's population was engaged in food production'; by contrast, today 'less than 10 per cent of the population supplies the world with 100 per cent of ... major food items'.[91] As to genetic erosion, Rangnekar suggests the use of indicators, such as the 'pronounced concentration on a limited range of variations as parental material' and the 'domination of active cultivation by a few varieties', as proxies to establish the levels of genetic erosion in a particular agro-ecosystem. He also emphasizes that 'the examination of genetic uniformity across dominant varieties in time and space is essential'.[92] Esquinas-Alcazar finds that of more than 7,000 known species that have been used in agriculture 'barely ... 150 species are now cultivated' and 'most of mankind now lives off no more than 12 plant

---

[87]   A.B. Damania *et al.* (eds) (1997), 'Jack R. Harlan (1917–1998)—Plant Explorer, Archaeobotanist, Geneticist and Plant Breeder', in *The Origins of Agriculture and Crop Domestication. Proceedings of the Harlan Symposium, 10–14 May 1997*, Aleppo, Syria: IPGRI.

[88]   J. Esquinas-Alcazar (2005), 'Protecting crop genetic diversity for food security: political, ethical and technical challenges', *Nature*, 6/12, 946–53.

[89]   H. Demsetz (2002), above note 29.

[90]   Ibid. at p. 667.

[91]   Ibid. at p. 665.

[92]   D. Rangnekar (2000), above note 49.

species'.[93] Moreover, genetic diversity—and its erosion—should be measured not only between species, but also within species (i.e. their intra-specific diversity) and over time. Although the loss of crop-biodiversity is difficult to quantify, all indicators show that this diversity is suffering a tremendous reduction, which is prominently due to the replacement of more heterogeneous traditional varieties and landraces with modern uniform varieties.[94] Thus, to the extent that specialization may require the use of genetically uniform varieties, it seems to contribute to the erosion of *in-situ* crop diversity.[95]

2.3.2 Technology, specialization and intellectual property

As to the relationship between specialization and institutional change—in particular, the creation and allocation of property rights—Demsetz

---

[93]   J. Esquinas-Alcazar (2005), above note 88. Based on FAO (1998), *The State of the World's Plant Genetic Resources for Food and Agriculture*, Rome, Italy: FAO.

[94]   Chapter 1 of *The State of the World's Plant Genetic Resources for Food and Agriculture*, under 'Genetic Erosion', states:

> Country Reports indicate that recent losses of diversity have been large, and that the process of 'erosion' continues. Of major concern is the irreversible loss of genes, the basic functional unit of inheritance and the primary source of the variation in the appearance, characteristics, and behaviour among plants. Gene complexes and species can also be lost, and in effect become extinct. ... The chief contemporary cause of the loss of genetic diversity has been the spread of modern, commercial agriculture.

FAO (1998), ibid., pp. 13–4. A previous study also reveals that 'most varieties can no longer be found in either commercial agriculture or any US genebank. For example, of the 7098 apple varieties documented as having been in use between 1804 and 1904, approximately 86% have been lost. Similarly, 95% of the cabbage, 91% of the field maize, 94% of the pea, and 81% of the tomato varieties apparently no longer exist.' C. Fowler (1994), *Unnatural Selection. Technology, Politics and Plant Evolution*, International Studies in Global Change, Vol. 6, Yverdon, Switzerland: Gordon and Breach Science Publishers; and K.D. Rubenstein *et al.* (2005), 'Crop Genetic Resources: An Economic Appraisal', Economic Information Bulletin Number 2, US Department of Agriculture (May 2005). Finally, for a description of the state of cultivated systems and their impact on ecosystem services see: Millennium Assessment (2005), *Ecosystems and Human Well-being: Current State and Trends—Cultivated Systems*, Millennium Ecosystem Assessment, Vol. 1, Washington: Island Press, at Chapter 26.

[95]   J. Esquinas-Alcazar reminds us that the 'Green Revolution' has made it possible to meet the demand for homogeneity that is necessary for industrial food production; 'however, this has been at a high price: the loss of innumerable heterogeneous traditional farmer's varieties'. J. Esquinas-Alcazar (2005), above note 88.

argues that: first, 'the single most important force behind our growing use of private ownership has been the productivity gains that results from specialization' and second, 'high productivity ... creates a societal interest in arrangements that encourage effort and facilitate some sharing of the gains from this effort'.[96] To the extent that 'modern farming ... yields returns greatly in excess of the amounts needed to sustain the persons doing the farming ... [it] creates a demand for social organization that ... provides for "social sharing" of the yields obtained from this investment'.[97] With the recent integration of socialist and communist economies into the world trading system and the consequent adoption of minimum intellectual property standards, such as those contained in the WTO–TRIPs Agreement, patents and plant variety rights have globally become one of the most important 'institutions' through which the 'social sharing'—to use Demsetz terminology—of yields from research and development (R&D) investment in agriculture can be obtained.[98]

Dutfield considers the origins of IP protection in agriculture and explains that protecting 'products of new technological fields or products of old technological fields that have hitherto been unprotected' may proceed from 'redefining existing rights so as to encompass the novel material' to the 'creation of new rights'.[99] He also notes that the protection of innovation in the fields of organic chemistry, pharmaceutical sciences and biotechnology has followed—what Cornish calls—the route of 'accretion' (i.e. the expansion of existing rights).[100] On the contrary, the subject matter of plant breeding (i.e. plant varieties) has mainly followed a *sui generis* route to IP protection by 'emulation' of already established IPR systems.

A number of key scientific and technological discoveries have prompted agricultural development in modern Europe and North America. Such discoveries were followed by the adoption of new and stronger forms of

---

[96]   H. Demsetz (2002), above note 29, p. 663.

[97]   Ibid.

[98]   M. Blakeney provides an overview of different legal and technological means by which breeders can stimulate agricultural innovation and capture returns from R&D investments by restricting others from using their varieties without due remuneration. M. Blakeney (2005), 'Stimulating Agricultural Innovation', in K.E. Maskus and J.A. Reichman (eds), *International Public Goods and Transfer of Technology under a Globalized Intellectual Property Regime*, Cambridge: Cambridge University Press.

[99]   G. Dutfield (2003), *Intellectual Property Rights and the Life Science Industries: a Twentieth Century History*, Aldershot, UK: Ashgate, at Chapter 7.

[100]   W.R. Cornish (1993), 'The International Relations of Intellectual Property', *Cambridge Law Journal*, 52/1, 46–63.

IPR protection. At the beginning of twentieth century, the two most important steps forward in the rising science of plant breeding were the application of Mendel's laws of heredity to improve the genetic makeup of plants and the development 'pure lines' or self-pollinating corps. These crops can 'breed true to type and contain consistent and identifiable traits that can be transferred to other plants'.[101] Their importance resides in the fact that they allow for particular combinations of genes to be transferred from the first generation of improved plants to their progeny without losing associated desirable traits. However, plant breeding is a relatively long process and the creation of a new variety takes from seven to ten years on average.

A traditional way to improve plants is to cross parents with desired traits and to select within their progeny the plants that have retained those characteristics. For self-pollinating plants, such as wheat, rice and sorghum, the introgression of particular traits can usually be realized by back-crossing. This means that the progeny resulting from a first cross must be crossed back with one of the parent lines to reduce the presence of the other parent's undesired characteristics in the final variety. This process must be repeated several times to obtain a new plant variety that is stable (i.e. that maintains its distinctive characteristics from one generation to the other).

Although back-crossing is normally deleterious for sexually-reproduced plants, such as maize, millet, cereals and pulses, in the 1920s a US public sector plant breeder discovered that for some species the 'cross-breeding of inbred pure lines' gives rise to hybrid plants with increased yield vigour. An important corollary is that this vigour decreases exponentially when the progeny of hybrid plants is used for further propagation. These two characteristics of hybrids allowed private seed companies to emerge and make lucrative profits, which would not have been foreseeable without the particular form of biological protection that derives from hybridization.[102]

The establishment of the American Seed Trade Associate at the end of the nineteenth century which lobbied for limiting saving and free distribution of seeds by the Government in the US, and the decision of

---

[101]   G. Dutfield (2003), above note 99.

[102]   However, in the US, 'the separation of farming from breeding and the undermining of the customary practice of seed saving' cannot be explained only by reference to these important advancements in scientific breeding, because the economies of scale that derived from mechanized harvesting and land consolidation had already made less attractive for farmers to produce directly all the seeds that they needed. C. Fowler (1994), above note 94.

the US Department of Agriculture to invest in hybrid seed technologies promoted the growth of the modern seed industry.[103] However, while 'in North America and Europe ... the profession of farming became a separate one from crop improvement ... in many other parts of the world this separation has barely taken place'.[104] Some authors, therefore, criticize hybrid technologies because not only they prevent seed saving, but also 'eliminate all opportunities to improve crops through selective breeding'.[105]

Conventional breeding techniques, such as crossing and selection, may be supplemented by so-called second generation biotechnologies, which include tissue and cell culture. The advantage of these techniques is that they can 'regenerate large numbers of plants that are genetically identical and free from diseases'.[106] However, the most important developments in modern plant science, especially as to their intellectual property implications, have come with the advent of third generation biotechnologies and the creation of genetically modified organisms (GMOs). Actually, modern biotechnologies allow the introgression of foreign genes into plants from other kingdoms. For instance, the insect resistance trait of varieties known as 'BT' corn and cotton was derived from a soil microbe called *Bacillus Thuringiensis* through the transfer of a foreign gene that is responsible for the expression of that trait. The possibility to transfer genes from genetically distant organisms is a remarkable scientific progress because it overcomes natural barriers between unrelated species.

Cell fusion, direct gene transfer, genomics, proteomics and plant system biology provide additional tools that can be employed in modern crop improvement.[107] In particular, a common distinction may be drawn between enabling and traits technologies.[108] The first category includes

---

[103]   'Several of the world's major-twentieth century seed companies first came to prominence through their successful breeding of hybrid corn varieties. These include Pioneer Hi-Bred, DeKalb, Pfister, and Funk.' G. Dutfield (2003), above note 99.

[104]   Ibid.

[105]   J.P. Berlan and R.C. Lewontin (1998), 'Cashing in on Life—Operation Terminator', *Le Monde Diplomatique*, available at: http://mondediplo.com/1998/12/02gen (accessed 10 January 2008).

[106]   G. Dutfield (2003), above note 99.

[107]   R. Fears (2007), 'Genomics and Genetic Resources for Food and Agriculture', Background Study Paper No. 34, FAO, Rome, Italy; P. Oldham (2004), 'Global Status and Trends in Intellectual Property Claims: Genomic, Proteomics and Biotechnology', CESAGen, Cardiff, UK.

[108]   Graff *et al.* (2003), above note 45.

research tools that are used to create transgenic crops, such as: 1) transformation methods related to the transfer of genes into plant cells; 2) selectable markers to detect whether a particular transformation event has successfully occurred; and 3) constitutive promoters that regulate the expression of specific genes and associated traits.

Traits technologies are very important in functional genomics because they 'provide the genetic basis for new functionalities'.[109] Thus, this category includes: tissue-specific and developmental stage-specific promoters that limit the expression of foreign genes to specific plant organs or tissues to eliminate the non-desired effects of transgenies; targeting sequences useful to drive proteins into specific subcellular locations; and sequences that confer novel traits to plants. Other types of gene promoters are: inducible promoters, whose typical characteristic is that 'their performance is not conditioned by endogenous factors, but rather to external factors that can be artificially controlled', such as chemical compounds and synthetic promoters.[110] Most of these technologies have been in use for some time in private companies and it is likely that they are associated with various IPR restrictions, including patents and trade secrets.[111]

2.3.3 Agro-biodiversity, intellectual property and genetic erosion

With respect to the impact of patents and plant breeder rights on plant breeding from the standpoint of how the use of crop diversity might be influenced, the literature points out that 'human societies adopt a low-biodiversity agro-ecosystem because of scale economies ... path-dependency and lock in effects'.[112] A further inference is that institutional

---

[109] Ibid.

[110] WIPO (2006), 'Progress Report on Work towards the Assessment of Patent Data Relevant to Agricultural Biotechnology and the Availability and Use of Material from the International Network of *Ex-Situ* Collections under the Auspices of FAO and the International Treaty on Plant Genetic Resources for Food and Agriculture: a Draft Patent Landscape Surrounding Gene Promoters relevant to Rice', IT/GB-1/06/Inf.17.

[111] For instance, in the case of marker assisted selection, Henson-Apollonio points out that not only particular genes, but also 'processes/methods, reagents, and equipment [may] be covered by patent claims, both in industrialized countries and also in many developing countries such as China, India and Brazil'. V. Henson-Apollonio (2006), 'The Impacts of IPRs on MAS Research and Application in Developing Countries', paper given at the 19th Session of the Genetic Resources Policy Committee of the CGIAR, El Batan, Mexico, 22–24 February 2006.

[112] D. Rangnekar (2000), above note 49.

factors such as patents and plant breeders rights 'might be actively designed by the beneficiaries of [a] particular techno-economic trajectory' to lock in that trajectory.[113]

Modern high-yielding varieties whose creation is encouraged by patents and plant breeders' rights are bred from a narrow circle of parental materials and are genetically uniform. As Halewood *et al.* note, these varieties are 'the product of a formal crop-breeding process undertaken with clear breeding objectives set out at the beginning of the process' and 'are continuously reproduced (i.e. maintained) from the same known and stable parents, so the system for their production is "closed" with no new genes being introduced'.[114]

Productivity gains that arise with the specialization and mechanization of agriculture depend to a large extent on crop uniformity (and its stability over time). In particular, uniformity ensures that each individual plant that is sown is presented with the same characteristics that allow for its mechanical harvesting, including uniform ripening time and sufficient strength to be picked up by machines. In this respect, some have argued that modern varieties are actively 'designed to be harvested by machines and respond to chemical inputs'.[115]

Low-diversity agro-ecosystems can be highly productive under the stable environmental conditions for which they are designed. Crop varieties that are used therein are expressly selected to respond to the regular administration of external inputs so as to increase yields. For this reason, they perform better than traditional varieties; however, in order to obtain this result, they must be grown in controlled environments or greenhouses.[116]

---

[113] Ibid.
[114] M. Halewood *et al.* (2007), above note 73.
[115] G. Winter (1992), above note 16.
[116] In a recent report, the International Life Science Institute stresses that:

The goal of domestication is to produce crops with uniformity and desirable agronomic traits, and not necessarily to have plants with increased fitness. Natural selection creates resilient biological systems with properties that adapt to a variety of environmental conditions and ensures the continuation of the species ... conventional plant breeding and domestication of many crops often creates gene combination that would not survive without ongoing human intervention.

International Life Sciences Institute (2007), 'Nutritional and Safety Assessments of Foods and Feeds Nutritionally Improved through Biotechnology: Case Studies: Executive Summary of a Task Force Report by the International Life Sciences Institute, Washington, DC ' *Journal of Food Science,* 72/9, R131–7.

However, modern varieties show increased yield variability when their growing environment cannot be externally controlled. In particular, they are more sensitive to variations in climate, soil type, pests and pathogens evolution than heterogeneous plant populations. This is because the genetic variability of traditional varieties and landraces is insurance on yield performance and guarantees that under unfavourable external conditions some resilient plants will develop.[117] Thus, the stability of yields and the genetic stability of a plant variety—intended as the stability of its relevant and uniform characteristics across generations[118]—are two distinct concepts, whose relationship is of direct proportionality when the growing conditions can be controlled, while they are inversely proportional in the opposite case.

In many countries, climate change, desertification, increased water scarcity, unavailability or non-affordability of agricultural inputs, such as pesticides, fertilisers, water and fuel, may reasonably cast doubts regarding the need for pursuing uniformity as a breeding goal of any agricultural research programme that seeks to target these problems. Bearing in mind the evolutionary dynamics of cultivated species and the important role played by farmers, Esquinas-Alcazar notes that 'a genetic resource ceases to evolve as the natural processes of selection and adaptation are halted'.[119]

Both hybridization and the focus on genetic purity of varieties may lead to homogeneous populations with decreased chances of on-farm selection.[120] Although a few examples of registered varieties encompassing a

---

[117] M. Halewood *et al.* (2007), above note 73, at p. 175, states:

The stability of the genetic structure of a landrace ... is different from the stability of yield. Yield stability, which is often associated with wide adaptability, is an attribute that several authors use to describe landraces. ... yield stability is a consequence of ... [the] genetic diversity within the landrace. First, wide adaptability, as represented by genetic heterogeneity, will enable a population to yield under a wide range of environmental conditions. Second, environmental conditions that fluctuate from year to year will tend to favour different genotypes in different years.

[118] See UPOV 1991, Article 9, which states: 'The variety shall be deemed to be stable if its relevant characteristics remain unchanged after repeated propagation or, in the case of a particular cycle of propagation, at the end of each such cycle.'

[119] J. Esquinas-Alcazar (2005), above note 88, pp. 946–53.

[120] Rangnekar argues that 'the farmer got locked into a new mode of production based on genetically uniform varieties and chemical inputs ... farms have been transformed, from mixed crops to single crops, from multi-lines to single varieties, where the variety is genetically homogeneous'. D. Rangnekar (2000), above note 49.

distinct plant population—instead of a pure line—exist,[121] in a growing number of countries, the requirement for uniformity under the 1991 Union for the Protection of New Plant Variety (UPOV) Act is a factor that contributes to genetic erosion. Indeed, breeders may not ignore that if they want to obtain a plant variety protection certificate, they will have to meet a relatively high uniformity standard. Thus, they are encouraged to breed for uniformity.

In the context of plant patenting, the reproducibility requirement is 'fulfilled when additional specimens from the first unique specimen could be obtained as a result of a reproduction process'.[122] This also entails a remarkable degree of genetic uniformity as a condition for the patentability of plant-related materials.

The above discussion raises the following crucial question: to what extent can the social benefits that derive from specialization and the kind of technological change encouraged by patents and plant variety rights balance the associated social and environmental costs?

2.3.4   Distributional implications of crop germplasm enclosure

2.3.4.1   The politics of enclosure

Libecap observes that 'the problem of "producing" property rights reduces to one of creating effective agreements on any proposed institutional reorganization ...' and such agreements must be able to provide 'politically acceptable allocation mechanisms to assign gains from institutional change, while maintaining its production advantage'.[123] However, it may also be argued that 'the existence of such a mechanism is not obvious', because the transition from a less efficient property regime to a more efficient one 'is likely to be costly'.[124] At least in theory, these

---

[121]   M. Logan (2007), 'Agro-biodiversity in Nepal: Wise Insurance', IDRC News, No. 17, available at: www.idrc.ca/en/ev-110870-201-1-DO_TOPIC.html (accessed 10 February 2008).

[122]   Van Overwalle explains that the reproducibility requirement 'stemmed from the industrial-applicability requirement in Belgium and Germany and the enabling-disclosure requirement in the United States'. See G. Van Overwalle (1999), 'Patent Protection for Plants: a Comparison of American and European Approaches', *The Journal of Law and Technology* 39, 143–94, at pp. 156–9.

[123]   D.G. Libecap (2003), 'Contracting for Property Rights', in T.L. Anderson and F.S. McChesney (eds), *Property Rights: Cooperation, Conflict, and Law*, Princeton, NJ: Princeton University Press, 142–67.

[124]   S. Banner (2002), above note 85, pp. 359–71.

costs arise as a consequence of the need to value 'rights under the old regime' and assign 'rights under the new one'.[125]

Among the scholars, who have analysed the mechanisms through which the transitions between property regimes may occur, some favour 'consensual social norm theories', while others share a less optimistic view that is grounded in so-called 'distributional' or 'interest group theories'. The former theories are based on the idea that 'consensus for institutional change may emerge if those potentially harmed in the proposed definition of rights are compensated'.[126] At the other end of the spectrum, interest group theories postulate that 'societies reallocate property rights when some exogenous political realignment enables a powerful group to grab a larger share of the pie'.[127]

As regards the creation of plant variety rights, industry interests played a crucial role during the 1957 Paris Diplomatic Conference of the International Association of Plant Breeders (ASSINSEL). In particular, the European agenda tabled by ASSINSEL lead to the adoption of the UPOV Convention in 1961.[128] In the 1980s, with the advent of genetic engineering and new molecular techniques, industry turned to patenting for the protection of plant-related inventions, because patents provide a more stringent control both over the technology and the genetic material.[129]

Dutfield highlights that interest group politics should 'strongly discourage any expectation that patents and PBRs ... finely balance the interests of existing owners, users, and the public, while optimally encouraging wealth-enhancing innovation'.[130] Winter is also explicit in showing that 'the promotional impetus towards patenting' in biotechnology was 'based on the professional interest of patent lawyers ... the relevant industries and its governmental support'.[131] Thus, the design and interpretation of patent and plant variety protection laws has always been influenced by well-organized interest groups.

2.3.4.2   The relationship between specialization, concentration and wealth-shifting effects

This chapter has already highlighted the importance of concentration as a form of organizational structure that allows for coordination between

---

125   Ibid.
126   D.G. Libecap (2003), above note 123.
127   S. Banner (2002), above note 85.
128   M. Blakeney (2005), above note 98.
129   Ibid.
130   G. Dutfield (2003), above note 99, at p. 243.
131   G. Winter (1992), above note 16.

separate specialized harms of relevant industries. The present section reviews some theoretical insights that explain how vertical and horizontal integration may increase the political influence of such industries and the redistribution impact in their favour.

Demsetz argues that 'specialization creates identifiable groups between which wealth can be shifted' and 'empowers pressure groups' that 'seek and sometimes get wealth from persons who either belong to no specialized group or belong to a politically weaker specialized group'. Therefore, it 'makes wealth redistribution (in favour of the most specialized pressure groups) and protectionism easier'.[132]

However, Demsetz has a positive view of the above transition, as he believes that 'continued growth in specialization will cause redistribution to wane', because increases in 'the number of specialized activities' would eventually lead each activity to 'wield less political force'. He also considers the role of risk, which is 'to make persons more hesitant to accept the dependency that comes with specialisation', and concludes that wealth created by specialization 'buffers the adverse effects of risks'.[133] While the relationship between specialization and wealth redistribution is convincingly explained, Demsetz's conclusions do not appear to be persuasive if questions are framed in terms of whose risks and wealth the focus is on.

Banner's theoretical contribution to this debate, beyond Demsetz's insights, is twofold: to explore 'how society overcomes the obstacles that might block a transition to an (allegedly) more efficient property regime'— i.e. mainly the problem of costing 'old rights and assigning new ones'; and to suggest various potential mechanisms 'by which efficiency gets translated into political action'.[134]

His analysis starts by considering the transition costs, which arose 'in North America, Australia and New Zealand, as British and American governments purchased or simply occupied large blocks of lands', eliminated indigenous functional property systems and subdivided the land between settlers.[135] The key point that he makes is that 'if done with

---

132   H. Demsetz (2002), above note 29, p. 663.
133   Ibid.
134   S. Banner (2002), above note 85, pp. 359–71.
135   A right is allocated on a functional basis when a person has the right to use particular resources which may be 'scattered in a variety of different spaces', as opposed to the right to use resources that are located in a particular area. Examples are the rights to fish, graze animals, catch birds, cultivate fields or gather plants in different places with 'productive resources allocated by use, not space'. Ibid.

a rigorous attention to the valuation and allocation of everyone's interests', the costs of the transition 'might have easily eaten up the efficiency gains from the switch'.[136]

The allocation of private property rights to commonly managed lands during the colonial period is an interesting case, which holds some truth also in relation to the efficiency and wealth redistribution effects associated with the commodification of crop diversity.[137] There is a strong indication that all enclosure movements had in common 'significant distributional consequences' with 'clear winners and losers'.[138] In the area of IPR regulation, Dutfield notes that 'the differences between the gains for some and the losses for others are bound to be great when the biggest right holders have ... a firm grip on the regulatory system to the partial or total exclusion of other holders, users and those representing consumers' interests'.[139]

Wallace and Mayer criticize the expansion of patent law, which now covers gene-based inventions, because of its effects 'on innovation in public health and agricultural systems'.[140] Their argument is that 'scientific knowledge that can be made the subject of a patent application is being favoured above the acquisition of other knowledge'. In agri-food research, the possibility of DNA patenting coveys most funding and attention towards the use molecular techniques for crop improvement, while less expensive tools are available for the benefits of farmers and consumers.[141] Expressing a related concern, Jefferson, asks the following question:

---

[136] Ibid.

[137] Banner explicitly states that 'in their distributional effects, enclosure and the parallel colonial schemes were a bit like free trade today, with diffuse gains for most and concentrated gains for some coming at the expense of concentrated losses for others'. Ibid.

[138] In the above case of land redistribution, Banner argues that:

... the expected payoffs to the winners were large enough to provide them with an incentive to bear a disproportionate share of the administrative costs of reorganization. ... The political economy of the transition thus tended to pit an oligarchy against a large number of relatively powerless farmers. ... By skewing the payoffs of the reorganization in favour of the powerful, these programs facilitated the reallocation of property rights.

A corollary of the above is that 'the more concentrated political power is ... the more unevenly the gains from the transition will be distributed'. Ibid.

[139] G. Dutfield (2003), above note 99.

[140] H. Wallace and S. Mayer (2007), 'Scientific Research Agendas: Controlled and Shaped by the Scope of Patentability', in C. Waelde and H. MacQueen (eds), *Intellectual Property: The Many Faces of the Public Domain*, Cheltenham, UK: Edward Elgar.

[141] Ibid. 'The perceived economic value of patenting DNA sequences is one factor which leads to the identification of individual gene functions being

> We've got a system where virtually any concept in the life sciences and nanotechnology that you come up with, no matter how good you are, is likely to be come up with by someone else within days, months, at best years, but certainly not decades. Where is then the justification for a very long exclusionary right?[142]

For instance, it has been suggested that weakening rights may be appropriate when there is a 'fall in the average life cycle of new products' or when R&D costs decrease.[143]

2.3.5   Internalizing externalities from agricultural research and breeding

Earlier in this chapter it was explained that with Demsetz, law and economics theorists have postulated that property rights, including IPRs, can cause private and social returns to converge, a process that is also known as 'internalization of externalities'.[144]

---

prioritised over and above other potentially more useful knowledge.' Tansey and Rajotte stress that 'the current focus on biotechnology, which is partially driven by IP, is skewing the overall research effort away from other approaches to improve farming, especially for poor and marginalized farmers, from better water management to more appropriate equipment to integrated pest management techniques'. G. Tansey and T. Rajotte (eds) (2007), *The Future Control of Food. A Guide to International Negotiations and Rules on Intellectual Property, Biodiversity and Food Security*, London, UK: Earthscan, at Chapter 8. Finally, as regards agro-biotechnology research, Dutfield underlines that:

> ... there are some reasonable doubts that the first wave of products coming out of this research is much better than the more conventionally developed existing ones or that such products do not have drawbacks of their own. ... Public expenditure on the life sciences ... is likely to have spurred innovation over the years far more than the existence of patents.

See G. Dutfield (2003), above note 99, at p. 243.

[142]   Speech by R. Jefferson, Chief Executive Officer of the Australian-based CAMBIA Biological Open Source Initiative, in J.F.B. Wilbanks *et al.* (2007), 'Could the key to feeding the world be locked up in a company fridge somewhere?', Alfred Deakin Innovation Lecture, 29 December 2007, available at: www.abc.net.au/rn/scienceshow/stories/2007/2122486.htm (accessed 10 January 2008).

[143]   G. Dutfield (2003), above note 99, at p. 21.

[144]   Proponents argue that such process should lead to the ideal situation in which hypothetical agents would reflect in their management decisions the entire value generated by their productive activities as well as their costs. This would promote the efficient allocation of private investment and the efficient management of resources. H. Demsetz (1967), above note 1, pp. 347–59.

'Technological externalities' occur when third parties, who have not transacted with the agent that is producing them, enjoy some direct benefits (i.e. positive externalities) or pay some costs (i.e. negative externalities) arising from the agent's activities.[145] These externalities are believed to affect net social welfare. In some cases, their internalization could be worthwhile by excluding non-paying users.[146]

In agricultural research and breeding, legal restrictions on the use of plant genetic resources may generate higher levels of appropriable returns. However, spillovers in most cases are good for society, while 'extending property rights to internalize externalities may distort market allocation in a manner that is detrimental to social welfare'.[147] Thus, the social value of providing open access to PGRFA and related agricultural technologies may exceed private returns in terms of aggregate surplus, i.e. consumer surplus plus producer surplus. In this case, legal requirements that may produce a complete internalization of positive externalities such as those related to the patenting of crop diversity should not be taken as a given.

2.3.6 Plant genetic resources as non-traditional infrastructural resources

The FAO International Treaty on Plant Genetic Resources for Food and Agriculture defines PGRFA as 'any genetic material of plant origin of

---

[145]   On the distinction between technological and pecuniary externalities, see: A.M. Lemley and M.B. Frischmann (2007), 'Spillovers', *Columbia Law Review*, 107 (1), 257–301, at p. 262.

[146]   However, Frischmann highlights that:

The market mechanism exhibits a bias for outputs that generate observable and appropriable benefits at the expense of outputs that generate positive externalities. This is not surprising because the whole point of relying on [private] property rights and the market is to enable private appropriation and discourage externalities. The problem with relying on [private property rights and] the market is that potential positive externalities may remain unrealized if they cannot be easily valued and appropriated by those that produce them, even though society as a whole may be better off if those potential externalities were actually produced.

M.B. Frischmann (2005), 'An Economic Theory of Infrastructure and Commons Management', *Minnesota Law Review*, 89, 917–1030, at pp. 988–9.

[147]   A.M. Lemley and M.B. Frischmann (2007), above note 145, at pp. 265–99. The authors argue that:

Courts and scholars must resist the easy answer of equating public and private value by internalizing externalities because spillovers aren't always bad, and more property rights aren't always good. Only if we understand when and why each can enhance social welfare can we hope to design legal rules that do more good than harm.

actual or potential value for food and agriculture'. It also defines 'genetic material' as 'any material of plant origin, including reproductive and vegetative propagating material, containing functional units of heredity'.

These definitions emphasize the tangible nature of PGRFA through the use of the term 'material'. At the same time, they narrow the classes of materials comprised in the definitions through a criterion based on their particular informational contents, i.e. the fact that they contain 'functional units of heredity'. As explained below, from an economic and legal point of view both the tangible (i.e. material) and intangible (i.e. informational) aspects of PGRFA are important.

Frischmann has argued that 'the same rationale for managing traditional infrastructure in an openly accessible manner applies to other resources that behave in the same economic fashion as traditional infrastructure, even though they are not generally considered infrastructure'.[148] Infrastructural resources can be defined in accordance with the following criteria:

1) they may be consumed non-rivalrously;
2) they are used primarily as inputs in downstream productive activities, whose outputs' demand determines the demand for infrastructural resources; and
3) they are generic inputs in the sense that they may generate a 'variance of potential downstream outputs', which can be private goods, public goods and non-market goods.[149]

The ensuing sections explain how plant genetic resources for food and agriculture match the above criteria.

2.3.6.1 Non-rival consumption of PGRFA

The first requirement which characterizes infrastructural resources, namely 'non-rivalry', depends on how their 'capacity' adjusts to consumption.[150] In other words, 'non-rivalrousness of consumption

---

[148] M.B. Frischmann (2005), above note 146, at p. 927.

[149] Ibid. at pp. 956–8.

[150] 'Capacity' means 'the potential or suitability for holding, storing, or accommodating; the facility or power to produce, perform, or deploy'. Available at: www.merriam-webster.com/dictionary/capacity (accessed 10 December 2008). Rivalry also determines the private or public nature of a resource. Instead, excludability depends on 'how costly it is to prevent someone else from consuming the resource'. Thus, the latter is an important factor that must be considered when

measures the degree to which one user's consumption of a resource directly affects another user's present consumption possibilities'.[151] On the one end, the direct consumption of pure private goods, such as rice (understood as a commodity/food), entirely exhausts another user's present consumption possibilities.[152] On the other, the consumption of pure public goods, such as information, never diminishes the possibility of other consumers to satisfy their needs.[153]

The issue of whether PGRFA should be considered as private goods or public goods depends on the purpose and modalities of consumption, since their value may derive from their informational contents, rather than from direct consumption. Besides, several transfers of PGRFA normally occur during the development of a new plant variety.[154] The prospective users of ABS and IPR systems may be either providers of PGRFA or recipients of such resources. This depends on whether PGRFA are an output from or an input into their research and breeding activities.

Initially, crop genetic diversity is an output from farmers' conservation and breeding efforts and may involve traditional agricultural practices. Besides, PGRFA can be sourced from national and international genebanks.[155] When these intermediaries are involved, the evaluation of seed samples may take place and passport and characterization data can be made available to recipients.

For agricultural scientists, crop genetic diversity is a partially non-rival input into research and breeding and an impure public good.[156] It follows that when adequate stocks are kept, the capacity of PGRFA to adjust to

---

decisions are made as to the design of legislation which creates legal mechanisms to correct supply-side market failures. However, the degree of excludability of a resource does not influence its public or private nature. Ibid. at pp. 964–5.

[151]   Ibid. at p. 945, note 99.

[152]   For instance, if someone eats a bowl of rice nobody else can benefit from its nourishment.

[153]   For example, genetic information which is obtained by sequencing the genetic code of rice is a pure public good.

[154]   The 'development cycle' comprises all R&D and breeding processes that take place before the new variety is ready for commercialization.

[155]   The enforcement of ABS restrictions on access to genetic resources operates when such resources leave the source country for the first time. Thus, it relies on their tangible nature. If genetic resources can be accessed from other sources, which do not require any benefit-sharing agreement, the costs of excludability may be very high. This is one of the arguments that justify the need for an ABS Protocol to the CBD.

[156]   The research use of a seed sample does not diminish the potential of other samples with the same genetic makeup to satisfy the scientific enquiries of other recipients.

consumption (understood as research and breeding) tends to be an infinite capacity, which is typical of pure public goods. The information that is derived from such research is also a pure public good. This shows that PGRFA 'may be consumed nonrivalrously' as required by Frischmann's definition of infrastructural resources.

To conclude, if adequate resources are available, seed samples can be reproduced to avoid so-called 'congestion problems' and the results of basic agricultural research can be widely disseminated to generate as many positive externalities as possible.[157]

2.3.6.2   Downstream productive uses as sources of value

Most of the value of PGRFA derives from their use as inputs into downstream productive activities. Thus, the demand for PGRFA (and their informational contents) depends on how useful they are to develop new and improved crops, and on the expected demand for those crops.

Before commercialization takes place, all outputs from R&D and plant breeding are intermediate research products, including *inter alia*: proprietary information derived from PGRFA; research tools, such as gene markers and express sequence tags; genes and gene fragments with identified properties of agronomic value; and advanced breeding lines created from elite germplasm. As for the initial seed sample, their value derives from downstream productive uses rather than from direct consumption. Thus, embodiments of intermediate research products can be PGRFA and meet the second requirement of infrastructural resources, i.e. that they are valuable because of their downstream productive uses.

2.3.6.3   PGRFA as generic inputs into agricultural research

Even though modern commercial plant varieties are 'rival' agricultural production inputs, they may always be used as partially non-rival research inputs. For instance, they may need to be locally adapted to specific agro-climatic conditions and soil characteristics. This can involve further

---

[157]   These principles underpin the mandate of the Centers of the Consultative Group on International Agricultural Research, which is to deliver international public goods. M. Halewood (2007), 'Searching for a Line in the Sand: Issues to Consider Concerning Financial Returns from Recipients of Centres' PGRFA under Development', paper given at the 13th CGIAR Executive Council Meeting, Rome, Italy, 16–17 October 2007.

breeding and development, including crosses and selection with local varieties to reflect consumers' taste.[158]

The benefits that derive from facilitating access to PGRFA 'may be substantial but extremely difficult to measure'.[159] This is a consequence of the variance and unpredictability of the potential downstream outputs of PGRFA's 'functional units of heredity', whose phenotypic expression depends on the interaction between the environment and human agricultural practices. Thus, in geographical areas different from those in which modern commercial verities are well adapted, gains from improved performance will always require training, experimentation and local adaptation. An enabling legal and policy environment for agricultural innovation should not prevent this from happening.

2.4 CONCLUDING REMARKS

This chapter has assessed the theoretical proposition that economic law reforms that provide for exclusion rights do not necessarily evolve in the direction of promoting efficient outcomes and benefits for the affected communities. In particular, interest group theories suggest the costs associated with the commodification of crop diversity are likely to be unfairly distributed with the developing world bearing a disproportionate amount of such costs, while minorities in industrialized countries appropriate most of the benefits.

Where formal seed markets have worked efficiently, plant intellectual property protection has accelerated technological change in terms of faster varietal turnover.[160] However, it has also influenced the distribution of benefits from research investments and innovation spillovers.[161] As a

---

[158] However, in the case of patented plant innovation, as well as in other technology fields, 'the buyer's *private* return to buying, changing, and reselling the good may be less than the seller is charging, even if the *social* return to the changed good would have been enough to justify the transaction'. This problem becomes acute when few players in highly concentrated markets adopt strategic behaviours with the aim to exclude undesired competitors from the market. A.M. Lemley and M.B. Frischmann (2007), above note 145, at p. 274.

[159] M.B. Frischmann (2005), above note 146, at pp. 956–7.

[160] The varietal turnover *per se* does not indicate an increase in genetic diversity; rather it 'is more a measure of the output of a plant breeding program'. K.D. Rubenstein *et al.* (2005), above note 94, at p. 41.

[161] A.M. Lemley and M.B Frischmann (2007), above note 145, at p. 275, argue that:

result, such spillovers are not available to less-developed countries and the public sector to the same extent as they were in the past.[162]

Against this backdrop, the commodification of crop diversity should not be expected to promote a shift towards a fairer global food system. Agricultural innovation is typically a cumulative process and PGRFA should be managed in a regulated openly accessible manner, because such 'non-traditional infrastructural resources' may generate higher social value and positive externalities if they are managed as regulated commons.[163]

The universe of pecuniary externalities we can safely ignore is quite a bit narrower in the innovation context than it is with traditional property. While the allocation of benefits between willing participants to most transactions may not matter, the same cannot be said when the government steps in to allocate rights among parties who would not otherwise transact, as it does by creating IP rights.

[162] For instance, Chang wonders whether 'countries have vested interests in imposing policies and institutions, which they themselves have not used during their own development, but which are beneficial for them once they have reached the technological frontier'. H. Chang (2002), *Kicking Away the Ladder: Development Strategy in Historical Perspective*, London, UK: Anthem Press, at p. 139.

[163] For instance, Levmore's definition of 'open access' may include a regime that provides for 'common-pool resources that are managed by a group or its agents ... with open access and restricted use'. This definition fits well the status of PGRFA that are included into the FAO Multilateral System. S. Levmore (2002), above note 85, pp. 421–51.

3. Plant intellectual property protection: patents and plant variety rights

3.1 INTRODUCTION

The main proposition of this book is that global institutional reforms governing the present and future allocation of wealth from crop diversity are insufficient—and in some respects inappropriate—to achieve international equity in terms of the way plant genetic resources are transferred, how agricultural research is conducted and its benefits are shared.

A corollary of the above proposition is that strong restrictions on access to plant genetic resources may augment the technological divide between those who have reached the technological frontier and latecomers who rely on the adaptation of foreign technologies and germplasm for their domestic food needs. Thus, the distribution of the benefits that arise from the use of crop diversity depends on the institutional arrangements that govern the legal entitlements to use plant genetic resources, related information and technologies.

This chapter explains how international plant-related intellectual property agreements fit together and focuses, in particular, on how the implementation of the TRIPs Agreement has served the commercial interests of technology producing and exporting countries. By doing that, it presents substantive patent standards relevant for the protection of gene-based inventions as well as *sui generis* plant variety rights under the UPOV Convention. At the national level, the overlap between biotechnological patents and plant variety rights is examined through a comparative study. The latter analyses US and EU plant-related IP legislation, describes the tensions between these different protection schemes and the way in which such tensions have been resolved in each jurisdiction.

3.2 WTO AGREEMENT ON TRADE-RELATED ASPECTS OF INTELLECTUAL PROPERTY RIGHTS

For the first time in history, the TRIPs Agreement introduces intellectual property rules into the multilateral trading system by requiring all WTO members to provide minimum standards of protection for a wide range of intellectual property rights (IPRs).[1] In doing so, the TRIPs Agreement incorporates provisions from several international intellectual property agreements administered by the World Intellectual Property Organization (WIPO). It also introduces a number of new obligations, particularly in relation to geographical indications, patents, plant variety rights, trade secrets, and measures governing how IPRs should be enforced.

The transitional period, which gave developing countries an extended deadline to implement the obligations of the TRIPs Agreement (with the exception of national treatment and most-favoured-nation treatment), expired in 1999.[2] Instead, the deadline for the Least-Developed Countries (LDCs) was due to expire in 2005.[3] However, in November 2005, WTO members eventually agreed on a further extension until 1 July 2013, which gives LDCs more time for implementation.[4]

The above decision confirms the importance of special and differential treatment provisions under the TRIPs Agreement. However, it does not

---

[1]   The TRIPs Agreement was negotiated during the 1986–94 Uruguay Round and entered into effect on 1 January 1995. It covers four fundamental strategic areas for the protection of IPRs, in particular: it establishes international substantive minimum standards for IP protection; it provides detailed international criteria for national enforcement of IPRs; it subjects any controversy as to compliance with minimum standards and enforcement to the WTO dispute settlement system; and it establishes common procedural requirements concerning the administration and maintenance of IPRs at the national level.

[2]   Article 65 of the TRIPs Agreement.

[3]   Article 66 of the TRIPs Agreement.

[4]   WTO TRIPs Council (2005), 'Extension of the Transition Period under Article 66.1 for Least-Developed Country Members', IP/C/40, WTO, Geneva (30 November 2005); and WTO (2005), *Poorest Countries Given More Time to Apply Intellectual Property Rules*, Press Release No. 424, 29 November 2005, available at: www.wto.org/english/news_e/pres05_e/pr424_e.htm (accessed 10 February 2009). In addition, the deadline for the implementation of pharmaceutical patents has been extended until 1 July 2016 by the 'Doha Declaration on the TRIPs Agreement and Public Health', WT/MIN(01)/DEC/2 (14 November 2001); WTO TRIPs Council (2002), 'Extension of the Transition Period under Article 66.1 of the TRIPS Agreement for Least-Developed Country Members for Certain Obligations with Respect to Pharmaceutical Products', IP/C/25, WTO, Geneva (1 July 2002).

amount to a positive normative discrimination between member states' obligations. Thus, there is no agreement in the WTO as to the need to depart from the 'one size fits all' approach in implementing the TRIPs Agreement, although many countries call for a more flexible approach that should be adjusted to their different stages of industrial and economic development.

3.2.1 Plant patenting under Article 27.3(b) of the TRIPs Agreement

The use of genetic resources in modern biotechnology applications has increased their economic, scientific and commercial value for a wide range of stakeholders. In particular, plant genetic resources can be modified by human intervention and take on characteristics that do not exist in nature. When these modifications result in a new biotechnological invention that involves an inventive step and is capable of industrial application, the invention may qualify for patent protection.

In particular, the first paragraph of Article 27 of the TRIPs Agreement calls on WTO Members to provide patent protection for both products and processes, and forbids discrimination among different fields of technology, including agriculture.[5] Therefore, this provision allows the patenting of plants and plant varieties as well as their genetic components.

However, the number of TRIPs-compatible options under Article 27.3(b) is huge in comparison with other provisions in areas where the TRIPs Agreement dictates in great detail the way in which national IP laws should be crafted. Thus, in theory, the implementation of Article 27.3(b) gives the opportunity to tailor developing countries' national laws to agriculture sector's needs.[6]

3.2.2 Exclusions from patentability and sui generis plant variety protection

WTO members also agreed that plants, animals and all essentially biological processes for their production may be excluded from

---

[5] Article 27.1 of the TRIPs Agreement states: 'Patents shall be available for any inventions, whether products or processes, in all fields of technology, provided that they are new, involve an inventive step and are capable of industrial application.'

[6] See, for instance, the pioneering work of D. Leskien and M. Flitner (1997), *Intellectual Property Rights and Plant Genetic Resources: Options for a sui generis system*, Issues in Genetic Resources No. 6, Rome, Italy: IPGRI.

patentability.[7] However, if they do so, they shall provide for the protection of plant varieties either by patents or by an effective *sui generis* system or by any combination thereof.[8] Therefore, countries are in principle free to choose their own effective *sui generis* regime for the protection of plant variety rights.

Besides, Article 8.1 permits the adoption of 'measures necessary to protect public health and nutrition'. However, such measures must be consistent with the TRIPs Agreement. Thus, this provision cannot easily derogate from the patentability requirements of Article 27. Likewise, when a WTO member excludes plants from patentability, the obligation to provide an effective *sui generis* system for the protection of plant varieties cannot be waived on the basis of Article 8.1.[9]

3.2.3   Disclosure of origin and the revision of Article 27.3(b) of the TRIPs Agreement

Article 27.3(b) constitutes an example of 'regime development through implementation', in so far as it presents a built-in mechanism for its review, which is triggered after a certain period of time.[10] The review process that started in 1998 is far from being completed and all burning issues are still on the negotiating table.

In 2001, paragraph 19 of the Doha Ministerial Declaration instructed the WTO TRIPs Council 'to examine, *inter alia*, the relationship between the TRIPS Agreement and the Convention on Biological Diversity, the

---

[7]   However, micro-organisms and micro-biological or non-biological process must be protected.

[8]   Article 27.3(b) of the TRIPs Agreement allows members to exclude from patentability 'plants and animals other than micro-organisms, and essentially biological processes for the production of plants or animals other than non-biological and microbiological processes. However, Members shall provide for the protection of plant varieties either by patents or by an effective *sui generis* system or by any combination thereof.'

[9]   Queen Mary Intellectual Property Research Institute (2004), 'The Relationship between Intellectual Property Rights and Food Security', DG Trade of the European Commission, at pp. 9–10.

[10]   Article 27.3(b) of the TRIPs Agreement states: 'The provisions of this subparagraph shall be reviewed four years after the date of entry into force of the WTO Agreement.' K. Raustiala and G. Victor (2004), 'The Regime Complex for Plant Genetic Resources', in *International Organization* (Spring 2004), available at: http://papers.ssrn.com/sol3/papers.cfm?abstract_id=441463 (accessed 10 February 2009).

protection of traditional knowledge and folklore, and other relevant new developments raised by members'.[11]

Under the above negotiating mandate, several developing countries supported the proposal to amend the TRIPs Agreement to include a mandatory obligation to disclose the origin of genetic resources and traditional knowledge in patent applications.[12] In fact, the latest proposal at the TRIPS Council on mandatory disclosure is that it be implemented through an amendment to Article 29 of the TRIPs Agreement, not Article 27.3(b). This proposal includes a requirement that the applicant shall submit evidence of compliance with the CBD prior informed consent and benefit-sharing provisions.[13] Besides, the formulation of the potential remedies for non-compliance varies in strength, with remedies that affect the validity of patents being preferred by the strongest proponents of the amendment, including, *inter alia*, India, Brazil, the African Group and LDCs.[14]

---

[11]   WTO (2001), 'Doha Ministerial Declaration' (WT/MIN(01)/DEC/1, 2001).
[12]   For a detailed analysis of proposed options for the implementation of disclosure requirements in patent application see: Chatham House (2006), 'Disclosure of Origin in IPR Applications: Options and Perspectives of Users and Providers of Genetic Resources', Final Report, IPDEV – Work Programme 8; J.D. Sarnoff and M.C. Correa (2006), 'Analysis of Options for Implementing Disclosure of Origin Requirements in Intellectual Property Applications', UNCTAD/DITC/TED/2004/14; L.A. Hoare and G.R. Tarasofsky (2007), 'Asking and Telling: Can "Disclosure of Origin" Requirements in Patent Applications Make a Difference?', *JWIP*, 10/2, 149–69.
[13]   WTO TRIPs Council (2006), 'Doha Work Programme—The Outstanding Implementation Issue on the Relationship between the TRIPs Agreement and the Convention on Biological Diversity', Communication from Brazil, India and others, WT/GC/W/564/Rev.2—TN/C/W/41/Rev.2—IP/C/W/474, Geneva (5 July 2006), at p. 2, para. 2. Under Article 29.*bis*, such proposal states:

> Where the subject matter of a patent application concerns, is derived from or developed with biological resources and/or associated traditional knowledge, Members shall require applicants to disclose the country providing the resources and/or associated traditional knowledge, from whom in the providing country they were obtained, and, as known after reasonable inquiry, the country of origin. Members shall also require that applicants provide information including evidence of compliance with the applicable legal requirements in the providing country for prior informed consent for access and fair and equitable benefit-sharing arising from the commercial or other utilization of such resources and/or associated traditional knowledge.

[14]   Ibid. at p. 2, para. 5, which states:

> Members shall ensure that administrative and/or judicial authorities have the authority to prevent the further processing of an application or the grant of a patent and to revoke, subject to the provisions of Article 32 of this Agreement,

However, to make disclosure of origin negotiations extremely complex, it is not only their relationships with demands and concessions on the creation of a multilateral register for wines and spirits as well as the extension of the protection of geographical indications to other products, but also the issue of 'parallelisms'. This expression refers to the proposed inclusion of any WTO TRIPs Council-related outcomes within the package conclusion of the Doha Round of horizontal trade talks on market access for agriculture and other industrial products.

To conclude, in the WTO TRIPs Council, there is a mounting pressure on the TRIPs/CBD amendment.[15] However, such pressure may not be the determinant factor in increasing the likelihood that WTO members reach consensus on some soft form of disclosure requirements, which must be acceptable by their strongest opponents as well as proponents.[16] Besides, it appears very difficult that such a step forward will take place before, or in the absence of, the successful conclusion of negotiations under the WTO Doha Development Agenda.

3.3 UPOV CONVENTIONS FOR THE PROTECTION OF NEW VARIETIES OF PLANTS

As noted above, under Article 27.3(b) of the TRIPs Agreement, countries are free to choose their own effective *sui generis* system for the protection of new plant varieties. The UPOV Convention provides a legislative model, but unlike other relevant IPR instruments, such as the Berne and Paris Conventions,[17] it has not been mentioned in the TRIPs

---

or render unenforceable a patent when the applicant has, knowingly or with reasonable grounds to know, failed to comply with the obligations in paragraphs 2 and 3 of this Article or provided false or fraudulent information.

[15] K. Mara (2008), 'Push for TRIPs Changes Reaches Highest Level at WTO as Meetings Intensify', Intellectual Property Watch, 21 November 2008, available at: www.ip-watch.org/weblog/index.php?p=1329 (accessed 27 November 2008).

[16] Abbott argues that 'there is only a small segment of U.S. IP-dependent industry that has a genuine stake in the outcome, and "solidarity" among industry sectors may not be as valuable a commodity as its proponents would like to believe. Still, it is going to be very difficult as a domestic political matter for USTR to move on this issue.' F.M. Abbott (2008), 'Post-mortem for the Geneva Mini-Ministerial: Where does TRIPS go from here?' Information Note Number 7, ICTSD, Geneva.

[17] Berne Convention for the Protection of Literary and Artistic Works of 9 September 1886, available at: www.wipo.int/treaties/en/ip/berne/trtdocs_wo001.html (accessed 25 February 2009); Paris Convention for the Protection of

Agreement.[18] This is probably because when the TRIPs Agreement was negotiated, the 1978 UPOV Act was considered obsolete while the 1991 UPOV Act had not yet entered into force.[19] The result of this situation was that Article 27.3(b) provides a certain degree of flexibility to WTO members in deciding on the most effective *sui generis* legislation.[20] Thus, there are three possible TRIPs-compliant forms of intellectual property protection for plant varieties: patents, *sui generis* protection, or any combination thereof.

3.3.1 Patents versus plant variety rights

In comparison with the patent system, *sui generis* plant variety protection presents similarities as well as elements that remarkably differ. Under the UPOV Convention, the object of exclusive rights in plant varieties is the propagating material.[21] Thus, plant variety rights do not cover within their subject matter technical processes for the production of protected varieties, while patents may afford such protection. In addition, specific genes or combinations of genes of protected varieties are outside the scope of protection, remaining available for further research and breeding.

As regards the nature and characteristics of rights granted under the two systems, the comparison between Article 28 of the TRIPs Agreement and Article 14 of the 1991 UPOV Act demonstrates that a close correspondence exists between them.[22] In fact, according to Article 28 of

---

Industrial Property of 20 March 1883, available at: www.wipo.int/treaties/en/ip/paris/trtdocs_wo020.html (accessed 25 February 2009).

[18]   The French acronym 'UPOV' stands for 'Union International Pour la Protection des Obtentions Végétales'.

[19]   J. Watal (2000), *Intellectual Property Rights in the WTO and Developing Countries*, The Hague, NL: Kluwer Law International, at p. 140.

[20]   WTO TRIPs Council (2002), 'Review of the Provisions of Article 27.3(b)', IP/C/W/369 (8 August 2002).

[21]   Article 1 (vi) of the 1991 UPOV Convention defines the term 'variety' as:

a plant grouping within a single botanical taxon of the lowest known rank, which grouping, irrespective of whether the conditions for the grant of a plant variety right are fully met, can be: 1) defined by the expression of the characteristics that results from a given genotype or combination of genotypes; 2) distinguished from any other plant grouping by the expression of at least one of the said characteristics; and 3) considered as a unit with regard to its suitability for being propagated unchanged.

[22]   See the table, which compares Article 28 of the TRIPs Agreement with Article 14 of the 1991 UPOV Act, in R. Jördens (2002), 'Legal and Technological

the TRIPs Agreement, a patent shall confer on its owner the right to prevent others from making, using, offering for sale, selling or importing the patented product.[23] Likewise, under UPOV-like legislation, the holder of a plant variety protection certificate has the right to exclude others from producing or reproducing, conditioning for the purpose propagation, offering for sale, selling, exporting, importing and stocking propagating material of the protected variety for any of the above mentioned purposes.[24] These rights may also cover the harvested material that is obtained through the unauthorized use of propagating material, when the title holder has had no reasonable opportunity to exercise his rights in relation to the propagating material itself.[25]

However, the requirements for protection under UPOV are easier to meet than those that apply to patents. This is because plant breeders' rights are specifically crafted to accommodate the peculiar needs of plant breeding. Therefore, the criteria of distinctness, uniformity and stability (DUS) are generally adapted to the mode of reproduction of the variety and are more flexible than patentability requirements.[26] Moreover, the novelty criterion is defined in terms of commercial novelty: a plant variety cannot be protected if it has been offered for sale in the relevant market prior to the date of application.[27] No other conditions are allowed under UPOV 1991.[28]

Development Leading to the Symposium: UPOV's Perspective', paper given at the WIPO–UPOV Symposium on the Co-Existence of Patents and Plant Breeders' Rights in the Promotion of Biotechnological Developments (the WIPO-UPOV Symposium I), 25 October 2002; and R.L. Helfer (2004), *Intellectual Property Rights in Plant Varieties: International Legal Regime and Policy Options for National Governments*, Rome, Italy: FAO, at p. 35.

[23]   According to Article 28.1(b) of the TRIPs Agreement, in the case of a process patent, the same rights extend at least to the product obtained directly by the patented process.

[24]   Article 14(1) of the 1991 UPOV Convention.

[25]   Article 14(2) of the 1991 UPOV Convention.

[26]   Protected plant varieties must be 'distinct' or clearly distinguishable from previously known varieties and 'uniform' in the sense that their characteristics can be predictable and previously defined. Finally, these characteristics must be 'stable' over generations. Therefore, remarkable differences exist between the requirement for repeatability under patent law and the lower thresholds required by the uniformity and stability requirements under *sui generis* plant variety protection.

[27]   Article 6.1 of the UPOV Convention establishes that a variety shall be deemed to be new if the variety has not been sold by or with the consent of the breeder: earlier than one year before the date of application, within the territory of the contracting party in which the application has been filed; and earlier than four years or, in case of vines, earlier than six years before the said date, outside the territory of contracting parties.

[28]   Article 5.2 of the UPOV Convention.

Interestingly, neither the equivalent of utility/industrial application, nor inventive step/non-obviousness is required. Thus, no definite amount of human intervention is necessary in order to qualify for protection. Therefore, in principle, plant varieties, including plants growing in the wild, can be eligible for protection simply if they are distinct from earlier known species. However, the requirements for uniformity and stability in UPOV-type systems exclude from protection local varieties developed by farmers, because they are more heterogeneous genetically and less stable. But these characteristics are those that make them more productive under adverse and instable environmental conditions. Therefore, the definition of lower standards of protection may be beneficial for farmers in developing countries.

3.3.2 Agricultural exemptions under UPOV

Another aspect that differs from patent law is that PVP systems normally envisage the existence of agricultural exemptions. This is because plant breeding is an activity that is incremental in nature: innovations in agriculture necessarily depend on the availability of the widest possible range of germplasm. Thus, access to both unimproved PGRFA and improved plant varieties is extremely important.

Appropriate exceptions to exclusive rights are established under *sui generis* plant variety rights legislation. The 1978 UPOV Act contains two broad fundamental exceptions to breeders' rights:

- the breeders' exemption allows breeders to use protected varieties as the starting material for breeding new ones, without any authorization or payment of royalties; and
- the farmers' privilege allows farmers to retain seeds for their own use and for non-commercial exchange.

On the twenty-fifth anniversary of the UPOV Convention, on 2 December 1986, Heinz argued that 'the balance of national legislation needs to be reconsidered in the light of profound mutation of all kind'.[29] The allusion was to the fact that some breeders were not satisfied because, on the one hand, the advancement of science had made agricultural

---

[29]   A. Heitz (1986), 'The History of Plant Variety Protection', *The First Twenty-Five Years of the International Convention for the Protection of New Varieties of Plants*, Geneva, Switzerland: UPOV, at pp. 53–96.

research more costly and, on the other, both the legal and biological protections had become easier to circumvent.

From the 1980s, on account of the rapid evolution of modern DNA recombinant technologies, the mapping and characterization of genomic information and the selection and modification of targeted genes have become routine subject to adequate financial resources.[30] This technological progress has increased the likelihood that the biotechnological insertion of genes with little added value into the germplasm of protected plant varieties be sufficient for the 'inventor' to claim patent protection.

Heitz expressed concerns regarding the changes to be introduced in the UPOV Convention in response to the above situation as follows:

> Should one, under such circumstances, extend breeders' rights beyond the exclusivity of mere marketing of seed and seedlings? And how is the resulting balance to be reconciled with the absolute necessity, which the founders of the 1961 Convention had duly taken into account, for developing countries to protect their self-supporting agriculture, of at least enable it to be modernised gently?[31]

The adoption of amendments to the UPOV Convention in 1991 extended the scope of protection beyond the propagating material of protected varieties to include also 'essentially derived varieties'.[32] This concept was introduced in the UPOV Convention as a bulwark to protect breeders against forms of 'cosmetic modifications' and plagiarism. However, the new legal regime does not impose limits on access to protected plant varieties for research and breeding.

According to Article 15.1 of the 1991 UPOV Act, neither the authorization of the right-holder nor the payment of royalties is required when acts involving the use of protected varieties are 'done for the purpose of breeding other varieties'. Acts done 'privately and for non-commercial purposes' or 'for experimental purposes' are also exempted. Two major implications can be identified. On the one hand, the plant

---

[30]   J. Donnenwirth *et al.* (2004), 'Intellectual Property Rights, Patents, Plant Variety Protection and Contracts: A perspective from the Private Sector', *IP Strategy Today*, No. 9, at pp. 26–9.

[31]   A. Heitz (1986), above note 29.

[32]   Article 14.5 of the 1991 UPOV Act. The exploitation of an essentially derived variety requires the authorization of the title-holder, who owns the variety from which the former is derived. The essential derivation criterion is met when the essential characteristics of the first plant are replicated in the second one. J. Watal (2000), above note 19, at pp. 142–3.

breeders' exemption is preserved intact. However, the authorization of the breeder of the 'original' variety as well as some economic compensation is required when a new 'essentially derived' variety is commercialized.[33]

On the other hand, the diffusion of improved varieties by farmers is restricted.[34] The 1991 UPOV Act limits the farmers' privilege to save seeds for replanting, and requires farmers to limit the amount of saved-seeds or to pay an equitable remuneration to the right-holder.[35] In addition, the informal sale and offer for sale of protected varieties is outside the scope of such privilege, because plant breeders' rights may only be limited 'to permit farmers to use for propagating, on their own holdings, the product of the harvest obtained by planting, on their own holdings, the protected varieties.'[36]

3.4 PLANT INTELLECTUAL PROPERTY PROTECTION IN EUROPE AND NORTH AMERICA

This section focuses on the North American and European legal experiences concerning the protection of plant-related innovation. In particular, this comparative analysis centres on the interface between patent and plant variety rights protection and shows a progressive restriction of agricultural exemptions in these jurisdictions.[37]

The regional focus is on Europe and North America because both have pursued the objective and to a large extent obtained that developing

---

[33] Whether or not a variety is essentially derived from a protected one is matter which is left to courts and it is not assessed by examiners in Plant Varieties Protection Offices.

[34] M.C. Correa (2000), *Intellectual Property Rights, The WTO and Developing Countries: The TRIPs Agreement and Policy Options*, London and New York: Zed Books, at pp. 195–8.

[35] The farmers' privilege is allowed at the option of UPOV member states 'within reasonable limits and subject to the safeguarding of the legitimate interests of the breeder'. Article 15 of the 1991 UPOV Act.

[36] Article 15.2 of the 1991 UPOV Act.

[37] Historically, *sui generis* plant variety rights legislation provides for a broad breeders' exemption that is necessary to preserve open access to breeding materials. On the contrary, the research exemption in patent statutes is rather narrow, and when patents and plant variety rights overlap, the breeders' exemption may not be invoked as a defence against patent infringement. The same applies to the seed-saving farmers' privilege, which normally does not appear in patent legislation. However, the 1998 Biotechnology Directive makes an exception in so far it has recognized such privilege.

countries (at various stages of development) harmonize their IP legislation on the protection of biotechnological inventions and plant varieties in accordance with higher standards that are typical of the former.

In particular, both the US and the European Union have painstakingly tried to export their models of IP protection globally. They have made significant progress in achieving this goal, the most remarkable success being the inclusion in 1994 of the protection of IPRs in the WTO Trade-Related Agenda.[38] Therefore, this comparative analysis illustrates the way in which countries that are innovators in agriculture have designed their IPR systems to encourage investment in R&D and biotechnology transfer in their countries.

Another reason to focus on countries, which have already implemented strong restrictions on access to PGRFA, is that the monetary benefits, which should flow to the FAO Multilateral System of Access and Benefit Sharing, depend precisely on the existence of such restrictions. Against this backdrop, the interface between the scope of biotechnological patents and plant breeders' rights (PBRs), and the legal issues arising from such coexistence are also analysed.[39]

In sum, the interface problem depends on the extent to which the breeders' and farmers' exemptions are recognized within the patent system as legitimate limitations of the patent holder's rights. In every jurisdiction, the practical solutions given to the interface problem determine whether a product that is PGRFA can be made available to others for further research and breeding. If such patented product cannot be made available without restrictions—as it is usually the case—a compulsory benefit-sharing payment to the financial mechanism established under Article 19.3(f) of the ITPGRFA is due when such product is commercialized.[40]

---

[38]　The US and European foreign policies on IPRs have been criticized for entailing 'the one-dimensional task of pursuing the economic interest ...' that these countries and their '... technology companies have in a strong, global patent system'. M.R.Taylor and J. Cayford (2003), 'American Patent Policy, Biotechnology and African Agriculture: The Case for Policy Changes', RFF Report (November 2003).

[39]　The *nature* of the interface problem is different in the US and in the EU because the demarcation between the two systems is dissimilar. However, in both cases, agricultural innovations are subject to concurrent forms of protection. Therefore, the different *approaches* that are used to solve the interface problem are examined.

[40]　See below Chapter 4, at section 4.2.1.2.

3.4.1   Cumulative protection of plant varieties in the US

In North America, recent case law has recognized the need to ensure full protection to patent holders against the privileges enjoyed by plant breeders and farmers under concurrent forms of *sui generis* plant variety protection.[41] Therefore, when plant germplasm falls within the scope of patent claims, the legitimate experimental use of such genetic material is restricted and a licence from the patent owner may be required. Likewise, when protected seeds are replanted a royalty has to be paid to the patent-holder.

Utility patents, plant patents and plant variety rights are cumulatively available in the US.[42] Thus, the US legal system provides three statutory schemes of IP protection for plant-related innovation.

3.4.1.1   *The 1930 Plant Patent Act*

The 1930 Plant Patent Act (PPA) was the first system to be specifically designed for the protection of plants.[43] In particular, it provides 'patent-like protection' for asexually reproduced plants other than tuber-propagated plants or plants found in an uncultivated state.[44] The requirements for protection are novelty, distinctiveness and non-obviousness. This means that protection can be granted only if the plant presents characteristics that make it different from any extant known variety. The applicant must provide the examiner with a graphic representation of the plant in order to substantiate the claimed differences.

The plant patentee has the right to exclude everyone else from asexually reproducing the plant or using, offering for sale and selling plants

---

[41]   See, for instance, the decision of the US Supreme Court in *Monsanto Co. v McFarling*, 302 F.3d 1291, 1299, 64 USPQ 2d 1161, 1166 (Fed. Cir. 2002), and the decision of the Supreme Court of Canada in *Monsanto Canada Inc. v Schmeiser*, [2004] 1 SCR 902; (2004), 239 DLR (4th) 271; 31 CPR (4th) 161; 320 NR 201; 2004 SCC 34.

[42]   In *J.E.M. Ag Supply Inc. v Pioneer Hi-Bred International*, 534 US 124 (2001), the US Supreme Court confirmed the compatibility of utility patents with concurrent plant-specific IP regimes.

[43]   The US Congress, with the enactment of this piece of legislation, intended 'to afford agriculture ... the same opportunity to participate in the benefits of the patent system as has been given to industry ...'. Senate Report No. 315 71st Cong. 2nd Sess. (1930).

[44]   35 USC at Sections 161–164; and S.D. Chisum (1978), *Chisum on Patents*, New York, US: Matthew Bender, at Vol. 1, Sec. 1.05[1].

asexually derived from the patented variety. As a consequence, the burden of proof in case of infringement is relatively high because the patent holder must demonstrate that the infringing variety has been *actually* derived from the protected one. Therefore, the independent breeding of a similar variety does not constitute infringement.[45] Moreover, US jurisprudence neither applies the 'doctrine of equivalents' to plant inventions protected by the PPA, nor does the PPA provide for a mechanism to expand the scope of protection, for example through the use of the concept of 'essential derivation' included in the 1991 UPOV Act.

Notwithstanding the name, little similarity exists between the legal regime that applies to plant patents and utility patents for plant-related inventions.[46] Thus, the nature and characteristics of the rights conferred by the PPA may be considered a hybrid form of protection that is more akin to a *sui generis* system than to utility patents.[47]

3.4.1.2   The 1970 Plant Variety Protection Act

In 1970, the Plant Variety Protection Act (PVPA) was enacted to provide plant breeders with intellectual property protection for 'sexually propagated or tuber propagated plant varieties'.[48] Plant varieties are eligible for protection when they are new, distinct, uniform and stable.[49]

The PVPA states that plant varieties must be new:

> ... in the sense that, on the date of filing of the application for plant variety protection, propagating or harvested material of the variety has not been sold, or otherwise disposed of, to other persons, by or with the consent of the breeder, or the successor in interest of the breeder, for purposes of exploitation of the variety (A) in the United States, more than 1 year prior to the date of filing; or (B) in any area outside the United States (i) more than 4 years prior to

---

[45]   See the US Court of Appeals for the Federal Circuit decision, *Imazio Nursery v Dania Greenhouses*, 69 F. 3d 1560, 36 USPQ 2d 1673 (CAFC 1995).

[46]   V. Henson-Apollonio (2002), 'Patent Protection for Plant Material', paper given at the WIPO-UPOV Symposium I, at p. 2.

[47]   C.R. McManis (2002), 'Are There TRIPs-Compliant Measures for a Balanced Co-existence of Patents and Plant Breeders' Rights? Some Lessons from the U.S. Experience to Date', paper given at the WIPO-UPOV Symposium I.

[48]   7 USC Section 2402(a) and 7 USC Section 2401(a)(9) (2000) define plant variety as 'a plant grouping within a single botanical taxon of the lowest known rank'.

[49]   Ibid. Section 2404.

the date of filing; or (ii) in the case of a tree or vine, more than 6 years prior to the date of filing.[50]

A variety must be distinct 'in the sense that the variety is clearly distinguishable from any other variety the existence of which is publicly known or a matter of common knowledge at the time of the filing of the application'.[51] The PVPA also provides a statutory definition of distinctness, which 'may be based on one or more identifiable morphological, physiological, or other characteristics (including any characteristics evidenced by processing or product characteristics) with respect to which a difference in genealogy may contribute evidence'.[52]

It must also be uniform, 'in the sense that any variations are describable, predictable, and commercially acceptable',[53] and stable, 'in the sense that the variety, when reproduced, will remain unchanged with regard to the essential and distinctive characteristics of the variety with a reasonable degree of reliability commensurate with that of varieties of the same category in which the same breeding method is employed'.[54]

The PVP certificate holder has the right to exclude others from selling, offering for sale, reproducing, importing, exporting, propagating and conditioning for the purpose of propagating the protected variety.[55] However, the farmers' saved seed exemption is retained to a larger extent than that allowed by the European Community Plant Variety Right Regulation. Actually, farmers can replant saved seeds on their own holdings without further limitations. However, in 1994 an amendment prohibited the selling of saved seeds.

In accordance with the 1991 UPOV Act, the private use of protected varieties does not constitute an infringing act under the PVPA.[56] Besides, a relatively broad research exemption allows breeders to use protected varieties for breeding new ones with some limitations deriving from the 'essential derivation' criteria.[57] Moreover, compulsory licences can be granted in the public interest by the US Department of Agriculture (USDA) for a two-year period.[58]

---

[50]   Ibid. Section 2402(a)(1).
[51]   Ibid. Section 2402(a)(2).
[52]   Ibid. Section 2401(b)(5).
[53]   Ibid. Section 2402(a)(3).
[54]   Ibid. Section 2402(a)(4).
[55]   Ibid. Section 2422(4).
[56]   Ibid. Section 2541(e).
[57]   Ibid. Section 2544 and Plant Variety Protection Act Amendments of 1994, Pub. L. No. 103–341, 108 Stat. 3136–7.
[58]   Ibid. Section 2404.

3.4.1.3   Utility patents and plant-related inventions

Finally, the US Patent and Trademark Office (USPTO) has started granting utility patents for plant-related inventions under 35 USC Section 101, which states: 'Whoever invents or discover any new and useful process, machinery, manufacture, or composition of matter, or any new and useful improvement thereof, may obtain a patent therefore, subject to the conditions and requirements of this title.'[59]

The possibility of obtaining an intellectual property right in the form of a patent on a living organism was not obvious until the 1980s. In the *Diamond v Chakrabarty* case, the US Supreme Court held that a living genetically-modified micro-organism could be regarded as a patentable invention under 35 USC Section 101.[60] The issue under discussion was whether a human-made micro-organism could fall within the scope of patentable subject matter as a 'manufacture' or 'composition of matter'. The Supreme Court clarified that 'the relevant distinction was not between living and inanimate things, but between products of nature, whether living or not, and human made inventions'. After *Diamond v Chakrabarty*, the USPTO decided to grant the first utility patent for a sexually reproduced plant in the 1985 *Ex parte Hibberd* case.[61]

More recently, the US Supreme Court has specifically decided a case in which the interface problem between different protection schemes is addressed. In *J.E.M. Ag Supply Inc. v Pioneer Hi-Bred International*, Pioneer Hi-Bred, a subsidiary of DuPont, filed a suit against the defendant, who was accused of having sold and offered for sale patented corn seeds in violation of the terms of the licence signed with the plaintiff.[62] According to the licence any use of the product other than the production of food or feed was prohibited.

The alleged infringer counterclaimed that Pioneer Hi-Bred's patents were invalid by making the argument that plants were outside the scope of the patentable subject matter under Section 101. The reason for that being that the Congress' intention was to provide plants with specific and exclusive regimes of protection, namely the PPA for asexually reproduced plants and the PVPA for sexually reproduced plants. The Supreme Court

---

[59]   35 USC 101.

[60]   447 US 303, 206 USPQ 193 (1980); and S.D. Chisum (1978), above note 44, Sec. 1.02[7][d].

[61]   227 USPQ 443 (Bd. Pat. App. & Int., 1985); and ibid., at Section 1.02[7][d][iii].

[62]   534 US 124 (2001).

eventually held that utility patents can be granted for plant inventions and are compatible with plant-specific IPR regimes.

3.4.2 Concurrent protection for plant varieties in Europe

In Europe, three pieces of legislation delineate the legal framework that applies to the protection of plant-related innovations: the 1973 European Patent Convention, Directive 98/44/EC on the Legal Protection of Biotechnological Inventions (the Biotechnology Directive), and Council Regulation 2100/94/CE on Community Plant Variety Rights.[63]

The Community system of plant variety rights came into effect on 27 April 1995. The Community Plant Variety Office (CPVO) can grant a unique and uniform intellectual property right protecting plant varieties.[64] This form of protection is valid throughout the whole territory of the member states. The enlarged EU has implemented a model of legislation compliant with the 1991 UPOV Act, although it retains the prohibition of double protection contained in the 1978 UPOV Act. Actually, Article 1 of Regulation 2100/94/EC provides for 'a system of Community plant variety rights ... as the sole and exclusive form of Community industrial property rights for plant varieties'.

The EU system for plant variety protection coexists with national *sui generis* regimes. In particular, Article 3 of Regulation 2100/94/EC preserves 'the right of Members States to grant national property rights for plant varieties'. However, once a Community plant variety right is granted, national plant variety rights cannot be invoked. To this effect, Article 92 of Regulation 2100/94/EC prohibits cumulative protection with respect to both patents and national plant breeders' rights.

Thus, in Europe, plant varieties can formally constitute eligible subject matter of protection only under plant variety right legislation. However, according the authoritative opinion expressed by a Member of the Boards of Appeal of the European Patent Office, 'the European legal framework does not draw a clear demarcation between the two systems of protection and the overlap area remains broad.'[65] This lack of clarity originates from the fact that a growing number of patented inventions are 'embedded'

---

[63] The Biotechnology Directive is incorporated into the EPC by r. 23 b (1) EPC. OJ L 213 of 30.7.1998, at pp. 13–21. As regards Council Regulation 2100/94/CE, see: OJ L 227 of 01.09.94, at p.1.

[64] The CPVO is based in Angers, France, and its examination procedure is established by Regulation 1239/95/CE.

[65] R. Moufang (2003), 'The Interface between Patents and Plant Variety Rights in Europe', paper given at the WIPO–UPOV Symposium II; and R. Pavoni

into the germplasm of plant varieties protected by plant breeders' rights due to the rapid spread of modern biotechnological breeding techniques based on recombinant DNA methods.

Therefore, in a number of cases, even if plant varieties cannot qualify *per se* as patentable subject matter under the European Patent Convention and the 1998 Biotechnology Directive, the scope of protection granted to biotechnological inventions may encompass plant varieties.[66]

In particular, European Patent Law has evolved in a way that allows the express prohibition on the patenting of plant varieties to be overcome when the technical feasibility of the invention is not confined to a specific plant variety. In the 1999 *Transgenic Plant/NOVARTIS II* decision, the Enlarged Board of Appeal stated: 'A patent shall not be granted for a single plant variety but can be granted if varieties may fall within the scope of its claims.'[67] In other words, Article 53(b) of the EPC cannot be used to exclude the patenting of plants if specific plant varieties are not mentioned in the claims.

The 'more-than-a-single-variety approach' adopted in this decision is consistent with the 1998 Biotechnology Directive. In particular, Article 4.2 of the Directive states that plant inventions shall be patentable if the technical feasibility of the invention is not confined to a particular plant variety. This provision should be read along with Recital 31, which states:

> A plant grouping which is characterised by a particular gene (and not its whole genome) is not covered by the protection of new varieties and is therefore not excluded from patentability even if it comprises new varieties of plants.

(2000), 'Brevettabilità Genetica e Protezione della Biodiversità: la Giurisprudenza dell'Ufficio Europeo dei Brevetti', *Rivista di Diritto Internazionale* 83/2, 463.

[66]   Article 53(b) of the European Patent Convention provides that plant or animal varieties or essentially biological processes for the production of plants and animals do not constitute patentable inventions. In particular, in 1995, the EPO Board of Appeal maintained that: 'a product claim which embraces within its subject-matter plant varieties ... is not patentable'. *Plant Cells/Plant Genetic Systems,* T 356/93, OJ EPO 1995, 545, at para. 24; *Novartis AG,* T 1054/96, OJ EPO, 1998, 511, which states: 'In the view of the exception permitted under Article 27.3(b), the Board cannot see any possibility of conflict between the contracting States obligations under TRIPs and the provision of the EPC.' RICCARDO PAVONI, *'Brevettabilità Genetica E Protezione Della Biodiversità: La Giurisprudenza Dell'ufficio Europeo Dei Brevetti'*, (See also Article 4(1)(a) and (b) of the Directive 98/44/EC on the Legal Protection of Biotechnological Invention.

[67]   G 0001/98, OJ 2000,111.

As a result, the excluded material is only that which is protected by the UPOV Convention. Thus, huge differences exist between the level and scope of protection required by the European Patent Convention and that required by the 1998 Biotechnology Directive. For, this Directive goes well beyond the EPC, maintaining that plants, animals and their separate parts are eligible for patent protection.[68]

Plant varieties may also fall within the scope of patent claims when they are the direct product of a patented non-biological process. Such protection is mandatory under the TRIPs Agreement. For example, this is the case of a process patent that claims a non-essentially biological process for the production of plants. Finally, another relevant case may occur when a patented DNA sequence has been introduced in a plant variety in which it functions.[69] To conclude, in Europe the friction between plant variety protection and biotechnological patents may be no less intense than in the US.[70]

3.4.3   Experimental use exemption under patent law

In the area where the patent system and the PVP system interplay, the imbalance in their relative strength has several implications. The highest level of protection afforded by patents for biotechnological inventions threatens the existence and weakens the functionality of the breeders' exemption, which is an essential feature of any *sui generis* PVP system. The previous section pointed out that a compulsory breeders' exemption is set out under the 1991 UPOV Act, which provides the highest existing level of *sui generis* protection within the meaning of Article 27.3(b) of the TRIPs Agreement. This exemption significantly differs from the research exemption narrowly construed under patent law.

3.4.3.1   *Experimental use exemption in the US*

In the US, neither the US Patent Act provides for an applicable statutory research exemption, nor has a common law doctrine been construed allowing for a similar exception to override the rights granted to patent holders. The only statutory exemption in US law is the Hatch Waxman Act of 1984.[71] However, this exemption specifically applies only to

---

[68]   J. Watal (2000), above note 19, at pp. 153–4.
[69]   Article 9 of the Biotechnology Directive 98/44/EC.
[70]   R. Moufang (2003), above note 65, at p. 3.
[71]   (1984) 'Drug Price Competition and Patent Term Restoration Act', Public Law, 98–417 at Section 505(j) 21 USC 355(j).

experiments carried out on drugs or medical devices for the purpose of obtaining the Food and Drug Administration (FDA) approval.

In addition to the above statutory exemption, the US jurisprudence has crafted a common law defence in extremely narrow terms in the wake of the leading case *Madey v Duke University.*[72] In this case, the Court of Appeals for the Federal Circuit held that:

> Regardless of whether a particular institution or entity is engaged in an endeavour for commercial gain, so long as the act is in furtherance of the alleged infringer's legitimate business and is not solely for amusement, to satisfy idle curiosity, or for strictly philosophical inquiry, the act does not qualify for the very narrow and strictly limited experimental use defence. Moreover, the profit or non-profit status of the user is not determinative.[73]

Therefore, the experimental use exemption can hardly be invoked against the alleged infringement of patent rights over germplasm used in breeding programmes, regardless of their public or private nature. Thus, in the US, a licence agreement with the patentee is in any case required for gaining access to proprietary germplasm protected by a patent.

3.4.3.2 Experimental use exemption in the EU

In Europe, the existence of a research use exemption is a matter that is regulated by national patent laws. However, Article 27(b) of the Community Patent Convention (CPC) exempts 'acts done for experimental purposes relating to the subject matter of the patented invention'. Although the CPC was never given legal effect, a certain degree of harmonisation has been achieved through the members states' legislations.

In general, national laws provide some form of general research exemption, especially with respect to activities the result of which is to make improvements to a patented invention.[74] However, it is not clear the extent to which proprietary plant germplasm can be used for breeding purposes without an authorization from the patent holder. For instance, Moufang argues that the existence of a general research exemption 'does not mean that automatically all plant breeding activities will be exempted

---

    [72]   S.R. Eisenberg (2003), 'Patent Swords and Shields', *Science,* Vol. 299; and 64 USPQ2d 1737 (Fed. Cir. 2002).

    [73]   Ibid.

    [74]   T. Cook (2006), 'Responding to Concerns about the Scope of the Defence from Patent Infringement for Acts Done for Experimental Purposes relating to the Subject Matter of the Invention', *Intellectual Property Quarterly,* 3, 193–222.

from patent infringement'.[75] Instead, Straus expresses the opposite view that all breeding activities that are not prohibited under the CPVR Regulation should remain lawful also when patent protection applies to plant materials.[76] Thus, future case law is required to clarify the boundaries of existing exemptions.

3.4.4   The interface between patents and plant variety rights

The interface problem is now examined: how should patent claims that extend to plants affect the exercise of agricultural exemptions afforded by plant breeders' rights legislation? Two main approaches have been identified to address this issue.[77]

3.4.4.1   *North American approach to the interface problem*

According to the approach that characterizes US legislation, the interaction between utility patents and plant variety rights does not represent a problem. The traditional principle of independence between different IPR systems is deemed sufficient to strike an appropriate balance between these rights. Therefore, no special interface provision is required to regulate potential conflicts between different IPR regimes in the grey areas of the system.

Underpinning the principle of independence between IPRs is the assumption that these regimes confer only the right to exclude. Thus, all acts that do not expressly require the authorization of the title-holder can be freely performed with respect to the subject matter of protection. However, in the specific case of plant varieties, activities that are not prohibited under plant variety rights legislation can nonetheless infringe a patent, because the rights conferred by the latter are granted under a different protection scheme.

In North America, the peculiar situation resulting from cumulative IP protection for plant varieties is exemplified by the outcomes of two law suits involving *Monsanto Company* and respectively an American and a

---

[75]   See R. Moufang (2003), above note 65, at p. 6.

[76]   J. Straus (2002), 'Measures Necessary for the Balanced Co-existence of Patents and Plant Breeders' Rights—A Predominantly European view', paper given at the WIPO–UPOV Symposium I, at p. 8.

[77]   The Crucible II Group (2001), *Seedling Solutions. Options for National Laws Governing Control over Genetic Resources and Biological Innovations*, Vol. 2, Ottawa, ON: International Development Research Institute, IPGRI and Dag Hammarskjöld Foundation, at pp. 232–5.

Canadian commercial farmer. In the 2002 *Monsanto Co. v McFarling* decision, the Federal Circuit held that 'the right to save seed of plants registered under the PVPA does not impart the right to save seed of plant patented under the Patent Act'.[78]

The above decision was preceded by the 1998 *Percy Schmeiser v Monsanto Canada* case. In that case, a lawsuit was brought against a Canadian farmer by *Monsanto Canada* with the allegation that the farmer was infringing a Canadian patent owned by Monsanto US. The alleged infringing act was the cultivation of the company's 'Roundup Ready' canola without a licence.[79] This product, which is a genetically modified oilseed rape with herbicide tolerance, contains genes and cells claimed in the patent.

Mr Schmeiser's defence was based on the arguments that: 1) he was cultivating his own traditionally bred canola strains; 2) he made an extremely limited use of chemical herbicides; and 3) he did not knowingly acquire transgenic Monsanto seeds. He also argued that if the crops in his field were to be found to contain the technology patented by Monsanto, this was due to contamination by means of 'cross field breeding by wind or insects, seeds blowing by passing trucks, or dropping from farm equipment, or swaths blown from neighbours' fields'.

During the trial, experiments conducted by experts showed that 95–98 per cent of Mr Schmeiser's fields were planted with 'Roundup Ready' canola. The court held that:

- the case under question should be decided as a matter of patent law;
- the patent was valid and compatible with the Plant Breeders' Right Act;
- Mr Schmeiser, 'by growing seed known to be Roundup tolerant and selling the harvested seed', was guilty of making 'use of the invention without the permission of the plaintiff'.

The Federal Court of Appeal upheld the first instance decision. After that, Mr Schmeiser appealed to the Supreme Court.[80] In the final decision, the patent was held to be valid and Mr Schmeiser's use of

---

[78] 64 USPQ2d 1161, 1166.

[79] For a detailed account and analysis of this case see: P. Cullet (2005), 'Monsanto v Schmeiser: A Landmark Decision concerning Farmer Liability and Transgenic Contamination: Monsanto Canada Inc. v. Schmeiser', *Journal of Environmental Law,* 17/1, 83–108.

[80] See the Supreme Court of Canada decision of 21 May 2004, SCC 34, 239 DLR (4th) 271, 320 NR 201, [2004] 1 SCR 902.

patented cells and genes was qualified as an infringing act. An injunction was also granted against Mr Schmeiser, which prevented him from planting, growing, cultivating, harvesting, selling, marketing or distributing 'Roundup Ready' canola. However, the Supreme Court held that 'the award for account of profits had to be set aside' for the lack of evidence and 'causal connection between the profits the defendant were found to have earned through growing the herbicide resistant canola and the invention'.

Another relevant decision is *Monsanto Co. v Scruggs* by the US Court of Appeal for the Federal Circuit.[81] This patent litigation case involved the alleged infringement of Monsanto's patents that cover Roundup Ready soybeans and cotton. The facts of the case are that Scruggs initially purchased Roundup Ready soybean and cotton form seed companies without signing a licence agreement, as required by Monsanto.[82] After harvesting the plants, he replanted the seeds obtained from the harvest.

During the trial, Scruggs *inter alia*: denied infringement, sought a declaration of invalidity of such patents, and invoked the doctrine exhaustion. On appeal, the district court's summary judgment of infringement was upheld on several grounds. The Federal Circuit rejected Scruggs' argument that the patent claims did not read on his plants. Besides, it deemed inapplicable the first sale's patent exhaustion doctrine because:

> The new seeds grown from the original batch had never been sold. […] Without the actual sale of the second generation seed to Scruggs, there can be no patent exhaustion. The fact that a patented technology can replicate itself does not give a purchaser the right to use replicated copies of the technology. Applying the first sale doctrine to subsequent generations of self-replicating technology would eviscerate the rights of the patent holder.[83]

Another interesting aspect of this decision regards the Federal Circuit's rejection of Scruggs' assertion that Monsanto's licensing practices 'violate federal and state antitrust laws, and constitute patent misuse'. In particular, 'Monsanto's grower license agreements include an exclusivity

---

[81]   *Monsanto Co. v Scruggs, et al,* 459 F.3d 1328 (Fed. Cir. 2006).
[82]   In particular, 'Monsanto's restrictions on seed growers include: (1) requiring growers to use only seed containing Monsanto's biotechnology for planting a single crop ("exclusivity provision"); (2) prohibiting transfer or re-use of seed containing the biotechnology for replanting ("no replant policy"); (3) prohibiting research or experimentation ("no research policy"); and (4) requiring payment of a "technology fee".' Ibid. at p. 3.
[83]   Ibid. at pp. 8–9.

provision, a no replant policy, a no research policy, and the payment of a technology fee'.[84] In its decision, the Federal Circuit held that Monsanto's ...

> ... no replant policy simply prevents purchasers of the seeds from using the patented biotechnology when that biotechnology makes a copy of itself. This restriction therefore is a valid exercise of its rights under the patent laws. ... The no research policy is a field of use restriction and is also within the protection of the patent laws.[85]

Thus, in the US and Canada, when plant germplasm falls within the scope of patent claims, the legitimate experimental use of genetic material is restricted and a licence from the patent owner is required. Those who advocate this approach argue that it presents advantages in terms of legal certainty and strong *ex ante* incentives for private corporations to engage in agricultural R&D. However, drawbacks are not missing. One of them, is that the 'freedom to operate' in agricultural research is restricted.

3.4.4.2   IP management responses from international agricultural research

In the past, much of the patented inventions generated by public sector research institutions have been licensed under terms that did not allow the licensor to retain the rights to use these technologies to benefit the public at large. Besides, the ownership structure of the public sector IP is highly fragmented across many institutions[86] and several formal and non-statutory IP rights may be associated with improved varieties and breeding materials and processes in different jurisdictions.

Non-statutory IP rights may comprise, for instance:

> ... all unpatented inventions (whether or not patentable), trade secrets, know-how and proprietary information, including but not limited to (in whatever form or medium), discoveries, ideas, compositions, formulae, computer programs, ... databases, drawings, designs, plans, proposals, specifications, photographs, samples, models, processes, procedures, data, information,

---

[84]   Ibid. at p. 15.

[85]   Ibid at p. 17–18.

[86]   The public-sector IP portfolio in agricultural biotechnology accounts approximately for one-fourth of the IP in this research sector worldwide. D.G. Graff *et al.* (2003), 'The Public-Private Structure of Intellectual Property Ownership in Agricultural Biotechnology', *Nature Biotechnology*, Vol. 21, No. 9–2003.

manuals, reports, financial, marketing and business data, pricing and costing information ...[87]

They can also derive from the conditions embodied in material transfer agreements used to access plant genetic resources or other contractual obligations. The stringent enforcement of patent rights and the absence of interface provisions in the US has triggered various responses from public sector institutions, whose aim is to create institutional mechanisms to provide awareness on prior art and advice on the negotiation of licence agreements.

A paradigmatic example is that of the CGIAR International Agricultural Research Centres, which are currently facing the challenge of improving their capability to manage IPRs in a complex legal and policy environment.[88] For instance, the development of tools to identify and evaluate the status of self-generated IP assets will put CGIAR Centres in a better position to assess their current degree of freedom in different jurisdictions and their effective need to enter into partnership agreements with commercial entities and other research institutions.[89] The establishment of the Central Advisory Service (CAS) on Intellectual Property addresses these IPR-related concerns. The IPR audits carried out by CAS originally focused on third parties' proprietary IP inputs used by the Centres. However, the 'Revised 2003–2004 Plan of Work for CAS', whose eloquent title is 'Turning the Corner' calls on Centres to take a step

---

[87] 'Intellectual Property Ownership and Cross License Agreement', Find Law for Legal Professionals, available at: http://contracts.corporate.findlaw.com/ agreements/genuity/gte.ip.html (accessed 1 October 2009).

[88] Chapter 4, at section 4.2.2.

[89] A comprehensive study has been commissioned by the CGIAR on the use of other institutions' proprietary biological material and related information. A survey made up by 90 questions has been issued to the 15 International Agricultural Research Centres that form part of the CGIAR and the three Challenge Programmes. A first analysis of the results signals the 'present and possible future use of proprietary biological materials and related information', and considers 'how this may affect the conditions for the CGIAR Centres to produce international public goods'. C.G. Thornström (2005), 'Producing International Public Goods in a Proprietary Science World—The CGIAR Contribution', Bridges Monthly, 9 (1), available at: http://ictsd.net/downloads/ bridges/bridges9–1.pdf (accessed on 10 June 2006); C.G. Thornström (2005), 'Public Research in the Context of Proprietary Science—The Case of the Consultative Group on International Agricultural Research', paper given at Workshop on the Globalisation of Agricultural Biotechnology: Multi-Disciplinary Views from the South, 11–13 March 2005.

forward and to better identify and enhance self-generated IP assets in order to capitalize and distribute the results of their research efforts.[90]

Besides, collaborative experiences may be helpful to avoid the use of technologies that are not freely accessible. Even though the effectiveness of these approaches has not been tested fully in the realm of biosciences, they express the need for legal mechanisms that may be able to ensure that the use of plant-related IP does not restrict access to the genetic pool to the extent that incremental innovation is discouraged.

In the scientific community, it is debated how collaborative experiences between public–public and public–private organizations can provide biologists with freely available platforms of key technologies to overcome the problems that derive from the fragmentation of IP ownership. At least, two cutting-edge initiatives must be mentioned.

The first one is called Public Sector Intellectual Property Resource for Agriculture (PIPRA), an initiative promoted by a network of US elite universities, foundations and non-profit research institutions.[91] Its principal aim is 'to make agricultural technologies more easily available for development and distribution of subsistence crops for humanitarian purposes in the developing world'. In July 2004, PIPRA established its headquarters at Davis, University of California, in the US. A 'collective IP management strategy' is currently being developed by PIPRA and the purpose is to provide collaborative solutions to the public sector and small farmers in horticulture.[92]

The second experience draws inspiration from the open-source software movement and it is called BIOS, whose acronym stands for Biological Innovation for Open Society.[93] The leading institution is the Centre for the Application for Molecular Biology to International Agriculture (CAMBIA), a non-profit institute located in Canberra, Australia. The purpose of the BIOS initiative is to promote the application of biological technologies in a more democratic way to respond to the neglected needs of poor. In doing so, it tries to reform biological innovation activities and to adapt the instruments of biotechnology to the widest possible sphere of

---

[90]   CGIAR Central Advisory Service (CAS) on Intellectual Property (2002), 'Revised 2003–2004 Plan of Work for CAS—Turning the Corner'.

[91]   Public Sector Intellectual Property Resource for Agriculture (2003), 'Public Sector Collaboration for Agricultural IP Management', *Science,* Vol. 301, 174–5.

[92]   A. Krattiger *et al.* (eds) (2006), *Intellectual Property Management in Health and Agricultural Innovation. A Handbook of Best Practices*, Oxford, UK: PIPRA & MIHR.

[93]   The CAMBIA BIOS Initiative, 'Biological Innovation for Open Society', available at: www.bios.net/daisy/bios/bios/bios-initiative.html (accessed 10 November 2008).

diversified local conditions and priorities. The BIOS initiative is engaged in developing and validating 'new means for the cooperative invention, improvement and delivery of biological technologies'. The major donor of BIOS, the Rockefeller Foundation, is also funding PIPRA.

To conclude, the above initiatives have similar aims and their strategic objectives present many analogies, including: the sharing of IP data; the creation of patent pools; and the promotion of best licensing practices. However, their strategies on how to pursue these objectives may differ remarkably. With regard to access to biological innovation, PIPRA has emphasized the development of basic rules to share technologies among club members, while the BIOS initiative has privileged open access for all under conditions that guarantee open access to any improvements of the shared technologies and materials.

3.4.4.3 *European approach to the interface problem*

In Europe, the overlap between patents and plant variety rights may also conduce to problems related to the existence of legal restrictions on research and access to proprietary genetic materials. However, European plant-related IP law codifies specific interface rules to regulate such cases.

Thus, the European approach to the interface problem recognizes that the agricultural innovation system has functions that are broader than the mere creation of exclusive rights. Such rights may be subject to statutory exceptions and limitations that can be interpreted as self-standing positive rights. In particular, they may be invoked against the exclusive rights created by protection schemes different from those in which they usually operate. Two mechanisms have been devised in European law to determine the conditions under which agricultural exemptions may override the protection afforded by patents.

The first one is meant to ensure that the use of plant-related IP does not restrict access to the genetic pool to the extent that incremental innovation is discouraged. In particular, Article 12 of the 1998 Biotechnology Directive regulates a cross-compulsory licensing scheme between patents and plant variety rights. According to this scheme, breeders may obtain a non-exclusive compulsory licence for the use of a patented biotechnological invention when the acquisition or exploitation of plant variety rights would not be possible without infringing the patent. In such case, appropriate royalties must be paid to the patent holder. Moreover, as required by Article 31 of the TRIPs Agreement, the applicant must demonstrate that he has unsuccessfully applied for a contractual licence from the right holder and that the plant variety constitutes a 'significant technical progress of considerable economic interest' in comparison with the invention.

The above provision operates in combination with the compulsory exploitation right that is provided for in Article 29 of EC Regulation 2100/94 as amended by EC Regulation 873/2004. The conditions for the granting of compulsory exploitation rights have been modified because they were not entirely consistent with the 1998 Biotechnology Directive. Previously, it was envisaged that these conditions had to be grounded exclusively on the public interest, as required by the UPOV Convention. Now the 'significant technical progress of considerable economic interest' requirement has been taken over from patent law and applies in the context of the EC Regulation, too. Moreover, if the holder of a plant variety right has been granted a compulsory licence for the non-exclusive exploitation of a patented invention, a cross-licence under the same conditions can be granted to allow the patent holder to use the plant variety that contains the patented component.

Natural or legal persons can apply for a compulsory licence, including: private entities; member states; the European Commission; and any organization set up at the Community level and registered with the Commission. However, in accordance with Article 29.7 of EC Regulation 2100/94, the Community Plant Variety Office remains the only competent authority for grant of Community-wide plant variety rights. Moreover, the Administrative Council (which examines and controls all the activities of the CPVO) must be consulted before such decisions are taken.

The coverage of the licence may be limited to certain member states or extended to the whole territory of the Community. The CPVO may establish the acts permitted under the licence and fix reasonable conditions that take into account the interests of the right holder. These conditions may include time limitations and the payment of appropriate royalties and they may require the licence-holder to comply with certain obligations necessary for the effective exploitation of the licence. Moreover, if the circumstances underpinning the granting of the licence have changed after one year, any of the parties may request the cancellation or modification of the concerned decision.

However, if an appropriate research exemption is not included in the patent system, the compulsory cross-licensing scheme between biotechnological patents and plant variety rights might not create the expected balance between these two systems.[94] As explained above, under Article 31.1(i) of the TRIPs Agreement a compulsory licence can be

---

[94]   R. Jördens (2002), above note 22, at p. 7.

granted only if a new end-variety, which is bred using proprietary germplasm, constitutes 'an important technical advance of considerable economic significance' compared with the licensed technology. However, the above compulsory cross-licensing mechanism does not say anything about whether access to protected genetic materials during the development cycle is legitimate or not. Instead, it only operates once a new plant variety has been bred and its value determined. Besides, the proof that a new plant variety constitutes a 'significant technical progress' with respect to the patented invention that is used in it may be quite difficulty in practice.

To conclude, in Europe, some degree of flexibility for research conducted by using proprietary genetic materials is necessary to enable the provisions of the 1998 Biotechnology Directive and the Council Regulation on CPVR to be interpreted in accordance with their intended function. The mechanism described above has the potential to strike a balance between the protection of plant-related IP and the promotion of follow-on innovations, while providing an adequate reward to plant breeders.

The second mechanism provided for by the 1998 Biotechnology Directive in order to address the interface problem is to recognize the existence of a general right of farmers to replant saved seeds. Thus, the Directive extends the 'farm saved seed exemption' of Article 14 of EC Regulation 2100/94 beyond the scope of application of such Regulation. In particular, Article 11.1 of the Biotechnology Directive states that the sale or commercialization of plant-propagating materials for agricultural use 'implies authorization for the farmer to use the product of his harvest for propagation or multiplication by him on his own farm'.

The extent and conditions of this derogation correspond to those established in Article 14 of EC Regulation 2100/94. In particular, farmers can only replant seeds of the following agricultural species: fodder plants, cereals, potatoes, oil, and fibre plants. No quantitative restrictions are established. However, only small farmers are exempted from paying an equitable remuneration to the right-holder, while farmers who grow an area bigger than the area needed to produce 92 tons of cereals must pay a royalty 'sensibly lower' than the one normally charged by the title-holder. To conclude, in Europe the farmers' privilege operates in an identical manner irrespective of whether plant-propagating materials are protected by patents or plant variety rights.

3.4.4.4   *Responses from the private sector*

The interests of traditional plant breeders and those of agro-biotechnology companies do not converge as regards the question of the most desirable level of plant-related IP. This is because their IPR strategies adjust to different technologies and models of plant-related innovation.

Exponents of the biotechnology industry have argued that the UPOV Convention should be further strengthened. In particular, they have advanced the argument that an IP environment in which genes are strongly protected and plant varieties can be freely accessed for research and breeding encourages the creation of essential derived varieties with little added value.[95] According to the above proposition, strong IP protection for new plant varieties should promote investment in broad germplasm-development projects, instead of encouraging small genetic modifications on varieties that are already available.

They also allege that cross-licensing would curb any restrictions on the exchange of protected breeding materials. With stronger plant variety protection—the argument goes—more opportunities will arise to negotiate access to germplasm developed by other breeders.[96] Therefore, the initial genetic base from which improved varieties can be bred would not be narrowed down and the potential negative impact on agro-biodiversity should be avoided.

However, the majority of plant breeders who are represented by the International Seed Federation have expressed a different position. In particular, they believe that no amendment should be made to modify the 1991 UPOV Convention. During a Congress held in Bangalore, India, in June 2003, the International Seed Federation (ISF) adopted by a vast majority a Position Statement on Intellectual Property Rights, which states: 'ISF is strongly attached to the breeder's exception provided for in the UPOV Convention and is concerned that the extension of the protection of a gene sequence to the relevant plant variety itself could extinguish this exception.'[97]

In general, European plant breeders are against the use of compulsory licences. However, they suggest that a plant breeders' exemption, which

[95]   J. Donnenwirth *et al.* (2004), above note 30.

[96]   American Seed Trade Association (2004), 'Position Statement on Intellectual Property Rights for the Seed Industry'.

[97]   J.C. Gouache (2004), 'Balancing Access and Protection: Lessons from the Past to Built the Future', paper given at the ISF International Conference, 27–28 May 2004. The author calls for the full implementation of the UPOV Convention and underscores that when the experimental use of a protected variety is prevented, the concrete risk to 'lock up the genetic variability during the life of the patent' emerges. Therefore, the risk of creating monopolistic situations and slowing down genetic progress may increase. He also expresses concerns that the heterogeneity of granted claims over plant-related inventions in most cases does

could be drafted on the basis of those available under *sui generis* plant variety right legislation, should be introduced in the patent system.[98] At the international level, Article 30 of the TRIPs Agreement legitimizes the introduction of limited exceptions to the exclusive rights conferred by patents when certain conditions are met.[99] In *Canada—Patent Protection of Pharmaceutical Products*, the WTO Panel considered the interpretation of Article 30 of the TRIPs Agreement and the meaning of its limiting conditions.[100] In particular, it established that all three criteria which are specified in this Article must be met to qualify for an exception.[101] However, the TRIPs-compliant nature of plant-specific experimental use provisions can be also justified on the basis of Article 27.3(b), which expressly allows for the adoption of any combination between patents and *sui generis* plant variety rights.[102]

3.4.5   US and European foreign policies on plant intellectual property

US patent law policy is driven by the concern of boosting private investment in agricultural biotechnology research by providing strong *ex ante* innovation incentives. European countries seem to be more cautious in considering the effects of domestic patent law policy. However, in the field of external trade relations, Europeans are trying to emulate the US by demonstrating no less 'intellectual property fundamentalism' than the latter in many aspects of their foreign policies on IPRs.[103]

---

not reflect the differences in the nature of the inventive work of the breeder, but 'depend on the "creativity" of the patent attorney and on the reaction of the examiner'.

[98]   J. Straus (2002), above note 76, at p. 9; and M. Janis (2001), 'Sustainable Agriculture, Patent Rights, and Plant Innovation', *Indiana Law Review*, Vol. 9 /91.

[99]   Under 'Exceptions to the Rights Conferred', Article 30 of the TRIPs Agreement states: 'Members may provide limited exceptions to the exclusive rights conferred by a patent, provided that such exceptions do not unreasonably conflict with a normal exploitation of the patent and do not unreasonably prejudice the legitimate interests of the patent owner, taking account of the legitimate interests of third parties.'

[100]   WTO (2000), *Canada—Patent Protection of Pharmaceutical Products*, WT/DS114/R, WTO (17 March 2000).

[101]   'The three conditions are cumulative, each being a separate and independent requirement that must be satisfied. Failure to comply with any one of the three conditions results in the Article 30 exception being disallowed.' Ibid. at para. 7.20.

[102]   C.R. McManis (2002), above note 47, at p. 7.

[103]   G. Dutfield (2005), 'The US and Europe Are "Intellectual Property Fundamentalists"', Science and Development Network, available at: www.scidev.net/

The continuing controversy over the negotiations of the Substantive Patent Law Treaty (SPLT) in WIPO is just an example of the attitude of European countries, the US and Japan towards developing countries' requests to make the international IP standard setting-process more transparent and inclusive, and to integrate development goals in the WIPO agenda.[104]

Several countries are facing unprecedented pressure to adopt TRIPs-plus standards of IP protection that are included in bilateral and regional free trade and investment agreements. This pressure includes requests to:

- protect biotechnological inventions through patents;
- ratify the 1977 Budapest Treaty on the International Recognition of the Deposit of Micro-organisms for the Purposes of Patent Procedure; and
- ratify the 1991 UPOV Act for the protection of new plant varieties.

US trade negotiators have also made it routine to include provisions that require member countries to protect plant varieties through both plant breeders' rights and patents as, for instance, the Agreement establishing the Free Trade Area of Americas (FTAA).[105]

The immediate consequence of accepting similar TRIPs-plus obligations is to undermine the right of farmers 'to participate in making decisions on matters related to the conservation and sustainable use of plant genetic resources for food and agriculture' in accordance with Article 9 of the ITPGRFA. Developing countries that ratify agreements containing the above-mentioned IPR-related obligations curtail their freedom to comply with WTO–TRIPs standards in ways that are compatible with the promotion of societal objectives that can be in tension with the protection of biotechnological inventions.[106]

---

en/science-communication/opinions/the-us-and-europe-are-intellectual-property-funda.html (accessed 10 February 2009).

[104]   S. Musungu and G. Dutfield (2003), 'Multilateral Agreements and TRIPs-plus World: The World Intellectual Property Organization (WIPO)', TRIPs Issue Paper No. 3, Quaker United Nations Office and Quaker International Affairs Programme; and South Centre and CIEL IP Quarterly Update: Third Quarter 2004 and First Quarter 2005.

[105]   D. Vivas-Eugui (2003), 'Regional and Bilateral Agreements and a TRIPs-Plus World: The Free Trade Area of Americas (FTAA)', TRIPs Issue Paper No. 4, QUNO, QIAP and ICTSD.

[106]   A 2004 FAO study on IPRs in plant varieties has identified six policy objectives which require to be balanced with patent and PBRs protection. They are: 1) the conservation of genetic diversity; 2) the protection of Farmers' Rights;

Moreover, these agreements often provide for dispute-settlement mechanisms that allow not only states but also private entities such as multinational corporations to file a complaint to a panel of international arbitrators—for instance, under the ICSID Convention[107]—in order to challenge 'the legality of measures against covered investment including IP assets'.[108] Therefore, 'even where investment agreements fully accommodate the exceptions and flexibilities of multilateral IP instruments', measures that implement these instruments are 'open to challenge under the investor-to-state dispute settlement mechanisms'.[109]

3.5 CONCLUDING REMARKS

In the field of agriculture, the TRIPs Agreement leaves a remarkable degree of freedom for adjusting plant-related intellectual property legislation to domestic needs and promoting local innovation. However, the room for manoeuvre for developing countries may be quite narrow in practice.

Their freedom is restricted by two major factors. First, a growing number of developing countries have executed free trade and investment treaties with the US, the EU and other industrialized countries. In these treaties, they have agreed to provide patent protection for biotechnological inventions and make plant variety rights available in accordance with the 1991 UPOV Act. Second, UPOV, which advocates its 1991 Act as the most effective *sui generis* model law for the protection of plant varieties, discriminates against aspirant new members. In fact, since

---

3) the protection of traditional knowledge; 4) the regulation of access to plant genetic resources, 5) the prevention of 'biopiracy' and IPRs in unimproved plant materials; and 6) the preservation of plant breeders' research interests. R.L. Helfler (2004), above note 22, at p. 11.

[107] The International Centre for the Settlement of Investment Disputes (ICSID) is established by the Convention on the Settlement of Investment Disputes between States and Nationals of Other States, entered into force on 14 October 1966, available at: http://icsid.worldbank.org/ICSID/ICSID/RulesMain.jsp (accessed 21 February 2009).

[108] South Centre (2005), 'Intellectual Property in Investment Treaties: the TRIPs-Plus Implications for Developing Countries', South Centre Analytical Note, at p. 19.

[109] Ibid. at p. 19; M.C. Correa (2004), 'Bilateral Investment Agreements: Agents of New Global Standards for the Protection of Intellectual Property?', GRAIN, at p. 26.

1996 onwards, developing countries that implement a *sui generis* system of PVP compliant with the 1978 UPOV Act are not entitled to join the Union.[110]

Because strong patent and plant variety rights may fail to support crop diversity research and domestic innovation in countries that have not yet reached the technological frontier, lessons can be learned from the previous experience of now industrialized countries.

European plant-related IP laws codify specific interface rules to avoid overly restrictive rights on proprietary genetic materials. In particular, a compulsory cross-licensing mechanism has been devised to enable the commercial exploitation of new plant varieties containing third parties' patented inventions.[111] However, in most cases, when the licensing conditions are not regulated, it is doubtful whether the above provisions are sufficient to curb the monopolistic behaviours of large agro-biotech companies. The European system is also articulated in such a way that the 1998 Biotechnology Directive takes over the farmers' exemption from the EC Regulation on Community Plant Variety Rights.[112] On the contrary,

---

[110]   Article 37.3 of the 1991 UPOV Act. On the contrary, old UPOV members may opt not to bring their *sui generis* plant variety rights legislation into compliance with the latest Act, such as Norway. See R. Andersen (2005), 'Norway say "no" to UPOV 1991', Grain, 8 December 2005, available at: www.grain.org/bio-ipr/?id=458 (accessed 10 November 2008). Similarly, India also provides a relevant example because in 1999 the UPOV Council decided to accept '... an instrument of accession to the 1978 Act by India after the coming into force (24 April 1998) of the 1991 Act'. See UPOV (2003), 'Annual Report of the Secretary-General for 2002', C/37/2, Thirty-Seventh Ordinary Session of the UPOV Council, Geneva (23 October 2003), at paras 11–12. However, Rangnekar emphasizes that 'provisions for farmers' rights [in particular, the right to save, use, sow, re-sow, exchange, share or sell their farm produce including non-branded seeds of a protected variety] must be the most difficult element in negotiating India's accession to UPOV even under the 1978 Act'. D. Rangnekar (2006), 'Assessing the Economic Implications of Different Models for Implementing the Requirement to Protect Plant Varieties: A Case Study of India', produced for the European Commission under the project 'Impacts of the IPR Rules on Sustainable Development (IPDEV)', at p. 27.

[111]   The applicant should fulfil two conditions: the variety must constitute a 'significant technical progress of considerable economic interest' and the breeder must have unsuccessfully tried to obtain a contractual license from the patent holder. Identical conditions must be met by inventors who want to obtain a compulsory exploitation right to commercialize a biotechnological product that is contained in a plant variety for which a Community Plant Variety Right (CPVR) has been granted to a third party.

[112]   Therefore, farmers can enjoy the freedom to save and replant seeds under identical conditions regardless of whether such seeds are protected by plant variety rights or patents.

the interpretation of US plant-related IP laws relies on the principle of independence between different IPR systems. The consequence is that an action prohibited under a protection scheme (e.g. the patent system) cannot be permitted only because it is expressly allowed under a different protection scheme (e.g. a *sui generis* PVR system).

In sum, plant-related IP policies by industrialized countries have remarkably limited the options for designing *sui generis* plant variety right systems that can safely be adopted by developing countries without violating bilateral deals. However, the enactment of specific interface provisions between patents and plant variety rights, including the recognition of broad research and farmers' exemptions, may uphold the legal scope to implement important food security safeguards, which may require the use of protectable plant materials for domestic needs.

4. The international legal framework of access to plant genetic resources and benefit sharing

4.1 INTRODUCTION

Innovation, and in particular agricultural innovation, crucially depends on the balance between the realms of private property, common property and the public domain more than on a single component of such balance. This is because physical access to PGRFA for the purpose of breeding new varieties is important as much as the incentives that IPRs, such as patents and plant variety rights, may create to encourage private sector agricultural research. Besides, at the community level, customary arrangements, which provide access to PGRFA under a regime of common property, may establish mechanisms to monitor resource use by allowing community users to exploit common pool resources, while restricting access to outsiders.[1]

Aside from private and common property regimes, governments have implemented ABS-related restrictions on access to PGR to regulate the transfer and use of genetic materials and prevent their misappropriation. The legal basis of these laws is the principle that national sovereignty extends to all natural resources within national borders, including genetic resources. Thus, with the adoption of the Convention on Biological Diversity, the assertion of sovereign rights over genetic resources has also upset the balance between private property, public domain and other existing customary norms, which may provide indigenous and local communities and farmers with entitlements related to seeds and associated TK.

This chapter provides a review of the processes and deliberations within the ITPGRFA, the CGRFA and the CBD in efforts to promote benefit sharing, the sustainable use of PGRFA and farmers' rights. In the course

---

[1] E. Ostrom (1990), *Governing the Commons. The Evolution of Institutions for Collective Action*, Cambridge, UK: Cambridge University Press.

of the review, it analyses the challenges and opportunities within both the general and specific legal and institutional contexts. Based on the above analysis, it discusses ways forward within the international ABS legal framework relevant for crop diversity to ensure that such framework is a real instrument of intervention for sustainability and development. Finally, with the recent adoption of the 'Nagoya Protocol on Access to Genetic Resources and the Fair and Equitable Sharing of Benefits Arising from their Utilization' to the CBD, it considers the relationship between the ABS Protocol and the ITPGRFA.

4.2 THE FAO INTERNATIONAL TREATY ON PLANT GENETIC RESOURCES FOR FOOD AND AGRICULTURE

After seven years of negotiations, the FAO International Treaty on Plant Genetic Resources for Food and Agriculture was adopted by the FAO Conference on 3 November 2001. It entered into force on 29 June 2004 with 119 contracting parties as of March 2009.

The ITPGRFA should make an enormous contribution to international equity in terms of the way plant genetic resources are transferred and agricultural research is conducted. As part of the efforts to achieve the UN Millennium Development Goals 1 and 7, the ITPGRFA implementation should mobilize resources for the conservation of PGR and sustainable agriculture, while boosting research and domestic innovation capabilities in poor countries.[2] The importance of reducing inequalities is self evident and a more equitable distribution of the benefits arising from the use of crop diversity is an important tool to achieve this goal, including through the full implementation of farmers' rights under the Treaty.

The ITPGRFA provides an internationally agreed framework for the conservation and sustainable use of crop diversity and the fair and equitable sharing of benefits, in accordance with the CBD. In particular, it facilitates access to PGRFA through the Multilateral System (MLS) and sets out specific ABS rules in the Standard Material Transfer Agreement that implements it.

---

[2] Article 18 of the ITPGRFA.

4.2.1   The Multilateral System of ABS

Part IV of the ITPGRFA establishes a Multilateral System that facilitates access to 64 important crops and forages to ensure worldwide food security. The species of included crops are listed in Annex I of the ITPGRFA. These pooled resources must be used only for the purpose of utilization and conservation for research, breeding and training for food and agriculture. This means that national ABS laws that are consonant with the CBD may apply if recipients intend to make use of PGRFA for other purposes, 'such as chemical, pharmaceutical and/or other non-food/feed uses'.[3]

While the ITPGRFA encourages facilitating access to all plant genetic resources for food and agriculture,[4] only PGRFA that are under 'the management and control of the Contracting Parties and in the public domain' will be automatically included into the MLS.[5] This is the consequence of the fact that providers under the jurisdiction of contracting parties can only be obliged to provide access to materials that are: 1) under the direct or indirect management and control of the state; and 2) unencumbered by property rights or other legal entitlements such as those deriving from relevant customary laws.[6]

---

[3]   Article 12.3(a) of the ITPGRFA.

[4]   Article 11.2, second sentence, and in Article 11.3 of the ITPGRFA.

[5]   Article 11.2 of the ITPGRFA. In other words, not all the PGRFA listed in Annex I are automatically included in the Multilateral System. A WIPO Report stresses the difference between 'material which is covered in the MLS', namely Annex I listed material, and 'material which in included in the Multilateral System at a given time'. WIPO (2004), 'Preliminary Report on Work towards the Assessment of Patent Data Relevant to Availability and Use of Material from the International Network of *Ex-Situ* Collections under the Auspices of FAO and the ITPGRFA', CGRFA/MIC-2/04/Inf.5, FAO, Rome, at pp. 3–4. For example, materials in private collections, if not voluntarily included, are outside of the purview of the MLS.

[6]   If contracting parties were required by the ITPGRFA to give access to IP-protected materials, the ITPGRFA would possibly conflict with relevant international agreements such as the TRIPs Agreement and UPOV, and this is not the case.

Table 4.1. Crops covered under the FAO Multilateral System

Annex I

List of Crops Covered Under the Multilateral System

Food crops

Crop	Genus	Observations
Breadfruit	*Artocarpus*	Breadfruit only
Asparagus	*Asparagus*	
Oat	*Avena*	
Beet	*Beta*	
Brassica complex	*Brassica* et al.	Genera included are: *Brassica, Armoracia, Barbarea, Camelina, Crambe, Diplotaxis, Eruca, Isatis, Lepidium, Raphanobrassica, Raphanus, Rorippa,* and *Sinapis*. This comprises oilseed and vegetable crops such as cabbage, rapeseed, mustard, cress, rocket, radish, and turnip. The species *Lepidium meyenii* (maca) is excluded.
Pigeon Pea	*Cajanus*	
Chickpea	*Cicer*	
Citrus	*Citrus*	Genera *Poncirus* and *Fortunella* are included as root stock.
Coconut	*Cocos*	
Major aroids	*Colocasia, Xanthosoma*	Major aroids include taro, cocoyam, dasheen and tannia.
Carrot	*Daucus*	
Yams	*Dioscorea*	
Finger Millet	*Eleusine*	
Strawberry	*Fragaria*	
Sunflower	*Helianthus*	
Barley	*Hordeum*	
Sweet Potato	*Ipomoea*	
Grass pea	*Lathyrus*	

Crop	Genus	Observations
Lentil	*Lens*	
Apple	*Malus*	
Cassava	*Manihot*	*Manihot esculenta* only.
Banana/ Plantain	*Musa*	Except *Musa textilis.*
Rice	*Oryza*	
Pearl Millet	*Pennisetum*	
Beans	*Phaseolus*	Except *Phaseolus polyanthus.*
Pea	*Pisum*	
Rye	*Secale*	
Potato	*Solanum*	Section tuberosa included, except *Solanum phureja.*
Eggplant	*Solanum*	Section melongena included.
Sorghum	*Sorghum*	
Triticale	*Triticosecale*	
Wheat	*Triticum* et al.	Including *Agropyron, Elymus*, and *Secale*
Faba Bean/ Vetch	*Vicia*	
Cowpea et al.	*Vigna*	
Maize	*Zea*	Excluding *Zea perennis, Zea diploperennis*, and *Zea luxurians.*

Forages

Genera	Species
LEGUME FORAGES	
Astragalus	*chinesis, cicer, arenarius*
Canavalia	*ensiformis*
Coronilla	*varia*
Hedysarum	*coronarium*
Lathyrus	*cicera, ciliolatus, hirsutus, ochrus, odoratus, sativus*
Lespedeza	*cuneata, striata, stipulacea*
Lotus	*corniculatus, subbiflorus, uliginosus*
Lupimus	*albus, angustifolius, luteus*

Genera	Species
Medicago	*arborea, falcata, sativa, scutellata, rigidula, truncatula*
Melilotus	*albus, officinalis*
Onobrychis	*viciifolia*
Ornithopus	*sativus*
Prosopis	*affinis, alba, chilensis, nigra, pallida*
Pueraria	*phaseoloides*
Trifolium	*alexandrinum, alpestre, ambiguum, angustifolium, arvense, agrocicerum, hybridum, incarnatum, pratense, repens, resupinatum, ruepellianum, semipilosum, subterraneum, vesiculosum*
GRASS FORAGES	
Andropogon	*gayanus*
Agropyron	*cristatum, desertorum*
Agrostis	*stolonifera, tenuis*
Alopecurus	*pratensis*
Arrhenatherum	*elatius*
Dactylis	*glomoerata*
Festuca	*arundinacea, gigantea, heterophylla, ovina, pratensis, rubra*
Lolium	*hybridum, multiflorum, perenne, rigidum, temulentum*
Phalaris	*aquatica, arundinacea*
Phleum	*pratense*
Poa	*alpine, annua, pratensis*
Tripsacum	*laxum*
OTHER FORAGES	
Atriplex	*halimus, nummularia*
Salsola	*vermiculata*

4.2.1.1 The concepts of 'public domain', 'private property' and 'common property' in relation to the MLS

Wondering whether a certain sample of seeds is in the 'public domain' means to wonder whether those seeds have private property rights or other relevant legal entitlements over them in the relevant jurisdictions. Something is not in the public domain when there is property over it. Boyle has identified four distinct and well-understood ways in which the term 'property' is commonly used: 1) a property interest as any legal cognizable condition of market advantage; 2) those rights protected by a 'property rule' rather than a 'liability rule'; 3) a variable bundle of rights of interest in things (subject to almost unlimited state regulation and reformulation); and 4) any collection of privileges that includes market alienability, sole, absolute and despotic dominion and so on.[7]

Even though the conceptualization of private property, and the way it applies to PGR, may be differently understood in different legal systems (e.g. systems that establish property in written laws and other systems recognizing forms of property as customary rights), any form of property necessarily requires the owner to have some kind of control over the material. The concept of the public domain derives from, and is rooted in, the idea of public property, free for all to use, as opposed to private property. Therefore, whether certain materials are in the public domain depends on the extent to which the actual ability to obtain access to them is restricted by *proprietary* claims in the jurisdiction concerned.

The concept of 'public domain' may refer both to the substantive freedom of access to PGRFA considered as tangible goods and the formal freedom of access to PGRFA in relation to their formal status under IP law.[8] Even though in the modern world of plant breeding and genetic engineering 'the term public domain is generally used to refer to material that is not protected by IPRs ... and is thus "free" for all to use', the importance of the actual ability to obtain access to physical materials conserved in *in-situ* conditions suggests that the 'tangible aspect' of the public domain may also count in the glossing of Article 11.2 of the Treaty.[9] This is now made explicit by Article 5(d) of the SMTA, whose scope of application covers both IPR[10] as well as other relevant legal

---

[7]   J. Boyle (2003), 'Foreword: the Opposite of Property?' *Law and Contemporary Problems*, Vol. 66 /Nos 1 & 2, at p. 30.

[8]   In the study carried out by WIPO on patent data relevant to availability and use of germplasm, the following negative definition of the concept of public domain is given: 'When a PGRFA is directly covered by the claims of a national or regional patent that is in force in the relevant jurisdiction, it would in normal usage not be considered to be in the public domain within that jurisdiction, until the patent term has expired or the patent has lapsed, although this would not apply in jurisdictions where the patent was not in force.' See WIPO (2004), above note 5, at pp. 3–4.

[9]   In the common law tradition, the term 'public domain' was used to describe public lands. J. Boyle (2003), 'The Second Enclosure Movement and the Construction of the Public Domain', *Law and Contemporary Problems,* Vol. 66/No. 1 & 2, at p. 58.

[10]   For instance, in the case of patents, the latter entail the exclusive right to commercially exploit the knowledge (not part of prior art) of the utility of the material.

entitlements to regulate access to and use of PGRFA in accordance with common property regimes pertaining to traditional systems of customary law.[11]

Based on the above analysis of what 'public domain' means in relation to 'property rights', it may be argued that the latter shall be broadly understood as comprising not only the notion of 'private property rights' but also the notion of 'common property'. Under a regime of common property, local level collective action is usually regulated to allow community users to exploit common pool resources, while restricting access to outsiders.[12] Fenny *et al.* have argued that resource users' rights under common property regimes usually are non-exclusive and non-transferable rights of equal access and use.[13] They also highlight the differences with open access, as the successful exclusion of non-club members is the rule for the common property, rather than the exception. Therefore, from the perspective of outsiders, common property rights are similar to private property rights, because 'there is exclusion of non-owners', while 'who is in the resource management group and who is not' is usually defined.[14]

In conclusion, the notion of 'public domain' and, *mutatis mutandis*, those of 'management and control' that are relevant for identifying PGRFA included into the Multilateral System should take into account property rights and interests that may be broader than those identified by the private property rights paradigm.

---

[11] Article 5(d) of the SMTA, under 'Rights and Obligations of the Provider', states: 'Access to [PGRFA] protected by intellectual and *other* property rights shall be consistent with relevant international agreements, and with relevant national laws.' Emphasis added.

[12] E. Ostrom (1990), above note 1. According to Ostrom, several preconditions need to be in place for common property resource arrangements to provide stable and sustainable governance, including: defined boundaries; congruence between appropriation and provision rules and local conditions; effective participation, monitoring and conflict-resolution mechanisms; effective sanctions for the violation of community rules; and minimal recognition of rights to organize.

[13] D. Fenny *et al.* (1998), 'The Tragedy of the Commons: Twenty-Two Years Later', in J. Baden and D. Noonan (eds), *Managing the Commons*, Bloomington: Indiana University Press.

[14] B. Adhikari (2001), 'Literature Review on the Economics of Common Property Resources—Review of Common Pool Resource Management in Tanzania', report prepared for NRSP project R7857, University of York, at pp. 6–8.

4.2.1.2   The Standard Material Transfer Agreement

In June 2006, the adoption of the SMTA was an important outcome of the first session of the Governing Body of the ITPGRFA. In particular, the SMTA establishes the level, form and manner of equitable benefit-sharing payments to be made under the ITPGRFA. Under such international standard contract, recipients are free to transfer received materials to third parties without asking for the provider's prior informed consent. However, they must ensure that subsequent recipients are also bound by the standard conditions of the SMTA.[15] Thus, during the development cycle, a chain of SMTAs ensures that benefit-sharing obligations are passed onto any 'other person or entity' that develops a product (i.e. seeds) derived from the Multilateral System.

Under the ITPGRFA, benefit sharing is not limited to monetary benefits.[16] Therefore, the SMTA provides scope for sharing non-monetary benefits (Article 6.9), and encourages recipients to make voluntary payments into the trust fund administered by FAO for the purpose of implementing the ITPGRFA (Article 6.8). However, it also provides for compulsory payments under Article 6.7 and for an alternative payment scheme under Article 6.11. A description of these two benefit-sharing mechanisms will follow.

a   Compulsory benefit sharing

If certain legal requirements are met, compulsory benefit sharing of 1.1 per cent of incomes that derive from the sale of seeds must be paid by recipients to the Multilateral System.[17] The first requirement is that the commercialized 'Product'[18] must incorporate 'the Material' received from

---

[15]   Article 12.4 of the ITPGRFA states: 'the recipient of PGRFA shall require that the conditions of the MTA shall apply to the transfer of PGRFA to another person or entity, as well as to any subsequent transfer of those PGRFA'.

[16]   B. Visser *et al.* (2005), 'Options for Non-Monetary Benefit-Sharing—An Inventory', Background Study Paper No. 30, FAO, Rome, Italy.

[17]   Article 6.7 of the SMTA states: 'In the case that the Recipient commercializes a Product that is a Plant Genetic Resource for Food and Agriculture and that incorporates Material as referred to in Article 3 of this Agreement, and where such Product is not available without restriction to others for further research and breeding, the Recipient shall pay 1.1% [less 30%—to allow for sale cost recovery] of the Sales of the commercialized Product.'

[18]   The definition of 'Product' which is given in Article 2 of the SMTA excludes products other than PGRFA and other products used for food, feed and processing. Hence, the commercialization of bulk goods that are 'sold or traded as

the Multilateral System.[19] With regard to this 'incorporation requirement' a practical inquiry which needs to be addressed is: when does a product incorporate 'the Material or any of its genetic parts and components'?

Accessions normally amount to very small samples of seeds, which often need to be regenerated before research and breeding. If the above expression in quotes were literally interpreted to mean *direct* 'physical incorporation', then there would be few benefits to be shared, if any. As a point of legal interpretation this would lead to an absurd outcome and is unlikely to be upheld in any arbitration.[20] Therefore, the incorporation requirement should reasonably encompass the 'progeny' and 'unmodified derivatives' of the material.[21]

The second requirement is that payments are due only if the 'Product' (i.e. seeds) is not freely available for further research and breeding. In essence, this requirement entails the existence of a patented product (legal restrictions) or restrictions deriving from particular technologies, such as

---

commodities' shall not be considered. For instance, while the sale of grain as a reproductive material would be relevant under Article 6.7, the sale of flour obtained from that grain is not. Annex 2, para. 1(c) of the SMTA.

[19]   The SMTA does not provide a definition of the term 'the Material'. Thus, it is important to consider whether the latter expression refers only to the transferred material or includes also its progeny and unmodified derivatives.

[20]   Personal communication with Sam Johnston, UNU–IAS Senior Research Fellow, Yokohama, Japan (10 July 2007).

[21]   Article 4.3(e) of the UNIDROIT Principles provides that contract term must be interpreted taking into account 'the meaning commonly given to terms and expression in the trade concerned'. Most MTAs used by universities and research institutions across the world specify the meaning of the term 'the material'. Such definition generally comprises 'the provided material, its progeny and unmodified derivatives'. In contrast, 'modifications' are normally excluded. MTAs also specify that the concept of 'progeny' covers 'all unmodified descendants from the material', while 'unmodified derivatives' are 'all substances created by the recipient that constitute an unmodified functional subunit or product not changed in form or character and expressed by the provided material'. Thus, 'unmodified derivatives' may include genetic components or gene sequences obtained from MLS materials through isolation and purification. Compare the relevant definitions of the following MTAs: 1) The Biodefense and Emerging Infections Research Resources Repository (2004), *Material Transfer Agreement*; 2) The University of Rochester Medical Center (2004), *Material Transfer Agreement (Biological Materials)*; 3) The Johns Hopkins University (2006), Standard Terms and Conditions for The Johns Hopkins University, *Material Transfer Agreements*; 4) The University of Basel—Office of Technology Transfer (2006), *Material Transfer Agreement between the University of Basel and For-Profit Organizations*; and 5) The Hong Kong University of Science and Technology (2006), *Material Transfer Agreement*.

Genetic Use Restriction Technologies (GURTs),[22] or certain licensing practices.[23] Thus, Article 6.7 of the SMTA not only seems to legitimize the patenting of seeds that incorporate materials accessed from the Multilateral System, but also creates a strong link between benefit sharing and the patenting of biotechnological products and processes.[24]

However, interpretative problems may arise because the SMTA prohibits recipients to claim 'any intellectual or other property rights that limit the facilitated access to the Material … or its genetic parts or components, in the form received from the Multilateral System'.[25] This poses the difficult question of assessing whether the changing patent landscape surrounding PGRFA covered by the Multilateral System may limit, in practice, their availability and use.[26] In other words, it is questionable whether patent claims to the 'progeny' and 'unmodified

---

[22]   The use of GURTs was discussed at the Eighth Conference of the Parties to the UN Convention on Biological Diversity in Curutiba, Brazil, 20–31 March 2006. Further information can be found at: www.cbd.int/programmes/areas/agro/gurts.asp (accessed 10 July 2007).

[23]   For instance, the *Biotechnology Law Report* (2006) describes Monsanto's practice to license its insect-resistant technology (Bollgard/Roundup Ready cotton) to producers, who are obliged to sublicense the technology to customers with certain restrictions. In particular, seeds cannot be 'saved from one years' crop to sell or give to others or to plant another crop. Purchasers are also barred from doing research on seeds.' These restrictions would give rise to benefit sharing. Patent Litigation (2006), 'Monsanto's Patent and License Agreement Again Upheld', *Biotechnology Law Report,* 25/5, 564–7.

[24]   Article 5(d) of the SMTA provides that intellectual and other property rights must be respected.

[25]   Article 6.2 of the SMTA seems to confer some sort of protection to the positive dimension of the public domain. However, the meaning of the expression 'genetic parts and components' that is used in connection with the words 'in the form received' is not clear. In general, genebanks do not provide 'genetic parts and components', but samples of seeds called accessions (i.e. 'distinct, uniquely identifiable samples of seeds representing a cultivar, breeding line or a population, which is maintained in storage for conservation and use'. N.K. Rao *et al.* (2006), *Manual of Seed Handling in Genebanks*, Handbooks for Genebanks No. 8, Rome: Bioversity International. Thus, a reasonable interpretation is that the terms 'genetic parts and components, in the form received' should correspond to the well-known concept of 'unmodified derivatives'.

[26]   See, for instance, WIPO (2006), 'Progress Report on Work towards the Assessment of Patent Data Relevant to Agricultural Biotechnology and the Availability and Use of Material from the International Network of *Ex-Situ* Collections under the Auspices of FAO and the ITPGRFA: a Draft Patent Landscape Surrounding Gene Promoters relevant to Rice', IT/GB-1/06/Inf.17, First Session of the Governing Body of the ITPGRFA, Madrid (12–16 June 2006).

derivatives' of materials transferred through the SMTA should be allowed. This is because such claims can restrict access to germplasm, genome sequences and their functional characterisations, which—some argue—'may be deemed to be international public goods' under the ITPGRFA.[27]

Another important provision is Article 6.10 of the SMTA, which regulates the assignment of IPRs.[28] In particular, it links the transfer of IPRs to the transfer of the recipient's benefit-sharing obligations to the assignee (i.e. 'one to whom a right, property', interest, title or claim 'is legally transferred').[29] Interestingly, this Article applies also to cases where there is no transfer of material either 'in the form received' or as a 'PGRFA under development' (i.e. as a derivative).[30]

Therefore, Article 6.10 of the SMTA gives self-standing relevance to IPR claims that cover the use of information obtained from MLS materials. In other words, the 'incorporation requirement' under Article 6.7 can be fulfilled, if the practical application of such information is necessary to manufacture the product and it results in legal restrictions on access to such product.[31]

On the contrary, it would be legally absurd to provide for the transfer of benefit-sharing obligations, which could not be performed if there is no transfer of PGRFA. To conclude, the incorporation into a proprietary product of patented information, which results from R&D carried out on MLS materials, may give rise to benefit-sharing payments *per se*.

---

[27] R. Fears (2007), 'Genomics and Genetic Resources for Food and Agriculture', Background Study Paper No. 34, FAO, Rome, Italy.

[28] Article 6.10 of the SMTA states: 'A Recipient who obtains [IPRs] on any Products developed from the Material or its components, obtained from the Multilateral System, and assigns such [IPRs] to a third party, shall transfer the benefit sharing obligations of this Agreement to that third party.'

[29] J. Simpson (ed.) (2007), *Oxford English Dictionary*, Oxford, UK: Oxford University Press.

[30] Article 6.4 applies to the first case, while the second case falls within the scope of application of Article 6.5 of the SMTA.

[31] Patented inventions that constitute PGRFA derived from a crop covered by the Multilateral System 'might cut across to applications in other crops, which might be either inside or outside' the Multilateral System. See WIPO (2006), above note 26. This is because, under the patent law doctrine of equivalents, 'variations', which 'are of a nature similar enough to be equivalent to the patented invention', may fall within the coverage of patent claim. V. Henson-Apollonio (2006), 'The Impacts of IPRs on MAS Research and Application in Developing Countries', paper given at the 19th Session of the Genetic Resources Policy Committee of the CGIAR, El Batan, Mexico, 22–24 February 2006.

b   The alternative payment scheme

The development and commercialization of a new plant variety normally may take more than ten years during which recipients are not required to make payments under Article 6.7 of the SMTA. Against this backdrop, the most innovative aspect of the alternative payment scheme is that it may provide an immediate flow of financial resources to the Multilateral System. This is because it derogates to both requirements of Article 6.7 of the SMTA. However, it also offers numerous advantages to plant breeders.

In sum, the alternative payment scheme provides that recipients may voluntarily choose, at their option, to make crop-based payments in accordance with Article 6.11 of the SMTA.[32] This Article states that payments must be calculated at the discounted rate of 0.5 per cent of the overall sales of seeds pertaining to the same crop species obtained from the Multilateral System by the recipient.[33] For example, if the latter is a breeder that receives rice accessions, payments must be calculated on the basis of his/her overall sales of rice.[34]

The alternative payment scheme, which was initially known as the African Proposal, is justified on several grounds. On the one hand, its proponents emphasized that it can simplify the system, increase transparency and reduce monitoring costs.[35] They also argued that this option would offer a way to implement the second part of Article 13.2(d) (ii) of the ITPGRFA, which calls for promoting voluntary contributions. On the other, recipients may want to use it for two main reasons. The first one is obvious: the discounted rate is considerably lower than the rate of

---

[32]   This payment scheme is also regulated by the provisions contained in Annexes 3 and 4 of the SMTA. As regards its voluntary nature, the African Proposal from which it is derived clearly points out that it 'is "voluntary" in the sense that it would allow the Recipient to choose it or to be subject to the standard mandatory payment provision, but it would not exempt him from payments that are due under the Treaty, nor would it leave payments at his discretion.' FAO (2005), 'African Proposal', Working Group on the Drafting of the Standards Material Transfer Agreement, CGRFA\IC\CG-SMTA-1, Hammamet, Tunisia (21 July 2005).

[33]   Article 6.11(d) of the SMTA states: 'The payments to be made are independent of whether or not the Product is available without restriction.'

[34]   It is apparent that benefit sharing under Article 6.11 would be theoretically larger than under Article 6.7 in terms of the numbers of relevant transactions upon which payments can be calculated.

[35]   'Monitoring the utilization of particular samples will not be needed, as payments would apply in respect of all products of a certain crop or crops.' FAO (2005), above note 32.

Article 6.7 of the SMTA. The second reason is that they will have to comply only with a single benefit-sharing obligation, no matter how many SMTAs they have entered into, because cumulative payments are expressly excluded (SMTA Article 6.11(f) and Annex 3, at para. 5). Moreover, even if recipients have previously assumed—or will assume—an obligation to make payments at the full rate of 1.1 per cent under Article 6.7, that rate is automatically reduced. However, recipients must expressly opt for crop-based payments.[36] The period of validity of this option is ten years.[37]

4.2.1.3   The third party beneficiary

During the negotiation of the SMTA, the contracting parties of the ITPGRFA agreed that they should not be directly responsible for enforcing the provisions of the SMTA. They also noted that providers of PGRFA 'may have neither the capacity nor the willingness to monitor and/or enforce compliance by recipients with the terms of the Standard Material Transfer Agreement'.[38] This is not surprising because benefits flow to the Multilateral System rather than to the source of the material (i.e. the provider). Moreover, recipients may subsequently transfer PGRFA to third parties who will not have a contractual link with the initial source.

The designation of FAO as the 'third party beneficiary' under the SMTA provides an institutional solution to this problem.[39] This feature of the SMTA is totally unique and without precedent in international law. In

---

[36]   Annex 4 of the SMTA contains a template form that the recipient must fill in, sign and notify to the Governing Body. In addition, the use of click-wrap and shrink-wrap SMTA is excluded for this modality of payments.

[37]   Article 6.11(b) of the SMTA provides that such period is automatically renewed if the recipient does not notify the Governing Body of his decision to opt out at least six months before the expiry of the ten-year period. At the end of this period, if the recipient has opted out, payments must continue to be made at the discounted rate of 0.5 per cent of the sale of any 'Products', which fulfil the requirements of Article 6.7 of the SMTA. See Annex 3, para. 4 of the SMTA.

[38]   FAO (2006), 'Third Party Beneficiary, including in the Context of Arbitration', CGRFA/IC/CG-SMTA-2/06/Inf.4, Alnarp, Sweden (24–28 April 2006).

[39]   The Governing Body of the ITPGRFA adopted the Standard Material Transfer Agreement and invited: 'The Food and Agriculture Organization of the United Nations, as the Third Party Beneficiary, to carry out the roles and responsibilities as identified and prescribed in the SMTA, under the direction of the Governing Body in accordance with the procedures to be established by the Governing Body at its next session.' FAO Resolution 2/2006, at para. 8.

a presentation to the Council of UPOV, Stannard described it as 'the unusual situation of payments to an international body administering a global pooled good, as the result of a contract under private law'.[40] In sum, FAO is the legal person who represents the Governing Body and can act on its behalf in the context of dispute settlement.[41] Therefore, FAO is empowered with legal standing (i.e. the right to act or being heard as a litigant) and monitoring rights to protect the interests of the Multilateral System.[42]

Third party beneficiary's rights must be recognized by the substantive law applicable to the SMTA in order to be enforceable.[43] In general, national law may or may not recognize the validity of third parties' rights of contractual nature. However, the UNIDROIT Principles expressly recognize that the parties to a contract are free to confer rights on a third party under Articles 5.2.1 and 5.2.2.[44] Therefore, it is not surprising that Article 7 of the SMTA includes the UNIDROIT Principles among the sources of applicable law.[45]

4.2.2   The International Network of ex-situ collections under the auspices of FAO

4.2.2.1   The establishment of the International Network

The uncertainty of the legal status of *ex-situ* germplasm collections and the lack of appropriate arrangement to ensure their safe conservation were the two reasons that, in 1989, pushed the CGRFA to call for the development of the International Network of *ex-situ* collections under the auspices of FAO. The legal basis for the establishment of the International Network is to be found in Article 7.1(a) of the IUPGR, which provides that international arrangements complementing the IUPGR should be developed to promote:

---

[40]   C. Stannard (2006), 'Presentation by the FAO on the ITPGRFA', C/40/17, UPOV Council, Fortieth Ordinary Session, Geneva (19 October 2006).

[41]   Articles 8.1 and 8.2 of the SMTA.

[42]   Article 8.3 of the SMTA.

[43]   The applicable law or *lex causae* is the substantive law that governs a contract.

[44]   M.J. Bonell (2004), 'UNIDROIT Principles 2004—The New Edition of the Principles of International Commercial Contracts adopted by the International Institute for the Unification of Private Law', *Uniform Law Review,* 2004/1, 5–40.

[45]   FAO (2006), above note 38; and C. Chiarolla (2008), 'Plant Patenting, Benefit Sharing and the Law Applicable to the SMTA', *JWIP,* 11(1), 1–28.

An internationally coordinated network of national, regional and international centers, including an international network of base collections in gene banks, under the auspices or jurisdiction of the FAO, that have assumed the responsibility to hold, for the benefit of the international community and on the principle of unrestricted exchange, base or active collection of plant genetic resources.

Article 7.2 of the undertaking adds that:

Within the context of the global system, any Governments or institutions that agree to participate in the Undertaking may, furthermore, notify the Director-General of FAO that they wish the base collection … to be recognized as part of the international network … under the auspices of the jurisdiction of FAO. The centre concerned will, where requested by FAO, make materials in the base collection available to participants in the Undertaking, for purposes of scientific research, plant breeding or genetic resource conservation, free of charge, on the basis of mutual exchange, or on mutually agreed terms.

The negotiation of the Agreements between FAO and the Centres of the Consultative Group on International Agricultural Research started in 1992 and was ready for signature two years later. In 1994, the Director-General of FAO upon recommendation by the CGRFA invited governments and the International Agricultural Research Centers (IARCs) of the CGIAR to bring their base collections under the auspices of the FAO. Finally, on 26 October 1994 12 Centres of the CGIAR and the FAO signed the Agreements.

4.2.2.2   *The legal status of designated germplasm in the International Network*

Article 3 of these Agreements regulates the status of designated germplasm, providing that the Centre must hold it 'in trust for the benefit of the international community, in particular the developing countries'. Moreover, the Centre 'shall not claim legal ownership over the designated germplasm, nor shall it seek any intellectual property rights over that germplasm or related information'. Article 9 establishes that samples of designated germplasm and related information shall be made available directly to users or through FAO, for the purpose of scientific research, plant breeding or genetic resources conservation, 'without restriction'. Finally, with regard to the subsequent transfer of designated germplasm and related information to any other persons or entities, Article 10 of the Agreement provides that the Centre shall ensure that such other persons or entities, and any further entities receiving samples of the designated germplasm, are bound by the conditions set out in Article 3.

In addition, FAO and the CGIAR Centres have promulgated a 'First Joint Statement' clarifying their common understanding concerning certain provisions of the Agreements.[46] In particular, it states that Article 3 should 'not prevent the Centres from using instruments such as material transfer agreements when they are designed to ensure the materials distributed remain in the public domain'. Besides, 'the words "without restriction" ... should be interpreted consistently with the [CBD] and as not in any way affecting the rights of countries of origin under this Convention', further clarifying that in the case of 'the transfer of samples of designated germplasm, the requirements of Article 10 will be satisfied by arrangements, such as material transfer agreements, that require the recipient not to seek intellectual property protection on the material and to pass on the same obligation to subsequent recipients'.

At the 1998 renewal of the FAO–CGIAR Agreement, the CGIAR Centres and FAO issued a 'Second Joint Statement' that addresses the issue of enforcement of the conditions established in the interim Material Transfer Agreements used by IARCs.[47] The Statement recognizes that the CGIAR Centres cannot guarantee that recipients will abide by the terms of the MTA that prohibit them, or any subsequent recipients, from taking out intellectual property rights over the material received. However, the CGIAR Centres and FAO committed themselves 'to taking appropriate remedial action, in accordance with agreed procedures, in case of suspected violation of MTAs'.[48]

The 'Second Joint Statement' also outlines the steps that the Centres may undertake when they become aware that a possible violation has taken place. This agreed procedure includes the following remedial actions: 1) the request of an explanation; 2) the request that the recipient desist in its effort to obtain IPRs over the materials, or renounce to such rights if they have already been granted; 3) the notification to the proper regulatory body in the relevant country of the possibility that the MTA has been violated and that the grant of IPRs may have been inappropriate; 4) and the notification to the International Plant Genetic

---

[46]   SGRP (2003), *Booklet of the CGIAR Centre Policy Instruments, Guidelines and Statements on Genetic Resources, Biotechnology and Intellectual Property Rights*, Version II, at p. 8.

[47]   Ibid. at p. 13.

[48]   FAO (1999), 'Progress Report on the International Network of Ex Situ Collections under the Auspices of FAO', Eighth Regular Session, Annex 2, CGRFA-8/99/7, Rome, Italy (19–23 April 1999), at para. 16.

Resources Institute (IPGRI) and the CGRFA of the possible violation of the MTA. Moreover, the Centres in cooperation with FAO reserve the right to take action, including legal action, to enforce MTAs and preserve the integrity of the Agreements with FAO.

A concrete example of the violation of IPR-related provisions of the FAO–CGIAR Agreement is the famous *Enola Bean Patent Case*.[49] In 1999, US national Larry Proctor obtained utility patent 5,894,079 from the US Patent and Trademark Office.[50] The International Center for Tropical Agriculture (CIAT) of the CGIAR, alerted of the potential abuse from Mexican farmers, found out that the patented variety was identical to at least six well-known bean varieties stored in its genebanks. In 2000, CIAT requested the USPTO to re-examine the patent. The fact that it took seven years for the patent to be revoked, during which Proctor continued to enjoy fully his rights, is an alarming signal of a dysfunctional patent system that has led itself to being abused.

4.2.2.3 *The agreements between the governing body of the ITPGRFA and the CGIAR Centres*

The Multilateral System also includes the *ex-situ* collections of CGIAR, which are supporting components of the Treaty.[51] In particular, 11 CGIAR Centres and the Tropical Agricultural Research and Higher Educational Center (CATIE) have signed agreements with the Governing Body, whereby they have placed their collections within the Multilateral

---

[49] FAO (2007), 'Updated Information provided by the International Center for Tropical Agriculture (CIAT), regarding its Request for a Re-Examination of US Patent No. 5,894,079', Eleventh Regular Session, CGRFA-11/07/Inf.10, FAO, Rome, Italy (11–15 June 2007).

[50] In this patent, Proctor claimed to have developed a new bean variety, obtained from a Mexican variety known as *Phaseolus vulgaris*, which 'produces distinctly colored yellow seeds which remain relatively unchanged by season'. Then, Proctor threatened the Mexican farmers who traditionally exported their beans into the US to pay him royalties, if they did not want to be sued for patent infringement. Eventually, this resulted in considerable economic losses by these farmers, who suddenly saw their produce seized at the frontier with the US. A. Barba (2008), ' "Biopiracy" Thwarted as US Revokes Bean Patent', Science and Development Network, 13 May 2008, available at: www.scidev.net/en/news/-biopiracy-thwarted-as-us-revokes-bean-patent.html (accessed 23 May 2008).

[51] The other supporting components of the ITPGRFA are described in Part V of the Treaty. They are: the Global Plan of Action for the Conservation and Sustainable Use of PGRFA (Article 14); International Plant Genetic Resource Networks (Article 16); and the Global Information System (Article 17).

System.[52] In concluding these agreements, the Centres have also recognized the authority of the Governing Body of the ITPGRFA to provide policy guidance relating to their collections, in accordance with Article 15 of the ITPGRFA.[53] As a consequence of these agreements, the legal status of materials in the International Network is now regulated by the provisions of the Treaty and its SMTA.[54] Besides, the issue of whether the SMTA needs to be modified for its use with non-Annex I crops has been discussed by the Governing Body of the ITPGRFA at its third meeting in June 2009. No substantial changes have been made to the SMTA and such Agreement is currently been used for the transfer of non-Annex I crops.[55]

4.2.3 Farmers' rights and TK protection under the ITPGRFA

Agricultural Traditional Knowledge (TK) contributes to the conservation of crop diversity in developed and developing countries alike.[56] As the erosion of genetic resources for food and agriculture advances, the entire body of agricultural TK, which applies to those resources, becomes irrelevant. Thus, the erosion of agro-biodiversity and the extinction of agricultural TK are inextricably related and mutually reinforcing processes, which require immediate action and appropriate legal frameworks to be halted.

---

[52] The Agreements between FAO, acting on behalf of the Governing Body of the ITPGRFA, and the Centres of the CGIAR, which were signed on 1 January 2007, available at: www.planttreaty.org/art15_en.htm (accessed 25 February 2009).

[53] CGIAR (2007), 'Submission by the International Agriculture Research Centres of the CGIAR to the Group of Technical Experts on an Internationally Recognized Certificate of Origin/Source/Legal Provenance (Addendum)', Lima, Peru (22–25 January 2007), UNEP/CBD/GTE-ABS/1/3/ADD2.

[54] FAO (2007), 'Consideration of the Material Transfer Agreement to Be Used by the International Agricultural Research Centers of the CGIAR and other Relevant International Institutions, for Plant Genetic Resources for Food and Agriculture not Included in Annex 1 of the Treaty', IT/GB-2/07/13 Rev 1, FAO, Rome, Italy (29 October–2 November 2007).

[55] FAO (2009), 'Report of the Third Session of the Governing Body of the International Treaty on Plant Genetic Resources for Food and Agriculture', GB-3/09/Report, Tunis, Tunisia (1–5 June 2009), at paras 38 and 39.

[56] The expression 'traditional knowledge' means 'knowledge, innovation and practices of indigenous and local communities and farmers' embodying traditional lifestyles relevant to the conservation and sustainable use of biological diversity. CBD (2009), 'Submission by NATURAL JUSTICE', Answers to the questions posed to the Expert Group on TK associated with GR as specified in COP decision IX/12, Hyderabad, India (16–19 June 2009) at: www.cbd.int/abs/submissions/absgtle-03-natural-justice-en.pdf, at pp 1–4.

In industrialized countries, the diversity of traditional agro-ecological systems is being replaced at an increasing rate by less diverse and more intensive agricultural production systems. However, it is in poor countries where the protection of agricultural TK is a matter of priority, because most farming and pastoral communities depend on traditional knowledge, innovation and practices for their survival. This is because these communities often have limited access to modern agricultural research and breeding technologies and to their products.

The indigenous and local communities (ILCs) and farmers have for a long time used their local know-how, techniques and technologies to preserve and develop seeds for food crops, and have managed their food crops and animal breeds sustainably. Their TK embodies useful information on how to preserve seeds, plants and cater for food and agricultural crops, which they have developed and acquired over long periods of time. The seeds we have today are partly a result of the contribution that agricultural TK and its custodians have made to society. However, these ILCs and farmers have not been adequately recognized for their contribution.[57] In addition, TK systems that embody such useful agricultural knowledge are being threatened today by numerous factors, including those associated with a changing climate, from decreasing precipitations and floods to soil and genetic erosion. At the same time, it is the evolution of such TK systems and their adaptation to new environmental conditions that makes life possible for those at the bottom of the pyramid in poor countries.

In order to recognize the contribution of ILCs and the farmers, and to prevent TK from loss and misappropriation, various treaties and processes have provided within their scope a framework or a platform for protecting agricultural TK and enhancing the role of its custodians. The ITPGRFA is the first international treaty to legally recognize farmers' rights, including their TK component, and to establish a Multilateral System (MLS) of access and benefit sharing (ABS), whose benefits shall flow primarily 'to farmers in all countries, especially in developing countries, and countries with economies in transition, who conserve and sustainably utilize PGRFA'.[58]

---

[57] As Brush points out, 'defining knowledge rather than genetic resources as the subject matter of Farmers' Rights is problematic because farmers' knowledge is local, widely shared, changeable, and orally transmitted'. B.S. Brush (2007), 'Farmers' Rights and Protection of Traditional Agricultural Knowledge', *World Development*, 35 (9), 1499–514.

[58] Article 13.3 of the ITPGRFA.

4.2.3.1   Farmers' rights protection

The sole express reference that the ITPGRFA makes to the protection of farmers' rights and traditional agricultural knowledge is contained in Article 9. Thus, the analysis of this Article deserves special attention.

Article 9 of the ITPGRFA recognizes 'the enormous contribution that the ILCs and farmers of all regions of the world, particularly those in the centres of origin and crop diversity, have made and will continue to make for the conservation and development of PGR that constitute the basis of food and agriculture production throughout the world'. Besides, Article 9.2 provides that the implementation of farmers' rights at the national level may include the following elements:

1)   the protection of TK relevant to PGRFA;
2)   the right to equitably participate in sharing benefits arising from the utilization of such resources; and
3)   the right to participate in making decisions on matters related to the conservation and sustainable use of PGRFA.

Finally, it states that: 'nothing in this Article shall be interpreted to limit any rights that farmers have to save, use, exchange and sell farm-saved seed/propagating material'.

However, the ITPGRFA leaves their implementation entirely up to national governments pursuant to Article 9.2, which provides that 'the responsibility for realizing Farmers' Rights, as they relate to PGRFA, rests with national governments'. In international negotiations, it may therefore appear as a paradox that the emphasis on national governments' responsibility to enact these rights is being used by some countries to defeat the emerging convergence of interests regarding the adoption of additional standards and measures to promote farmers' rights, including the protection of agricultural TK.

The recent adoption of a resolution on the implementation of farmers' rights by the ITPGRFA's Governing Body in June 2009 may not be seen as a tremendous breakthrough in the negotiations. Nonetheless, it highlights that a cross-cutting coalition of countries, supported by civil society's groups and farmers' organizations, has successful raised the attention on this issues and obtained that it be included on the agenda of the next session of the Governing Body (GB). Besides, the GB has set the ground for inter-sessional work on this item by:

1)   inviting 'each Contracting Party to consider reviewing and, if necessary, adjusting its national measures affecting the realization of Farmers' Rights', to protect and promote these rights;

2)   encouraging 'Contracting Parties and other relevant organizations ... to submit views and experiences on the implementation of Farmers' Rights ... involving, as appropriate, farmers' organizations and other stakeholders';

3)   requesting 'the Secretariat to convene regional workshops on Farmers' Rights ... aiming at discussing national experiences on the implementation of Farmers' Rights';

4)   requesting 'the Secretariat to collect the views and experiences submitted by Contracting Parties and other relevant organizations, and the reports of the regional workshops as a basis for an agenda item for consideration by the GB at its Fourth Session, and to disseminate relevant information through the website of the Treaty'; and

5)   appreciating 'the involvement of farmers' organizations in its further work ...'.[59]

4.2.3.2 Key challenges for the protection of PGRFA-related TK

The ITPGRFA presents two critical challenges for the protection of agricultural TK. The first one relates to the issue of whether the benefit-sharing mechanism of the Multilateral System will make available additional resources for the protection of PGRFA-related TK. This challenge is twofold, namely to ensure that the benefits arising from the use of PGRFA in the Multilateral System are: 1) generated in measure and forms that are adequate to support the activities relevant for the protection of agricultural TK, especially at the community level, including the issue of the *provision and availability of funds*; and 2) effectively delivered to the ILCs and farmers, who contribute through their traditional knowledge, innovation and practices to conserve and develop such PGRFA.

The second challenge regards the issue of whether (and how) the ABS norms of the FAO Treaty can provide enough flexibility for their mutually reinforcing coexistence with other systems of (international, national and/or community-level) norms, which regard the implementation of access to and use of PGRFA-related TK under terms that recognize the

---

[59]   Resolution 6/2009 on the implementation of Article 9—Farmers' Rights, Appendix A.6 of FAO (2009), above note 55.

right of indigenous and local communities and farmers to PIC and MAT.[60] This challenge presents two interlinked aspects, namely to implement the ITPGRFA's framework in a way that: 1) recognizes and respects the right of ILCs and farmers to give their prior informed consent before access to TK relevant to PGRFA (within the scope of the Multilateral System) is granted (i.e. the issue of *access to TK*-related PIC); and 2) provides scope for involving the ILCs and farmers, through their representatives, in the negotiations of the mutually agreed terms applicable to the use and transfer of such TK alongside the provisions of the SMTA (i.e. the issue of *use of TK*-related MAT).

4.2.3.3   Ways forward

Several measures may be taken to promote and protect traditional agricultural knowledge, innovation and practices of ILCs and farmers' rights under the ITPGRFA.

a   Reviewing the benefit-sharing conditions of the SMTA

The second paragraph of Article 13.2(d)(ii) of the ITPGRFA provides that

> the Governing Body may, from time to time, review the levels of payment with a view to achieving fair and equitable sharing of benefits, and it may also assess

---

[60]   Even though Article 15 of the CBD does not explicitly refer to PIC and MAT of indigenous and local communities for the use of their TK, their applicability has been emphasized in para. 26(d) of the Bonn Guidelines. Besides, access to TK shall be subject to PIC and MAT in accordance with Article 8(j) of the CBD, which states that parties shall promote the wider application of knowledge, innovation and practices of indigenous and local communities with 'the approval and involvement' of their holders and encourage the equitable sharing of the benefits arising from the utilisation of such knowledge, innovation and practices. In other words, 'the question no longer remains whether or not the CBD supports the right of ILCs to give PIC for the use of their associated TK and negotiate MAT, but rather how we can best ensure that ABS agreements with ILCs capture the spirit of Article 8(j) and affirm the rights of ILCs therein'. Thus, under the CBD, the conclusion of an ABS agreement, including its MAT, envisages bilateral negotiations between, on the one hand, the prospector or potential user of genetic resources and related TK and, on the other, the ABS focal point in the relevant country as well as the holders or custodians of such resources and TK—whenever identifiable—in accordance with national legislation, customary law and other relevant instruments such as 'bio-cultural community protocols'. CBD (2009), above note 56.

... whether the mandatory payment requirement in the MTA shall apply also in cases where such commercialized products are *available without restriction to others for further research and breeding*.[61]

At its third meeting, the Governing Body has decided to postpone such review to its fourth meeting. Aside from the discussion on whether 1.1 per cent (less 30 per cent) of sales (i.e. gross incomes from commercialization) is the most appropriate level of payments to be made to the benefit-sharing Fund of the Treaty, it would improve the current situation if parties could agree on removing the (above emphasized) access restriction requirement. The consequence would be that the Treaty's benefit-sharing mechanisms would become generally applicable to all transactions concerning the sales of seeds derived from the Multilateral System (*vis-à-vis* the present situation where only a not-well-identified share of transactions concerning MLS-derived patented seeds, GURTs and other PGRFA subject to licensing restrictions are subject to mandatory payments). Therefore, the proposed measure not only would make immediately available a larger amount of resources for supporting crop development projects and participatory plant breeding, implementing farmers' rights and protecting their TK, but would also increase transparency and legal certainty in the Multilateral System.

Besides, the level of mandatory benefit sharing under the Treaty is relatively low, for instance in comparison with an average VAT tax that for the decade 1996–2006 was above 19 per cent in EU 25 countries.[62] Such percentage corresponds to the level of payments that all of us make on the sales of any products that we buy in the EU, including seeds. Against this backdrop, the measure suggested above may not seriously be said to prejudice the financial stability of seed industries, breeders and consumers alike, while it would show their solidarity and commitment to sustainability, development and international equity. On the other hand, whenever the proposed revision of the benefit-sharing conditions of the SMTA might lead to inequitable outcomes, the Governing Body has the power 'to establish different levels of payment for various categories of recipients who commercialize such products [and] ... to exempt from such payments small farmers in developing countries and in countries with economies in transition'.[63] These safeguard measures, which are explicitly envisaged under the Treaty, should persuade all stakeholders to finally

---

[61]   Emphasis added.
[62]   European Commission (2006), *VAT Rates Applied in the Member States of the European Community*.
[63]   Article 13.2(d)(ii), second paragraph, of the ITPGRFA.

drop their reservations to the urgently needed revision of the Treaty's benefit-sharing conditions to ensure it can meet its benefit-sharing objective.

b   Implementing access to PGRFA-related TK under terms that
    recognize the right of ILCs and farmers to provide their prior
    informed consent and to negotiate mutually agreed terms for the
    use of their TK

The FAO Treaty and its SMTA already provide a mechanism that is suitable for implementing access to PGRFA-related TK under terms that recognize the right of ILCs and farmers to provide their prior informed consent and to negotiate mutually agreed terms for the use of 'PGRFA under development' and associated TK. However, this mechanism needs to be fine-tuned taking into account the special needs and capacities of ILCs and farmers in the context of their informal systems of seed production and crop improvement.

While the SMTA and its provisions have been drafted having in mind scientific plant breeding as reference, they do provide scope for protecting farmers' TK, innovation and practices relevant to PGRFA. In the effort to operationalize the relevant provisions of the Treaty and its SMTA, the Governing Body may decide to clarify the condition under which access to 'materials being developed by farmers' and associated TK shall require their prior informed consent in accordance with Article 12.3(e) of the Treaty, while ensuring that the use of such materials and associated TK is regulated by mutually agreed terms with the providing communities and farmers, alongside the terms of the SMTA.

4.3   CROP DIVERSITY AND THE ABS PROTOCOL TO THE CBD

Much of the genetic variability in today's cultivated crops largely benefited from free availability of plant genetic resources. The 1960s saw the first 'Green Revolution'. This was made possible by the wide sharing of such resources worldwide. With increasing privatization of both resources and knowledge during the past two decades, the entry into force of the Convention on Biological Diversity and the recent adoption of the ABS Protocol, issues of access to genetic resources, benefit sharing and IP protection have considerably changed the initial scenario of free access.[64] For instance, Parry investigates 'how 'bio-informational' resources are being collected and transacted in the global economy'.[65] She argues that:

> ... the ability to create new highly transmissible bio-informational proxies that, unlike many of their historical counterparts [i.e. raw genetic materials], actually prove fungible for them in processes of research and development ... as well as the creation of a new regulatory paradigm ... have together enabled collectors to create a burgeoning and lucrative market economy for these bio-informational commodities. If this trade is to be an equitable one, benefit sharing agreements must provide a mechanism that enables supplying countries to share in the profits that are generated from the many successive uses that are made of the bio-informational resources that have been collected within their borders.

During the negotiations of the CBD, developing countries with a rich endowment in natural resources and crop diversity bargained with developed countries offering access to their genetic resources in return for 'debt relief, royalties, technology transfers and research data'.[66] However, the implementation of CBD's third objective has proven to be particularly problematic.[67]

Eager to participate in the sharing of benefits arising from the use of genetic resources and associated traditional knowledge (TK), biodiversity-rich countries have started the development of national and

---

[64] The UN Special Rapporteur on the Right to Food has portrayed 'a marked paradigm shift ... from a system seeking to foster food security on the basis of the free exchange of knowledge to a system seeking to achieve the same goal on the basis of private appropriation of knowledge'. UN (2004), 'Report by the Special Rapporteur on the Right to Food, submitted in accordance with Commission on Human Rights Resolution 2003/25', E/CN.4/2004/10.

[65] P. Bronwyn (2004), *Trading the Genome: Investigating the Commodification of Bio-Information*, New York: Columbia University Press, at pp. 250–52.

[66] M. Blakeney (2002), 'Access to Genetic Resources, Gene-based Invention and Agriculture', Study Paper 3b, UK Commission on IPRs, at 27–9; and M. Chandler (1993), 'The Biodiversity Convention: Selected Issues of Interest to the International Lawyer', *Colorado Journal of International Environmental Law and Policy* 4, 141–76.

[67] UNU-IAS reports that only 50 countries either have 'adopted or are in the process of adopting measures to exercise and secure their sovereign rights over genetic resources'. UNU-IAS (2003), 'User Measures: Options for Developing Measures in User Countries to implement the Access and Benefit Sharing of the Convention on Biological Diversity', at p. 14; W.B. Chambers (2003), 'WSSD and an International Regime on Access and Benefit Sharing: Is a Protocol the Appropriate Legal Instrument?', *RECIEL,* 12/3, 310–20, at p. 316.

regional ABS regimes. Although their implementation does not appear to have generated the expected benefits so far,[68] such laws were perceived as a factor stopping long-running cross-boundary movements of PGR with potential negative consequences on agriculture and food security.[69]

However, in 2002 the perceived failure of the so-called 'grand bargain' and, in particular, poorly regulated access, lack of fair and equitable benefit sharing, and claims of misappropriation of genetic resources were all factors that contributed to the UN World Summit on Sustainable Development (WSSD) call for action to 'negotiate within the framework of the CBD, bearing in mind the Bonn Guidelines, an international regime to promote and safeguard the fair and equitable sharing of benefits arising out of the utilization of genetic resources'.[70]

Following the call, the Conference of the Parties of the CBD at its seventh meeting in 2004 decided to mandate the Working Group on ABS, with collaboration of the Working Group on Article 8(j), to negotiate an international regime on access and benefit sharing with the aim of adopting an instrument/instruments to implement the provisions in Articles 15 and 8(j) and the three objectives of the Convention.[71]

---

[68] IUCN reports that 'Since 1993, considerable, although still insufficient, progress has been made in implementing CBD obligations and principles especially through national laws and obligations. However, the effectiveness of national and regional measures has proven to be limited resulting in WSSD's call for an international framework'. IUCN (2006), IUCN Position Paper for CBD COP 8, Curitiba, Brazil (20–31 March 2006).

[69] Managers of CGIAR Centres frequently attribute the significant decline in the rate of acquisition of new materials by most of the Centres' genebanks in recent years 'to the highly politicised nature of access and benefit sharing issues at international, national and regional levels'. M. Halewood and R. Sood (2006), 'Genebanks and Public Goods: Political and Legal Challenges', paper prepared for the 19th session of the GRPC, El Batan, Mexico (22–24 February 2006).

[70] Paragraph 44(o) of the Johannesburg Plan of Implementation; L. Siegele (2008), 'How Many Roads? Negotiating an International Regime on Access and Benefit Sharing', paper given at SOAS LEDC/FIELD Lecture Series, IALS, London, 31 January 2008.

[71] See para. 1 of CBD COP Decision VII/19D. Article 8(J) of the CBD states:

Each Contracting Party shall ... subject to its national legislation, respect, preserve and maintain knowledge, innovations and practices of indigenous and local communities embodying traditional lifestyles relevant for the conservation and sustainable use of biological diversity and promote their wider application with the approval and involvement of the holders of such knowledge, innovations and practices and encourage the equitable sharing of the benefits arising from the utilization of such knowledge, innovations and practices.

For an overview of the developments leading to the international ABS regime

Against the backdrop of the recent adoption of the 'Nagoya Protocol on Access to Genetic Resources and the Fair and Equitable Sharing of Benefits Arising from their Utilization' (the ABS Protocol) at the tenth meeting of the Conference of the Parties of the CBD, this section considers the relationship between the ABS Protocol and the ITPGRFA. In particular, the legal requirements that may be established to implement the ABS Protocol will need to be mutually supportive of and coexist alongside the ITPGRFA. Thus, it might be crucial to assess whether lessons learned from the FAO Multilateral System's mechanism may advance discussions on related cross-sectoral issues in genetic resources that are considered by the CBD and its ABS Protocol.

4.3.1   The status of PGRFA under the ABS Protocol

CBD COP Decision VIII/4 established that the negotiation of an international regime on ABS under the CBD must be concluded 'at the earliest possible time before the tenth meeting of the Conference of the Parties'.[72] The importance of the ITPGRFA for the international ABS regime negotiations stems from two main facts.

First, to date the ITPGRFA is the only legally-binding international instrument—besides the ABS Protocol—that implements the ABS principles of the CBD. Second, while the ABS Protocol may cover all benefit-sharing instances not expressly regulated by the ITPGRFA, it should not preclude the potential expansion of the FAO Multilateral System.[73]

---

negotiations see: J.T. Hodges and A. Daniel (2005), 'Promises and Pitfalls: First Steps on the Road to the International ABS Regime', *RECIEL*, 14/2, 148–60.

[72]   CBD COP Decision VIII/4A, para. 6. In addition to renewing the mandate of the Working Group (WG) and setting the above timeframe for the negotiation, this Decision, in section C, established a Group of Technical Experts on an internationally recognized certificate of origin/source/legal provenance, which met in Lima, Peru, from 22 to 25 January 2007. CBD (2007), UNEP/CBD/WG-ABS/5/7, Lima, Peru (January 2007). The Group of Technical Experts: considered the possible rationale, objectives and the need for an internationally recognized certificate of origin/source/legal provenance; defined the potential characteristics and features of such an internationally recognized certificate; analysed the distinction between the options of certificate of origin/source/legal provenance and implications for achieving the objectives of Articles 15 and 8(j); and identified associated implementation challenges.

[73]   'The important contribution' of the ITPGRFA and its relevance for the negotiation of the international regime on ABS is emphasized by COP Decision VII/19D.

In particular, the draft ABS Protocol provided two alternative options to exclude from its scope: 1) genetic resource contained in Annex I of the ITPGRFA provided they are used for the purposes of the ITPGRFA; or 2) genetic resources under the Multilateral System of the ITPGRFA, both current and as may be amended by the Governing Body of the ITPGRFA.[74] The exclusion under the first option is narrower than the second one, since the latter makes no reference to purpose-of-use-related requirements for the actual inclusion of PGRFA into the Multilateral System. On the other hand, it envisages the potential expansion of the Multilateral System's coverage to other crops and forages not currently listed in Annex I. Besides, Article 3.*bis*, paragraph 4 of the draft ABS Protocol, states:

> This Protocol is the instrument for the implementation of the [ABS] provisions of the Convention. Where a specialised international [ABS] instrument applies that is consistent with, and does not run counter to the objectives of the Convention and this Protocol, this Protocol does not apply for the Party or Parties to the specialised instrument in respect of the specific genetic resource covered by and for the purpose of the specialised instrument.

In the final ABS negotiations, a common understanding emerged that the finalization of the Protocol would entail the deletion of both the alternative options for the express exclusion of PGRFA from the Protocol's scope under letter c) of draft Article 3. On the other hand, the above provision on 'relationship with other instruments', as contained in Article 3.*bis,* would be retained. When the ABS Protocol was adopted, such a common understanding eventually prevailed as the agreed solution that was built into it. Therefore, it is important to examine its legal implications.

Although the ITPGRFA and its MLS are not directly referred to in Artcle 3.*bis*, there is no doubt that the former is in fact the only existing 'specialised ABS instrument' consistent with the CBD. Article 3.*bis* is drafted in broad terms that allow for the voluntary use of the SMTA,

---

[74]   Article 3, not numbered para. 2, letter c) of the 'advanced unedited' text (UNEP/CBD/WG-ABS/9/ING/1), as amended by the Interregional Negotiating Group (ING) on 18–21 September 2010. The ING was established by the *Ad Hoc* Open-ended Working Group on ABS at its resumed ninth meeting (Montreal, 10–16 July 2010). The text developed by the ING was considered by the ABS Working Group, when it resumed its ninth meeting in Nagoya on 16 October 2010. Then, the tenth meeting of the Conference of the Parties (COP) to the Convention on Biological Diversity (CBD) finalized negotiations and adopted the ABS Protocol.

including for the transfer of non-*Annex* I PGRFA. In particular, this Article provides scope for using the SMTA for the transfer of materials held in the *ex-situ* collections of the CGIAR, including non-Annex I PGRFA, in accordance with the relevant decision of the ITPGRFA's Governing Body.[75] It also allows for the transfer of PGRFA from providers under the jurisdiction of an ITPGRFA party to recipients under the jurisdiction of non-parties.[76] Thus, the solution that was eventually adopted in the ABS Protocol appears neither to affect the rights and obligations of any Party deriving from existing international agreements nor to prevent parties from developing new specialized ABS agreements.

4.3.2   Lessons learned from the ITPGRFA

The role of the Standard Material Transfer Agreement under the ITPGRFA and 'the way it can be used to keep track of transfers of materials and to link their use to benefit-sharing is a very useful precedent' for the ABS Protocol's Parties to consider.[77] The CGIAR Centres suggested that 'the SMTA functions as a certificate of source, with the source or origin of the PGRFA being the Multilateral System itself'.[78] Thus, the SMTA functions not only as an essential mechanism for the implementation of the MLS, but also as a certificate of source or compliance with the ITPGRFA.

The report of the Expert Group on an internationally recognized certificate has emphasized that 'transfers to third parties should require maintenance of the link with the certificate and the [MAT] applying to the resources'.[79] The Expert Group has also noted that 'additional implementation challenges and costs may be related to the coexistence of genetic resources inside and outside the system'.[80] Therefore, the complementarity between the SMTA and 'an internationally recognized certificate of compliance' under the ABS Protocol may contribute to reduce costs from materials being exchanged outside the system.

---

[75]   IT/GB-2/07/Report, para. 68.

[76]   This interpretation is supported by the utilization of the expression '... this Protocol does not apply for the Party or Parties to the specialised instrument ...', where specific reference is made to either 'Party or Parties' *vis-à-vis* a single reference to 'Parties'.

[77]   SGRP (2007), 'A *de facto* Certificate of Source: the Standard Material Transfer Agreement under the International Treaty', at p. 3.

[78]   CGIAR (2007), above note 53, at p. 3.

[79]   CBD (2007), above note 72, at paras 26 and 41.

[80]   Ibid.

As regards the issue of 'derivatives', this term is not defined by the ITPGRFA or the SMTA. Fowler *et al.* 'sought to bring clarity to these issues by proposing how the "germplasm and related information" covered by the FAO-CGIAR Agreements should be interpreted and by describing a number of options for minimum requirements for taking out [IP] protection on derivatives and components of designated germplasm'.[81] However, the authors point out that 'the FAO, the CGIAR and the international community … may choose to retain the *status quo* in which the question of what can and cannot be done with designated germplasm is left unanswered'.[82] They also note that 'choosing not to deal with the subject is itself a choice, though perhaps not the best one'.[83]

In the context of the ABS Protocol negotiations, a critical question was whether an 'incorporation requirement' akin to the one used under the ITPGRFA to trigger benefit sharing from the sale of PGRFA derived from the FAO Multilateral System could be employed to identify derivatives for the Protocol's benefit-sharing purposes. Unfortunately, the application of the 'incorporation requirement' beyond plant breeding proves difficult. This is because the creation of new plant varieties inherently reduces to an activity that makes use of multiple genetic parts and components containing 'functional units of heredity'. On the contrary, many gene products at the sub-organisms level, non-DNA molecules and proteins do not contain such 'functional units of heredity'. For instance, this might be the case with natural product discovery in the pharmaceutical sector.

Therefore, in order to comprise categories of products whose discovery would not occur without the use of genetic resources, even though such products may not *physically* contain 'functional units of heredity', Article 2 of the ABS Protocol defines a 'derivative' as 'a naturally occurring biochemical compound resulting from the genetic expression or metabolism of biological or genetic resources, even if it does not contain functional units of heredity'.

4.3.3 A note of caution

Rose provocatively questioned whether 'the paper used over [the] seven years of negotiations' that were necessary to develop the ITPGRFA was

---

[81]   C. Fowler *et al.* (2004), 'The Question of Derivatives. Promoting Use and Ensuring Availability of Non-Proprietary Plant Genetic Resources', *JWIP*, 7/5, 641–63 at pp. 663–4.

[82]   Ibid.

[83]   Ibid.

'worth the trees'.[84] Besides, Koester argues that 'when faced with the question 'have we really accomplished anything?' the only answer is: what would be the condition of our biodiversity if these conventions did not exist?'[85] Koester's point is an important one, which is relevant with the view to assessing the outcome of the ABS Protocol negotiations.

As regards Rose's opinion on the FAO Treaty, 'the answer is yes', it was worth it, because the ITPGRFA 'will operate to ensure availability of PGRFA, simplify transfers, promote fairness in benefit sharing, and direct some benefits towards PGRFA conservation'.[86] If all the above is being accomplished thanks to multilateral cooperation on crop diversity conservation, that is indeed a great success. However, to the extent that the ITPGRFA sets global rules that impact on scientific research and plant breeding, the former can be considered a success story only because the affected scientific community eventually endorsed the proposed solutions or at least they could leave with them.[87]

In the same vein, it will be necessary to ensure that the regulation that is proposed under the ABS Protocol gives due consideration to the practical ways in which trans-national collaboration actually takes place in the research community.[88] One of the risks is that 'legislation and practice that seeks to implement the CBD do not unduly restrict the legitimate use of genetic resources, discouraging scientific research'.[89] In this respect, it might be appropriate to increase implementation efforts to distinguish between commercial and non-commercial research, and to set facilitated

---

[84]   G. Rose (2003), 'International Law of Sustainable Agriculture in the 21st Century: The International Treaty on Plant Genetic Resources for Food and Agriculture', *The Georgetown International Environmental Law Review,* XV/4, 583–632.

[85]   V. Koester (2002), 'The Five Global Biodiversity-Related Conventions: A Stocktaking', *RECIEL,* 11/1, 96–103, at p. 103.

[86]   G. Rose (2003), above note 84.

[87]   The CGIAR Centres report that over the first eight months of 2007 'a total of 97,669 samples were distributed under the SMTA' and 'only three potential recipients have refused explicitly to accept materials under the SMTA'. FAO (2007), 'Experience of the CGIAR with the implementation of the agreements with the Governing Body, with particular reference to the SMTA', IT/GB-2/07/Inf. 11, FAO, Rome, Italy (29 October–2 November 2007), paras 7–8.

[88]   See the risks highlighted by K.S. Jayaraman (2008), 'Entomologists stifled by Indian bureaucracy. "Biopiracy" concerns thwart insect hunters', *Nature,* 452, 7.

[89]   UK Commission on IPRs (2002), 'Integrating Intellectual Property Rights and Development Policy', London (September 2002), Chapter 4.

access conditions for those who do not seek access for commercial purposes in accordance with Articles 6(a) and 9.4 of the ABS Protocol.[90]

However, the difficulties involved in distinguishing public non-commercial research from private for-profit research should be fully taken into account. Therefore, the tensions of public research organizations concerning the need to strike a balance between their public role, as providers of public goods, and the necessity to make use of the IP system, including for securing access to intellectual assets as public goods for development, must be fully acknowledged. Such necessity may arise for several reasons, including *inter alia*: to increase research budgets through licensing revenues; to facilitate the transfer of technology for further development and commercialization; defensive protection; and freedom-to-operate-related purposes such as using IP assets as bargaining chips to access third parties' technologies.

While the above tensions blur the distinction between commercial and non-commercial research, their acknowledgment should not lead to the denial of the opportunity to define these concepts in a way that makes them fit for purpose in the context of the ABS Protocol's implementation. A basic principle that may provide guidance in defining such concepts could be that they should be flexible enough to regulate differently different situations. Besides, national courts routinely face the above definitional challenge, for instance when they need to determine the scope of application of the research exemption under patent laws.[91] Therefore,

---

[90]   Under 'Special Considerations', Article 6 of the ABS Protocol states:

In the development and implementation of its access and benefit-sharing legislation or regulatory requirements, each Party shall: (a) Create conditions to promote and encourage research which contributes to the conservation and sustainable use of biological diversity, particularly in developing countries, including through simplified measures on access for non-commercial research purposes, taking into account the need to address a change of intent for such research.

Under 'Traditional Knowledge associated with Genetic Resources', Article 9.4 states:

Parties, in their implementation of this Protocol, shall, as far as possible, not restrict the customary use and exchange of genetic resources and associated traditional knowledge within and amongst indigenous and local communities in accordance with the objectives of the Convention.

[91]   See, for instance, section 3.4.3.1 on the 'Experimental Use Exemption in the US' and, in particular, *Madey v Duke University*, 64 USPQ2d 1737 (Fed. Cir. 2002).

applicable patent law principles of domestic origin may be taken into account by analogy.

A possible approach is to draw the line between commercial and non-commercial research based on the principle of reciprocity. For instance, the Protocol's parties may include in their national legislation a rule that defines 'non-commercial research' on a case-by-case basis (for the purpose of applying 'simplified measures on access') in accordance with the criteria that define the patent law research exemption in the jurisdictions where the recipients/users undertake R&D activities. This mechanism could provide a balanced solution in that access to genetic resources would be easier for 'non-commercial research' defined in accordance with the scope of the restrictions that may be placed on access to the recipients/users' research products.

Another approach is to refer to relevant international standards. This chapter has noted that monetary benefits must be shared in the FAO Multilateral System when an IPR restriction limits the facilitated access to a derivative product that is a PGRFA. Thus, the intention to file an application for IP protection can be *per se* a useful element to draw the line between commercial and non-commercial research. However, patent applications do not necessarily indicate the intention to commercialize a product, including in the form of licensing. Therefore, it may be necessary to include exceptions to the straightforward application of such IP-protection-filing criterion, which could be based on relevant policy principles such as those provided by the 'Draft Policy of the Alliance of CGIAR Centres on Intellectual Assets'.[92]

Finally, if the potential for developing a commercial product exists, national legislation that implements the ABS Protocol should not prevent

---

[92]   GRPC (2009), 'Minutes of the Genetic Resources Policy Committee (GRPC)', 25th Session, Penang (17–19 March 2009), Appendix 4. This policy intends to provide guidelines for the management of the Centre's intellectual assets. In accordance with this proposal, the Centres 'will make their intellectual assets globally available without restriction' except 'when it is indispensable for the effective utilization or further improvement of Centres' intellectual assets'. In these cases, 'the Centres may grant limited exclusivity for commercialization in a defined market segment, for a limited period of time, provided they continue to make the intellectual asset available, for research and development in developing countries as well as for Advanced Research Institutions (ARIs) in support of the CGIAR mission'. The Centres may also seek or assert IPRs over such assets for the same reasons and subject to the same conditions about availability that are described above, and 'will not use their intellectual assets with the sole intention to raise income'. M.C. Correa (2009), 'Trends in Intellectual Property Rights relating to Genetic Resources for Food and Agriculture', Background Study Paper No. 49, FAO, Rome, Italy.

genetic resources, which have been acquired in accordance with non-commercial terms, from being used in a commercial research programme. This may occur under a new set of mutually agreed terms that reflect a new balance of benefit-sharing rights and obligations in accordance with Article 5.2(f)(iv) of the Protocol, which states: '... each Party requiring [PIC], shall take the necessary legislative, administrative or policy measures, as appropriate, to ... establish clear rules and procedures for requiring and establishing [MAT]. Such terms shall be set out in writing and may include, *inter alia* ... terms on changes of intent ...'.

4.4 CONCLUDING REMARKS

ABS-related restrictions on access to genetic resources could be understood as tools used by governments to internalize positive externalities that would otherwise be distributed in the form of benefits derived from unfettered access to genetic resources. Thus, ABS systems are government-led forms of commodification in the sense that materials covered by such systems do not usually form part of the public domain and the resulting benefits are shared bilaterally between transacting parties.

However, bilateral benefit-sharing mechanisms are not appropriate for crop research, because countries are enormously interdependent in terms of plant genetic diversity and several different breeding materials are necessary to breed a new plant variety. Thus, the ITPGRFA creates a Multilateral System of ABS that does not require *ad hoc* negotiations between providers and recipients of PGRFA, and reduces transaction costs. In particular, it uses a Standard Material Transfer Agreement to track individual accessions and ensure that some benefits flow back to the Multilateral System when a product based on MLS material is commercialized on the market.

As regards the link between IPR protection and benefit sharing, it is premature to make an evaluation of the impact of increasing levels of IPR protection on the diverse components of expected benefit-sharing flows from the Multilateral System. However, there is a strong correlation between restrictions on access to PGRFA, in particular patents, which are the strongest form of protection for plant-related inventions, and benefit sharing. By contrast, because of the breeders' exemption, *sui generis* plant variety protection systems do not generate benefits that can be captured in the form of compulsory payments to the MLS.[93]

Strong monopoly protection for intermediate products may be at odds with the ITPGRFA open access regime. Among other factors, the successful implementation of the MLS will depend on whether the increasingly global patenting of plant-related inventions will make it more cumbersome for poor countries to acquire and integrate new scientific and technical knowledge related to the conservation and sustainable use of PGRFA in their production systems. This highlights the need to protect the public domain status of materials included into the Multilateral System.

At its first meeting, the Governing Body of ITPGRFA established the level, form and manner of equitable benefit sharing payments to be implemented through the SMTA. These payments depend on: A) the incorporation of MLS materials into commercial plant varieties and B) the existence of research and breeding restrictions on their access, including IPRs restrictions. On the one hand, access to these plant varieties can be legally restricted (to meet the requirement under letter B above), only if they incorporate non-MLS patented technologies. By contrast, the SMTA should not allow patents to claim genetic components 'in the form received' from the Multilateral System, e.g. in the form of unmodified derivatives of MLS material and their progeny. On the other hand, the 'incorporation requirement' (under letter A above) should encompass the 'progeny' and 'unmodified derivatives' of the material transferred through the SMTA. Besides, the incorporation into a proprietary product of patented information that results from R&D carried out on MLS material can give rise to benefit-sharing payments *per se*, if the requirement under letter B above is met.

The importance of an effective global mechanism to monitor and enforce compliance with the SMTA is self evident. This is because the facilitated access conditions of the Multilateral System that are implemented through the SMTA also apply to non-contracting parties

---

[93] See section 3.3.2 on 'Agricultural Exemptions under UPOV' based on C. Chiarolla (2006), 'Commodifying Agricultural Biodiversity and Development-related Issues', *JWIP*, 9(1), 25–60. The breeders' exemption allows breeders to use protected varieties as starting materials for breeding new varieties without any requirement for an authorization or any payment of royalties (Article 14 of the 1991 UPOV Act). However, under Article 13(d)(ii) of the ITPGRFA, the Governing Body 'may assess ... whether the mandatory payment requirement in the MTA shall apply also in cases where such commercialized products are available without restrictions to other for further research and breeding'.

and their nationals, which are not directly bound by the ITPGRFA.[94] National laws, in turn, may differ on important issues, which are critical for the implementation of the SMTA. These issues range from the validity of the method of expressing acceptance of an SMTA to the enforceability of third party beneficiary's rights, from the scope of IPR protection that can be claimed by recipients over a derivative product, to the enforcement of benefit-sharing obligations.[95] Thus, in the context of dispute settlement, the predictable and uniform interpretation of the SMTA's standard terms and conditions guarantees the internal coherence of the Multilateral System. Because of this critical reason, the Governing Body of the ITPGRFA has decided that the law applicable to the SMTA should include only non-national and international standards without making any reference to national law.

However, substantive law of domestic origin could be used to supplement the interpretation of an SMTA in three exceptional cases. Arbitrators may apply 'mandatory' provisions of national origin in accordance with the relevant conflict rules of private international law. In addition, national law could also be used to fill a gap, when the UNIDROIT Principles do not provide a solution to a case, and such solution cannot be derived from the General Principles of Law or the ITPGRFA. Finally, in the case of transfer of 'PGRFA under development', providers may attach additional conditions, which relate to product development, in accordance with Article 6.6 of the SMTA. When this provision applies, the parties to an SMTA, in the exercise of their contractual freedom, may specify a national standard to regulate the

---

[94]   Third party transfers to nationals of non-contracting parties may occur in the case of materials held by the *ex-situ* collections of the CGIAR Centres, which have made clear that the Agreements with the Governing Body of ITPGRFA do not prevent them from sending materials held *in trust* to non-contracting parties. (2007), 'Agreements between FAO, acting on behalf of the Governing Body of the ITPGRFA, and the Centres of the CGIAR', signed on 1 January 2007, available at: www.planttreaty.org/art15_en.htm (accessed 6 October 2007).

[95]   For instance, with regard to the conclusion of the SMTA, Article 10 provides for three possible methods of acceptance: 1) signature; 2) 'shrink-wrap' SMTA; and 3) 'click-wrap' SMTA. In particular, this Article establishes that 'the provider and the recipient may choose the method of acceptance unless either party requires this Agreement to be signed'. Thus, the written form is not required for the conclusion of an SMTA. However, in many countries, the express acceptance by the parties to be bound by a contract must be proven in writing. Thus, an SMTA concluded in other forms could be void under national contract law. G. Moore and S. Moore (2005), 'Methods of Expressing Acceptance of the Terms and Conditions of MTAs: Shrink-Wrap and Click-Wrap Agreements', Background Study Paper No. 26, FAO.

supplementary matters that they have included in the SMTA. On the contrary, a choice a law clause, which specifies a particular national law with respect to the whole agreement or to some of its *standard* provisions, would jeopardize the SMTA implementation and should be void. In sum, only supplementary matters, but not standard terms, may be interpreted taking into account the national standards agreed by the parties, if any.[96]

As a consequence of economic law reforms certain commercial interests may prevail, while others may lose from harmonization processes and the opening up of new markets for biological information and materials.[97] The function of benefit sharing is precisely to compensate the losers from the international business regulatory game, linking economic law reforms with capacity building, information exchange and technology transfer. In agriculture, the SMTA is a fundamental mechanism for benefit sharing. In a dispute over the interpretation of a particular SMTA, the applicable law and, in particular, the balance between non-national, international and national standards will play an important role in defining both the scope and the impact of benefit sharing on international equity in agriculture.

ABS issues related to PGR that are not covered by the Multilateral System as well as non-food or feed uses of MLS crops may fall within the scope of the ABS Protocol under the CBD. As a consequence, legal requirements that may be established under the ABS Protocol need to be mutually supportive of and coexist alongside the ITPGRFA. However, to the extent that such ABS requirements (applicable to PGRFA not included into the MLS) will add complexity to the definition of the ownership status of PGR, as opposed to streamlining the widest application of the ITPGRFA's commons management principles, they risk acting as a barrier to agricultural research and plant-related innovation. Thus, the implementation of the ABS Protocol should not preclude the expansion of the list of food crops not yet included into the FAO Multilateral System of ABS.

As regards the issues of farmers' rights and TK protection, the FAO Treaty can be mutually supportive of other systems of international,

---

[96] However, monitoring the use of this type of clauses may be problematic because the additional conditions of Article 6.6 of the SMTA are likely to be kept confidential, unless the Governing Body expressly decides that they must be notified jointly with concluded SMTAs.

[97] Dutfield also notes that 'irrespective of whether the gains for the gainers of harmonisation are sufficient to compensate the losers for their losses' normally those who are better off do not compensate the losers. G. Dutfield (2006), 'Patents and Development: Exclusions, Industrial Application and Technical Effect', paper given at the WIPO Open Forum on the Draft Substantive Patent Law Treaty, Geneva, 1–3 March 2006.

national and/or community-level norms that implement access to PGRFA-related TK and associated resources under terms that recognize the right of ILCs and farmers to PIC and MAT. However, in the first place, the implementation of such right presents the challenge for customary right-holders to obtain the legal recognition of their *de facto* rights of customary nature under national laws.

In order to secure a more equitable distribution of wealth from crop diversity, several challenges needs to be addressed in relation to the benefit-sharing mechanism of the FAO Treaty and its Multilateral System. It is hoped that, having created such a flexible and forward-looking Treaty mechanism, the contracting parties, governments, development agencies and other relevant stakeholders alike will not ignore the rights that ILCs and farmers have under international law to share equitably the benefits arising from the use of crop diversity and associated TK for its conservation and development. Continuing business as usual will not provide the urgent actions needed to halt the erosion of agricultural biodiversity and the bio-cultural values that underpin such diversity.

5. Case study: the regulation of crop diversity in Viet Nam

5.1 INTRODUCTION

Viet Nam is a country with an economy in transition, which has recently undergone deep economic and legislative changes. These changes have modernized its national innovation and trading system with the aim of improving Viet Nam's competitiveness and its full participation in the global economy.

The positive impact of these reforms on economic growth, employment and income generation has also increased the pressure on natural resources and the environment.[1] The Government of Viet Nam, aware of the significant economic and cultural values of biodiversity, has developed a legal and policy framework for the management and protection of biodiversity. Such framework includes the regulation of access to genetic resources and the sharing of the benefits arising from their use.

This case study is designed to test the proposition that global institutional reforms, which govern the present and future allocation of wealth from crop diversity and, in particular, their implementation in the Vietnamese context, neither has legally recognized the need to afford a special treatment to PGRFA, nor has remarkably strengthened the important role that informal seed systems still play in the country.

In order to test the proposition outlined above it is necessary to analyse how IPR and biodiversity-related obligations are being enacted in Viet Nam to bring national legislation into harmony with international

---

[1] According to the World Bank, 'Viet Nam is one of the three borrowing countries achieving the highest quality outcomes for the period 2000 to 2004'. However, biodiversity and the livelihood of ethnic minorities appear to be particularly threatened by these developments. World Bank (2007), 'Country Report—Vietnam: Laying the Foundations for Steady Growth', IDA at Work, at p. 7.

requirements on plant genetic resources.[2] This chapter also highlights the reasons why it is challenging to design such national laws in a manner that duly takes into account the special nature of crop diversity and the domestic level of plant breeding and biotechnology capacity with the aim of defining the most appropriate balance between distributed innovation, on the one hand, and centralized control of plant-related innovation, on the other.

5.1.1   Criteria for the selection of the study country

The selection of the case study country is based on the following criteria. In Viet Nam, the most important industry is agriculture, which accounted for approximately one-fourth of its GDP in 2003.[3] It is also a country with an economy in transition, which has undergone deep economic law reforms and has modernized its national innovation and trading system.

On 11 January 2007, it became the 150th member of the WTO. As a consequence, Viet Nam has harmonized its national legislation on patents and plant variety rights protection. Besides, on 24 November 2006, it joined the Union for the Protection of New Varieties of Plants. Viet Nam's accession to these treaties is important for this study, because it entails the obligation to comply with international legal norms, including the 1991 UPOV Act.[4]

The Government of Viet Nam is also aware of the importance of biodiversity and is committed to its conservation through the development of an appropriate legal and policy framework. In 2003, as part of its efforts to implement the CBD, the Government started the elaboration of the 'Biodiversity Law',[5] which was adopted on 13 November 2008 and entered into force on 1 July 2009.[6]

---

[2]   The baselines, which are taken as reference points to identify the minimum standards applicable to international IPR and ABS obligations, are respectively Article 27.3(b) of the TRIPs Agreement and Article 15 of the CBD.

[3]   UNESCAP, 'Agricultural Background—Socialist Republic of Viet Nam', available at: www.unapcaem.org/ppt/vn-01.htm#bg (accessed 10 June 2008).

[4]   In particular, the 1991 UPOV Act entered into force on 24 December 2006. UPOV (2006), 'Viet Nam Accedes to the UPOV Convention', UPOV Press Release No. 70, Geneva (24 November 2006).

[5]   Government's Decision No. 35/2003/QD-TTg of 6 March 2003 to assign the Ministry of Natural Resources and Environment (MoNRE) to develop a Biodiversity Law; and IUCN (2008), *Leveraging legal mechanisms to safeguard biodiversity in Viet Nam*, 7 January 2008.

[6]   Article 77 of the 'Biodiversity Law of Viet Nam' (2008), No. 20/2008/QH12. The Law was passed on 13 November 2008 by the XII National Assembly of the Socialist Republic of Viet Nam at its 4th session.

Chapter 5 of the Biodiversity Law regulates issues of access to genetic resources and benefit sharing. These obligations will have a direct impact on domestic and transnational agricultural research, because several activities, including access to genetic resources, bioprospecting, the management of derivative intellectual property and the dissemination of biodiversity-based research products, will need to be carried out in accordance with the Biodiversity Law's ABS requirements and procedures.

Viet Nam is also a member of the FAO Commission on Genetic Resources for Food and Agriculture. While it has not yet ratified the International Treaty on Plant Genetic Resources for Food and Agriculture, such ratification is currently being considered by the Government. Against this backdrop, the Biodiversity Law should provide the scope to implement the ITPGRFA. This case study examines key issues, which have emerged during the drafting and consultation processes related to the Biodiversity Law; in particular the question of whether the development of the biodiversity legal framework gives due consideration to crop diversity and how to avoid that the use of plant genetic resources is unduly restricted in agricultural research and breeding.

Finally, Viet Nam has received a great deal of development and trade-related technical assistance from various national, regional and international agencies over the last 15 years. Such activities have focused on IP protection and enforcement[7] as well as on access and benefit-sharing issues.[8] This makes Viet Nam an interesting laboratory to observe how the interests, priorities and goals of different actors have played out in shaping, in collaboration with national stakeholders, the outcomes of the described law reform processes.

5.1.2 Methodology and sources of information

For both plant-related IPR protection and ABS, the analysis in this chapter follows a common pattern, which considers the following aspects of relevant legislative reforms.

---

[7] See: AgBiotech Vietnam, available at: www.agbiotech.com.vn/en/ (accessed 10 May 2008); K. Jensen (2008), 'Wrap-up of PIPRA's workshop in Vietnam', 2 January 2008, available at: http://blog.pipra.org/search/label/vietnam (accessed 10 May 2008); and The EC-ASEAN Intellectual Property Rights Cooperation Programme (ECAP II), 'Activities/Events at national level—Vietnam', available at: www.ecap-project.org/archive/index.php?id=135 (accessed 14 March 2011).

[8] CBD (2006), 'Capacity Building on Access and Benefit-Sharing (ABS) in Vietnam', available at: www.cbd.int/abs/project.shtml?id=30939 (accessed 10 May 2008).

The first component of this analysis is to study the legislative processes that have given legal recognition to restrictions on access to plant genetic resources through national obligations. The role of key national and international actors involved in these reform processes is duly considered as, *inter alia*, they contribute to: set the reform agenda; assess domestic capacity development needs in the relevant areas, including the need for legal technical assistance; and design technical assistance programmes in response to those needs.

The second component of this analysis is to consider the coverage of (and the scope of exemptions from) the rights conferred by the relevant legal instruments, including patent rights, plant variety rights, and veto rights of legal persons from whom prior informed consent must be obtained to access Vietnamese plant genetic resources.

The third component is to critically assess (to the extent that implementation has actually taken place and on the basis of available information) the expected impact of such exclusion rights on agricultural research in the context of sustainable development policies.

This case study is based on the analysis of primary and secondary sources, some of which were collected during three field-work research trips in the study country.[9] Primary sources include information collected through semi-structured interviews, informal discussions and official meetings, which were held to identify the key issues arising from the drafting and implementation of relevant national legislation.[10]

---

[9]   The first field-trip to Hanoi, Viet Nam, in October 2006, was to participate to the International Workshop on 'Exploring novel legal definitions of farmers' varieties in national initiatives to promote Farmers' Rights', which was organized by the Genetic Resources Policy Initiative (GRPI), a project jointly executed by Bioversity International and the International Development Research Centre. The workshop focused on plant variety protection, including the relevant features of the new Vietnamese plant variety rights system. The goal of the second and third field-trips to Hanoi, Viet Nam, held respectively in March and November 2007, was: to undertake research and semi-structured interviews alongside the provision of technical assistance for the development of the draft Biodiversity Law; and to participate to the 'International Workshop on the Biodiversity Law', which was organized by IUCN, UNDP and the Ministry of Natural Resources and the Environment of Viet Nam on 3 November 2007.

[10]   These research activities include meetings with officials and staff of: the FAO country office and the IUCN country office in Viet Nam; the Ministry of Natural Resources and the Environment; the Ministry of Agriculture and Rural Development; the Vietnamese Plant Variety Protection Office; managers and staff of public research institutes, including the Institute of Agricultural Genetics and the Viet Nam Academy of Agriculture Science.

Desk research was also important to assess the evolution of national legislation. Primary sources comprise the review of government documents as well as WTO and UPOV official documents.[11] Secondary sources, such as reports of UN development agencies, are utilized to provide the general background of the law reform process. Other secondary sources include: the website of technical assistance agencies and seed companies operating in Viet Nam as well as newspaper articles.

5.1.3 Legislative power and hierarchy between the sources of law

The legal system of Viet Nam has four levels of legislation. The first hierarchic level of legislation includes the Constitution, laws and ordinances. The Constitution of the Socialist Republic of Viet Nam was issued in 1992 and amended pursuant to Resolution 51/2001/QH10. Viet Nam has undertaken a deep process of economic and legislative reforms, named *do moi*, in accordance with the new Constitution.

In general, laws must be approved by the National Assembly, which is the institution with the highest powers under the Constitution.[12] The National Assembly exercises not only legislative, but also certain executive and judiciary powers and meets twice a year for a 30-day session. Ordinances, named *phap lenh*, hierarchically follow laws within the first level legislation; they are approved by the Standing Committee of the National Assembly through a process that is shorter and simpler than the one for the approval of laws.

The second level legislation can be enacted both by the Government and the Prime Minister, and includes government resolutions, government decrees, decisions of the Prime Minister, and instructions of the Prime Minister.

The third level legislation is enacted by the ministries and includes decisions, circulars and instructions of the ministers. The above legal

---

[11] These documents concern: 1) the TRIPs section of Reports of the Working Party on the Accession of New WTO Members; 2) notifications of relevant laws and regulations made to the WTO TRIPs Council in accordance with Article 63, para. 2 of the Agreement; and 3) reviews of legislation carried out by the WTO TRIPs Council, in response to written requests from other Members, in accordance with Article 63, para. 3 of the TRIPs Agreement; and 4) the UPOV (2006), 'Examination of the Conformity of the Intellectual Property Law of Viet Nam with the 1991 Act of the UPOV Convention', C(Extr.)/23/2, Twenty-Third Extraordinary Session of the UPOV Council, Geneva (7 April 2006).

[12] The legislative process in Viet Nam is regulated by: Articles 103 and 106 of the 1992 Constitution; Article 91 of the Law on the Organisation of the National Assembly; and Article 50 of the Law on the Promulgation of Legal Documents.

instruments normally have the same legal standing. Finally, the local government has the powers to enact the fourth level legislation. The local government structure is composed of: 64 provinces (corresponding to 64 Provincial People Committees), districts (corresponding to District People Committees), and commune/ward (corresponding to People Committees). These local authorities exercise their legislative powers through the decisions and instructions of People Committees.

5.2 IP REFORM AND PLANT INTELLECTUAL PROPERTY PROTECTION IN VIET NAM

In accordance with its Constitution of 1992, Viet Nam has undertaken a very deep economic and legislative reform, named *do moi*, which recognizes the need to develop a 'multi-component commodity economy functioning in accordance with market mechanisms under the management of the State and following a socialist orientation'. In sharp contrast with the Constitution of 1980, this reform has opened the door to a multi-sectoral economy marked by the progressive recognition of private property, including intellectual property, and the protection of foreign direct investments.[13]

5.2.1 The legal recognition of intellectual property

Until relatively recent times, the Socialist Republic of Viet Nam did not recognize private property rights over intellectual creations and inventions, which belonged to the State. The 1981 Ordinance on Innovation and Inventions is the first legal instrument to introduce the concept of IP protection in the Country. Under the 1981 Ordinance, inventions could be protected through either a certificate or a patent.

In theory, patents should confer exclusive rights on protected inventions. However, in practice, inventors could not benefit from such rights, because many socio-legal constraints were contributing to discourage individual entrepreneurship.[14] Therefore, in the early period of the Vietnamese intellectual property history, most inventors preferred the certificate system, which ensured at least a moral recognition and some remuneration for the services provided to the society. Interestingly,

---

[13]   A. Luu (2006), 'Vietnam Legal Research', GlobaLex, available at: www.nyulawglobal.org/globalex/Vietnam.htm#_edn9 (accessed 10 April 2007).
[14]   V.V. Dzung (2007), 'Vietnam Patent Law—Substantive Law Provisions and Existing Uncertainties', *Chicago-Kent Journal of Intellectual Property*, 6, 138–56.

inventions relating to food and agriculture were included into the category of subject matter exclusions for which only a certificate could be granted.

With regard to its participation to international IP agreements, since July 1976 Viet Nam has been a member of the World Intellectual Property Organization (WIPO) and, in December 1992, it acceded to the Patent Cooperation Treaty (PCT). After that, the negotiations for its accession to the World Trade Organization (WTO) gave a new impetus to the legislative reform process in the field of IPRs.[15]

In 1989 a new Ordinance on Industrial Property Rights strengthened the rights conferred by the patent system.[16] However, it was only with the Civil Code adopted in 1995 that a solid legal foundation for private ownership (including intellectual property rights) was established.[17] In addition, the implementation of the IP provisions of the Civil Code gave impetus for the establishment of a *sui generis* system for the protection of plant variety rights.[18]

5.2.2   Bilateral obligations to protect plant-related IP

Besides international treaties' obligations, estimates indicate that Viet Nam has 'signed trade agreements with around 76 countries'.[19] Some of

---

[15]   J. Kuanpoth (2007), 'Patents and Access to Antiretroviral Medicines in Vietnam after World Trade Organization Accession', *JWIP*, 10/3–4, 201–24, at p. 207.
[16]   The Ordinance was enacted by the State Council of Viet Nam on 11 February 1989. The term of protection for patents rights was limited to 15 years and it was not TRIPs compliant.
[17]   See Article 780 of the Civil Code of Viet Nam (1995), which states: 'Industrial property is the ownership by individuals and legal persons of inventions, utility solutions, industrial designs, trademarks, and of the right to the use of appellations of origin and other objects which may be provided by law.'
[18]   The Decree No. 13/2001/ND-CP on the Protection of New Plant Varieties has established the Plant Variety Protection Office (PVPO), which started its preliminary activities on 19 February 2002. However, it has started receiving PVP applications from 1 April 2004. See the website of the Vietnamese PVPO, at: http://pvpo.mard.gov.vn/english.asp?m=tn&ClassID=101 (accessed 10 January 2009).
[19]   H. Nguyen and U. Grote (2004), 'Agricultural Policies in Vietnam, Producer Support Estimates, 1986–2002', Discussion Paper No. 79, IFPRI, at pp. 37–9. The most important regional trade agreements include, *inter alia*: the Bali Treaty of the Association of Southeast Asian Nations (ASEAN), which was concluded in 1992 and came into force in July 1995; the Asia–Pacific Economic Cooperation (APEC) concluded in November 1998; and the Framework Agreement on Comprehensive Economic Cooperation between China and the ASEAN countries concluded in November 2002.

these agreements incorporate TRIPs-plus standards in the fields of patent and plant variety rights protection. In particular, Viet Nam has signed two important bilateral free trade agreements, respectively with Switzerland in 1999 and with the US in 2000, which have influenced the design of IP legislation in these areas.

Beyond TRIPs minimum standards of protection, the bilateral deal between Switzerland and Viet Nam provides for a best effort obligation to join the 1991 UPOV Act by 2002.[20] The free trade agreement (FTA) between the US and Viet Nam also provides that the latter must accede to the 1991 UPOV Convention.[21] However, the obligation to limit the scope of plant-related patent exclusions to the same extent that they are recognized in the 1998 EC Biotechnology Directive is even more compelling for its far-reaching impact on the interpretation of the Intellectual Property Law (2005).[22] In particular, Article 7.2(c) of the US–Viet Nam FTA states:

> The exclusion for plant varieties is limited to those plant varieties that satisfy the definition provided in Article 1(vi) of the UPOV Convention (1991). The exclusions for plant and animal varieties shall not apply to plant or animal inventions that could encompass more than one variety. Viet Nam must also provide patent protection on all forms of plants and animals that are not varieties, as well as on inventions that encompasses more than one variety.

This bilateral provision *de facto* impedes the adoption of patent-related measures to safeguard nutrition and food security in accordance with the principle that 'Members may, in formulating or amending their laws and regulations, adopt measures necessary to protect public health and nutrition, and to promote the public interest in sectors of vital importance to their socio-economic and technological development ...'.[23] In

---

[20]   GRAIN (2007), 'Bilateral Agreements Imposing TRIPS-Plus Intellectual Property Rights on Biodiversity in Developing Countries', Girona, Spain (February 2007). See also Article 2 and Annex 1 of the Switzerland–Viet Nam FTA (1999), 'Abkommen zwischen dem Schweizerischen Bundesrat und der Sozialistischen Republik Vietnam über den Schutz des geistigen Eigentums und über die Zusammenarbeit auf dem Gebiet des geistigen Eigentums'.

[21]   See Article 1.3 of Chapter 3 of the US–Viet Nam FTA (2000), 'Agreement between the United States of America and the Socialist Republic of Viet Nam on Trade Relations'.

[22]   On the 1998 Biotechnology Directive, see C. Baldock and O. Kingsbury (2000), 'Where Did It Come from and Where Is It Going? The Biotechnology Directive and Its Relation to the EPC', *Biotechnology Law Report*, 19/1, 7–17.

[23]   See Article 8.1 of the TRIPs Agreement; and R.J.L. Lettington (2003), 'Small-Scale Agriculture and the Nutritional Safeguard under Article 8(1) of the

particular, it curtails in a radical way the implementation of the flexibilities enshrined in Article 27.3(b) of the TRIPs Agreement.

As to the relationship between the EC and Viet Nam, their first Framework Cooperation Agreement was concluded in July 1995 and entered into force in June 1996, with a clause providing for an automatic extension after the initial five-year period.[24] 'The EC–Vietnam Cooperation Agreement provides reciprocal MFN treatment for goods and industrial property rights ... and confirms Vietnam's eligibility for the application of GSP'.[25]

Under the auspices of the Trans-Regional EU–ASEAN Trade Initiative (TREATI), which was launched in July 2003, a continuous negotiation for the ASEAN–EU FTA is being carried out in a Joint Committee, which met in Brussels, Belgium, from 30 January until 1 February 2008.[26] This negotiation has met with some criticism, including the claim that the FTA will 'deepen the spread of neo-liberalism in Southeast Asia—more privatization and more deregulation—with the goal of improving business opportunities for European TNCs in the region'.[27] The strengthening of IP protection and enforcement are key pillars of the EU strategy in Southeast Asia.

The European Parliament Resolution of 8 May 2008 on *Trade and Economic Relations with the Association of Southeast Asian Nations (ASEAN)* recalls the EU commitment to 'support the Doha

---

Uruguay Round Agreement on Trade-Related Aspects of Intellectual Property Rights: Case Studies from Kenya and Peru', UNCTAD-ICTSD Project on IPRs and Sustainable Development, Geneva, Switzerland (November 2003).

[24]   O.J. L. 136/28 of 07.06.1996. H. Nguyen and U. Grote (2004), above note 19, at p. 38.

[25]   French Embassy in Viet Nam, 'Country Fact File for Vietnam', available at: www.ambafrance-vn.org/IMG/doc/CountryFactFile_-_CFF2004V.doc (accessed 10 November 2008).

[26]   The latter is a 'framework for dialogue and regulatory co-operation between EU and ASEAN, with the purpose to enhance trade and investment relations between both partners'. Delegation of the European Commission to Malaysia, 'The Trans-Regional EU-ASEAN Trade Initiative' (updated 13 June 2006), available at: www.delmys.ec.europa.eu/en/special_features/The%20Trans-Regional%20EU-ASEAN%20Trade%20Initiative.htm (accessed 9 October 2008); T.N.S.A.Tengku (2008), *Flexible approach to drive EU-Asean FTA negotiations*, Bilaterals.org, 9 May 2008, available at: www.bilaterals.org/spip.php?article12075 (accessed 14 March 2011).

[27]   'EU-ASEAN News and Analysis', Bilateral.org (2008), available at: www.bilaterals.org/spip.php?rubrique151 (accessed 10 October 2008). See also Institute for Global Justice (2008), 'ASEAN-EU FTA will bring disaster and sovereignty losing', Bilaterals.org, 19 March 2008, available at: www.bilaterals.org/spip.php?article11687 (accessed 10 October 2008).

Declaration and the use of TRIPS flexibilities in favour of public health and of access to medicines in developing countries' and clearly recognizes the legal relationship between patent protection and access to essential medicines by stating that:

> Nothing in the agreement should create legal or practical obstacles to the maximum use of flexibilities set out in the Declaration amending the ... TRIPS agreement and access to medicines, and calls on the Commission negotiators to take full account of the points set out in its above mentioned resolution of 12 July 2007 on this topic.[28]

By contrast, in the above Resolution, nutrition and food security concerns are largely de-linked from the issue of access to plant genetic resources and intellectual property protection. While the European Parliament 'expresses concern about the consequences of higher rice prices, particularly for poorer households in rice-importing ASEAN countries', this statement does not have the prescriptive strength of the above health-related commitment so as to limit the potential introduction of harmful TRIPs-plus standards in the ASEAN–EU FTA.[29]

5.2.3 Capacity development needs in agriculture and IP-related technical assistance

Article 67 of the TRIPs Agreement sets out the terms under which developed country WTO members shall cooperate with developing and least-developed countries on providing technical and financial assistance for the implementation of the TRIPs Agreement. It states:

> In order to facilitate the implementation of this Agreement, developed country Members shall provide, on request and on mutually agreed terms and conditions, technical and financial cooperation in favour of developing and least-developed country Members. Such cooperation shall include assistance in the preparation of laws and regulations on the protection and enforcement of intellectual property rights as well as on the prevention of their abuse, and shall include support regarding the establishment or reinforcement of domestic offices and agencies relevant to these matters, including the training of personnel.

---

[28]   European Parliament (2008), 'European Parliament resolution of 8 May 2008 on Trade and Economic Relations with the Association of East Asian Nations (ASEAN)', at paras 13–14.

[29]   Ibid., para. 17.

In Viet Nam, IPR-related technical assistance has focused primarily on modernizing the IP system, its administration and enforcement. Specific activities included: regional and global workshops and seminars, IP public awareness-raising projects and custom technical cooperation. Estimates suggest that between 1996 and 2001 Viet Nam received technical assistance from eight different donor agencies.[30] In the period between 2001 and 2007, several countries and international organizations were involved in the delivery of IP-related technical assistance, including: France, Switzerland, the US, Japan, the Republic of Korea, Australia, the EU and the WTO.[31]

Thanks to the above assistance, the country has harmonized its national legislation on patents and plant variety rights in accordance with internationally agreed standards.[32] This is seen as a major success by IP-related technical assistance donors, whose mandate is to strengthen the legal protection of IP as well as enforcement measures.[33]

However, a growing body of literature has criticized mainstream IP-related technical assistance programmes, because they have shown the pitfall of being enforcement driven and 'one size fits all' in their approach.[34] In particular, attempts are being made to design and deliver

---

[30] T. Pengelly and M. Leesti (2002), 'Institutional Issues for Developing Countries in Intellectual Property Policymaking, Administration & Enforcement', Study Paper 9, UK Commission on IPR, London.

[31] WTO, 'Doha Development Agenda—Trade Capacity Building Database', available at: http://tcbdb.wto.org/advanced_search_results.aspx (accessed 10 October 2008). The search was performed with the following key words: Viet Nam and Trade-Related Intellectual Property Rights; The EC-ASEAN Intellectual Property Rights Cooperation Programme (ECAP II), 'Activities/Events at national level—Vietnam'.

[32] See, for instance: United States Trade Representative (2007), 'Statement by U.S. Trade Representative Susan C. Schwab on Vietnam Becoming WTO Member', available at: www.ustr.gov/about-us/press-office/press-releases/archives/2007/january/statement-us-trade-representative-susan-0 (accessed 10 February 2009).

[33] R. Sagar (2006), 'Identifying Models of Best Practices in the Provision of Technical Assistance to Facilitate the Implementation of the TRIPS Agreement', produced for the European Commission under its 6th Framework Programme for Research as part of the project 'Impacts of the IPR Rules on Sustainable Development (IPDEV)', at p. 34.

[34] For instance, Pengelly argues that 'the assessment of IP technical assistance requirements of a developing country should be based on what a developing country needs rather that on what a donor country wants, or is able to provide'. He also notes that 'the advice provided by certain technical assistance donors doesn't always fully take into account all the possible options and flexibilities to accommodate public policy objectives under the TRIPs Agreement'. T. Pengelly

TA programmes that are tailored to country-specific development needs. For instance, such programmes may emphasize patent-related flexibilities on the basis of the understanding that 'developing countries are at a fundamental disadvantage in the introduction or strengthening of patent rights standards because their starting point in terms of technology ownership, patent ownership and research and development is on average extremely low'.[35]

Thus, it might be useful to consider the extent to which the IP-related technical assistance, which was deployed during Viet Nam's accession to the WTO and immediately after it, has adequately matched the IP capacity building needs of the country by reference to its current levels of agricultural science and technology (S&T) capacity.

While the next section highlights key concerns regarding the design and delivery of IP-related technical assistance, the subsequent section considers emerging trends in agricultural S&T investment and the level of R&D capacity. After the examination of relevant IP Law provisions, section 5.2.8 concludes by assessing the post-WTO accession needs of Viet Nam as regards IP-related technical assistance and agriculture.

5.2.3.1   Key concerns regarding IP-related technical assistance

Because a multitude of technical assistance donors have operated in the country, their poor coordination may have resulted in the 'duplication of efforts or, at worst, waste of resources and conflicting advice on important policy and investment decisions', such as 'the right form of protection for intellectual property related to plant variety technologies'.[36]

The EC–ASEAN Cooperation Programme (ECAP II), which has played a crucial role in modernizing the Vietnamese IP system, has been blamed for having encouraged the use of TRIPs flexibilities only to a negligible extent, without sufficiently 'presenting policy alternatives or focusing on capacity building to enable developing countries to negotiate proactively on IP issues'.[37]

(2004), 'Technical Assistance for the Formulation and Implementation of Intellectual Property Policy in Developing Countries and Transition Economies', ICTSD, at pp. 46–9.

[35]   P. Cullet (2005), *Intellectual Property Protection and Sustainable Development*, New Delhi, India: LexisNexis Butterworths, p. 138.

[36]   T. Pengelly (2004), above note 34, at p. 50.

[37]   D. Matthews and V. Munoz-Tellez (2006), 'Bilateral Technical Assistance and TRIPs: The United States, Japan and the European Communities in Comparative Perspective', *JWIP*, 9/6, 629–53, at p. 643.

As a result, the EU and Viet Nam have now adopted—at least on paper—equivalent levels of IPR protection for plant-related innovation.[38] It is likely that the strategic policy goal to ensure improved market access for Vietnamese manufacturing products under the ongoing negotiations of the ASEAN–EU FTA has critically determined the acceptance by Viet Nam of its largest trading partner's requests.

As regards the US, IP technical assistance has focused on implementing the IPR chapter of the US–Viet Nam FTA (2000) and its TRIPs-plus standards. In a similar way to the EU–Viet Nam's relationship, the interests that the US has as the largest importer of Vietnamese products could reasonably have played a role in shaping Viet Nam's IP reform agenda.[39]

Against this backdrop, TA programmes have placed a strong emphasis on the adoption of the highest available plant-related IP protection standards, while neglecting alternative options under the TRIPs Agreement.[40] Besides, US technical assistance programmes have mainly used US legislation as the model for IP reform and training in the recipient country. While such a 'one size fits all' approach is not appropriate for the design of IP legislation in developing countries, the 'training' aspects of it could be useful to the extent that they are targeted to improve business education and awareness about IP for SMEs, whose plans are to operate in the US or to forge strong links with US enterprises and research institutions.

5.2.3.2 *Agricultural S&T investment and public sector R&D capacity*

The International Food Policy Research Institute reports that during the period between 1996 and 1998 the Vietnamese Government has spent

---

[38] However, such protection standards can be implemented in accordance with different needs and objectives.

[39] Such imports are estimated to amount to USD 3.9 billion per year. French Embassy in Viet Nam, 'Country Fact File for Vietnam', above note 25.

[40] US–Vietnam Trade Council, 'Intellectual Property Rights—Technical Assistance Programs', available at: www.usvtc.org/trade/ipr/ (accessed 10 October 2008). The introductory overview on the topic of IPRs cooperation by the US–Vietnam Trade Council makes clear that:

A business environment with a strong regime for the protection of intellectual property rights serves to attract inward foreign investment and assist in the development of a vibrant domestic industry while encouraging research & development and innovation. For American companies in Vietnam and Vietnamese companies operating overseas, strong IPR protection and enforcement is vital for … continuing investment in R&D.

VND 200–60 billion per year on agricultural research, which approximately amounts to USD 14–19 million using the 1998 exchange rate.[41] However, these sums include the expenditure for all agricultural sectors and are not limited to crop breeding.

In 2006, Decree 11/2006/ND-TTg concerning 'Key Programs and Application of Biotechnology in Agriculture to 2020' sets the goal to increase up to 70 per cent the production of biotechnologically improved varieties.[42] Besides, it established that the annual investments for agro-biotechnology research shall be increased up to approximately VND 100 billion (corresponding to USD 6.3 million). However, there are also indications that the Vietnamese government is encouraging public research institutes to diversify their sources of funding, while the expected budget cuts will increase from 20 per cent to 50 per cent of the current research expenditure respectively in 2010 and 2015.[43]

In terms of structural reform, a remarkable reorganization and consolidation is taking place in the public sector. In 2005, out of a total of 42 public agricultural research institutes, 32 were involved in agricultural R&D and 'were placed directly under [the Ministry of Agriculture and Rural Development] MARD or under state-owned enterprises under MARD's control'.[44] By the end of 2008, the Institute of Agricultural Genetics will merge with the Center for Plant Genetic Resources, which holds a genebank that includes both *in-vitro* and *in-vivo* conservation of PGR, and will form the Academy of Agriculture Science. This is a consortium established in 2005. Other mergers will follow, including ten research institutes located in the north and in the centre of the country,

---

[41] Over the same period, the Vietnamese Government has also spent VND 120–140 billion (i.e. USD 9–11 million) per year on training agricultural technicians, economists, specialists and workers and VND 3,000 billion (i.e. USD 216 million) per year on building and upgrading irrigation and drainage systems, dams, and technical infrastructure of institutes, colleges, etc. H. Nguyen and U. Grote (2004), above note 19, at pp. 29–30. The 1998 conversion rate between Vietnamese Dong (VND) and US Dollars (USD) is USD 1 = VND 13,900.0, available at: www.oanda.com/convert/classic (accessed 13 November 2008).

[42] The decree was adopted by the Prime Minister on 12 January 2006.

[43] L. Kilgour (2008), 'Building Intellectual Property Management Capacity in Public Research Institutions in Vietnam: Current Needs and Future Directions', *Minnesota Journal of Law, Science & Technology*, 9/1, 317–68, at p. 349. The author reports that 'Vietnam's annual R&D budget of $71.3 million (2005) represents 0.5 per cent of the country's GDP, placing its percentage investment third in Southeast Asia. This rate is far off the 2 per cent average of OECD countries.'

[44] G.J. Stads and N. Viet-Hai (2006), 'Vietnam—Agricultural Science and Technology Indicators', ASTI Country Brief No. 33, IFPRI, at p. 2.

and three institutes in the south. These institutes cover several research areas ranging from veterinary medicine and animal husbandry to mechanization and post-harvest, from agricultural economy to forest research.[45]

The Vietnamese R&D capacity in agricultural biotechnology was described as being 'largely at the stage of improving technology imported from advanced countries'.[46] Viet Nam is also the Asian county with the lowest degree levels among research staff and minimal private sector involvement in R&D.[47]

On the one hand, the overall 50 per cent cut of Government support for public research is likely to impinge upon all non-biotech crop development programmes. On the other, the USD 6.3 million of planned investment in agro-biotechnology research are unlikely to create a genuine competitive advantage for the national agricultural R&D sector, because of its technological dependence, the relatively strong IP policy framework in which it will operate, and the extremely limited or absent IP management capacity of public research institutes.[48]

In particular, in the absence of appropriate IP policy guidelines, the increasing need for funding can force them to sell off their crown jewels under terms that may not necessarily be favourable to them and their clients. Even though agricultural S&T capacity may be expected to benefit from increased foreign direct investment and public–private partnerships

---

[45]   This information is based on a semi-structured interview with a senior research manager at the Institute of Agricultural Genetics, Viet Nam Academy of Agriculture Science, Hanoi, Viet Nam (27 March 2007).

[46]   Nguyen argues that:

Conventional technologies such as *in vitro* micropropagation, virus elimination, somaclonal variation, anther culture, and haploid lines effectively improved crop productivity over the past decade. Gene transfer to breed disease and pest-resistant varieties, as well as plants tolerant to adverse environment conditions is being pursued. The development of transgenic crops for the potential control of viral and fungal disease is not completely developed, but already tested at laboratory levels. Various interesting genes have been cloned or imported from other countries and advanced techniques have been practiced extensively in research institutions.

T.V. Nguyen (2000), 'Agricultural Biotechnology in Vietnam', paper given at the Regional Conference on Agricultural Biotechnology, 29–30 June 2000.

[47]   G.J. Stads and N. Viet-Hai (2006), above note 44.

[48]   For instance, compare with Monsanto's spending of USD 1 billion in acquisitions and technology investments in 2008. Monsanto (2008), 'Monsanto Sees Record Sales in Fiscal Year 2008; Growth Serves as Strong Base for 2009', News Releases, 8 October 2008, available at: http://monsanto.mediaroom.com/index.php?s=43&item=650 (accessed 10 November 2008).

with technology providers, the resulting plant-related innovation may not be available as inputs into small and medium plant-breeding programmes, which may constitute the strength of a distributed agricultural innovation system based on adaptive learning.

5.2.4   The protection of plant-related inventions under the IP Law

The Intellectual Property Law was enacted in November 2005 and entered into force on 1 July 2006. The Vietnamese Patent Office is now established under the Ministry of Science and Technology (MOST) as part of the Department of Intellectual Property.

As regards the protection of plant intellectual property, paragraphs 5 and 6 of Article 59 of the IP Law (2005) respectively provide that 'plant varieties' and 'processes of essentially biological nature for the production of plants ... other than microbiological processes' shall not be patentable subject matter. This provision complies with both Article 27.3(b) of the TRIPs Agreement and Article 7.2(c) of the FTA between US and Viet Nam.

The number of patent applications related to biotechnology has shown a considerable growth between 1996 and 2002.[49] However, so far there is limited experience with patents granted on crops.[50] As seen above, product claims to inventions whose technical feasibility is not restricted to a single plant variety, such as claims covering plant species or families, seem to be permitted under Vietnamese patent law.[51] For instance, in 2004, the National Office of Intellectual Property (NOIP) has granted Syngenta Participations AG a patent for 'DNA comprising rice anther-specific gene and transgenic plant transformed therewith'.[52] However, examiners and court cases in Viet Nam need to clarify the boundaries of the subject matter exclusion by defining what it is meant by an 'essentially biological process' under Vietnamese patent law.[53]

---

[49]   Pham & Associates (2003), 'Vietnam: Patenting biotechnology inventions', *Managing Intellectual Property,* Supplement—Patent Yearbook 2003.

[50]   Semi-structured interview with a senior officer of the Plant Variety Protection Office (PVPO), Hanoi, Viet Nam (28 March 2007).

[51]   N.N. Dzung (2007), 'Vietnam Patent Law—Substantive Law Provisions and Existing Uncertainties', *Chicago-Kent Journal of Intellectual Property,* 6, 138–56 at p. 142.

[52]   Vietnamese patent No. 1–0004743. The PCT international application and related documents are available at: www.wipo.int/pctdb/en/wo.jsp?WO=2000026389 (accessed 15 March 2011). An example of a PCT international application is to be found at the end of this chapter at p. 192.

[53]   Pham & Associates (2003), above note 49.

Another aspect that may need to be clarified is the relationship between patent and plant variety protection. At first glance, the IP law does not provide a specific mechanism—i.e. an overlap provision—to deal with the case of a plant variety covered by patent claims. However, under 'Right to prevent others from using industrial property objects', paragraph 2 of Article 125 of the IP Law states: 'the owner of an industrial property object ... shall not have the right to prevent others from ... using the invention ... for personal needs or non commercial purposes or for evaluation, analysis, research or teaching, testing, ...' etc. Although, the extent to which agricultural exemptions are recognized under patent law must be clarified, this provision may allow seed saving 'for personal needs' as well as 'non commercial' research and breeding.[54]

Finally, the IP Law provides that the Ministry of Science and Technology can grant a compulsory licence if the patentee or the holder of an exclusive licence fails 'to perform the obligation to manufacture protected products or apply protected processes to satisfy the needs of national defense, security, disease prevention and treatment, and *nutrition for the people* and [to meet] other social needs'.[55] During the TRIPs Council review of legislation, the representative of Viet Nam explained that such needs are met 'if products or services, which apply the invention, are supplied with an adequate quantity and reasonable price so that people under demand' can afford them.[56]

5.2.5 Plant variety protection under the IP Law

On 24 November 2006, Viet Nam became the 63rd UPOV member by joining the International Union for the Protection of New Varieties of

---

[54] Namely, the farmers' and breeders' exemptions provided for in Part Four of the IP Law.

[55] Emphasis added. See Article 136 of the IP Law and Article 23 of Decree No. 103/2006/ND-CP of 22 September 2006.

[56] Article 23.2 of Decree 103/2006/ND-CP states:

When needs of national defence, security, disease prevention and treatment and nutrition for the people or other urgent social needs are satisfied by imported products or products manufactured by licensees of inventions under licensing contracts, holders of the exclusive right to use inventions shall not have to perform the obligation to manufacture protected products or apply protected processes mentioned in Clause 1 of this Article.

WTO TRIPs Council (2008), 'Responses from Viet Nam to the Questions Posed by Canada and Additional Questions Posed by the United States' (23 October 2008).

Plants.[57] The 1991 UPOV Act entered into force in Viet Nam on 24 December 2006.

5.2.5.1   The regulatory framework

Part Four of the Intellectual Property Law (2005) implements Article 27.3(b) of the TRIPs Agreement and provides for a *sui generis* system of plant variety protection that complies with UPOV 1991.[58] In particular, the IP Law (2005) regulates: the conditions for the protection of plant varieties (Chapter XI); the application process and the registration of the rights over plant varieties (Chapter XII); the contents of the rights conferred to the breeder and to the owner of the plant variety protection (PVP) certificate, if different from the breeder; the exceptions to such rights (Chapter XIV); and the transfer of the rights to a plant variety, including compulsory licensing (Chapter XV).[59]

The UPOV accession procedure provides that the acceding state shall request the advice of the UPOV Council on the conformity of its laws with the provisions of the 1991 UPOV Act.[60] In the document concerning the 'Examination of the Conformity of the Intellectual Property Law of Viet Nam with the 1991 Act of the UPOV Convention' the following comments were made:[61]

> Article 5(3) of the IP Law entitled 'Application of Laws' provides that 'where the provisions of the International Treaties to which the Socialist Republic of Viet Nam is party contravene the provisions of this Law, the former shall be applied.' Article 5(3) of the Law ... provides that, in case of conflict between UPOV 1991 and the IP Law, UPOV 1991 prevails. The general principle in Article 5 of the Law will remedy any *lacunae* or minor departures from the substance of the 1991 Act identified in this document.

---

[57]   See UPOV (2006), above note 4.
[58]   Intellectual Property Law (2005), No. 50/2005/QH11, available at: www.ecap-project.org/fileadmin/ecapII/pdf/en/information/vietnam/ip_law2005.pdf (accessed 3 January 2009).
[59]   The above English translation of the IP Law (2005) provided by the EC–ASEAN IPR Cooperation Programme (ECAP II) presents a material error, because while the numbering of the articles flows normally, Chapter XIII is missing. For the sake of clarity, this study refers to the number of chapters as they appear in the unofficial translation.
[60]   See Article 34.3 of UPOV 1991.
[61]   See UPOV (2006) above note 11, at para. 7.

The protection of new plant varieties in Viet Nam is also governed by the Implementing Decree on Plant Variety Rights.[62]

5.2.5.2 *Operations of the Plant Variety Protection Office and certificates granted*

In 2007, Viet Nam's list of plant species for which plant variety protection is available included a total of 38 species, namely: rice, corn, soybean, peanut, cotton, sugarcane, tomato, potato, watermelon, cucumber, kohlrabi, cabbage, chilli pepper, pumpkin, carrot, strawberry, onion, shallot, onion-shallot hybrids, bitter gourd, rose, chrysanthemum, gerbera, gladiolus, lilies, dianthus, marigold, grape, orange, mango, apple, banana, pomelo, papaya, dragon fruit, tea, rubber, coffee and ginger.[63]

As of 28 March 2007, the Plant Variety Protection Office of Viet Nam had received 23 applications for the protection of new plant varieties.[64] They are divided as follows: domestic applicants filed ten applications and, of these, five are for varieties developed by public sector institutions.[65] The rising private sector includes many small seed companies. At present, it is estimated that between 80 and 100 domestic companies operate in the country. The Southern Seed Company is the biggest domestic company in Viet Nam.[66] However, it is difficult to

---

[62]   Decree No 104/2006/ND-CP of September 2006 providing for the implementation of the Articles of the IP Law concerning plant variety rights protection. The Decree entered into force in November 2006 and repealed Chapter IV of the Ordinance on Plant Varieties (2004). Its structure (2006) reflects the structure of Part Four of the IP Law (2005). It has an introductory chapter on the allocation of state responsibilities for the administration of the plant variety rights system. In particular, Article 4 provides that MARD shall administer the Plant Variety Rights Office.

[63]   B.T. Huong (2008), 'Vietnam Biotechnology Update 2008', USDA Foreign Agricultural Service—Global Agriculture Information Network Report (11 July 2008), at p. 6.

[64]   The information contained in this section is based in part on a semi-structured interview with a senior officer of the Plant Variety Protection Office (PVPO), Hanoi, Viet Nam (28 March 2007).

[65]   The public sector includes numerous research institutes under direct Government control, such as the Centre for Hybrid Rice and the Agricultural University of Hanoi.

[66]   Decision No. 213/QD-TTg of 25 March 2002 converted the Southern Seed Company, a state enterprise under the Ministry of Agriculture and Rural Development, into a joint-stock company named Southern Seed Joint Stock Company. A Joint Stock Company under Vietnamese Law means that 20 per cent to 40 per cent of its capital is Government money, while the rest is private investment. The company's charter capital is VND 60 billion, of which the state's

evaluate whether any private domestic breeder has applied for PVP, especially if indirect government control is also considered, such as in the case of Joint Stock Companies.

The PVP Office also received 13 applications from foreign applicants. Monsanto,[67] Syngenta,[68] Bayer[69] and Bioseed Genetics International Inc.[70] have established offices in Viet Nam. The latter is an Indian company that formed part of GP Group (until 2007) and it was the first company to invest in the seed sector in Viet Nam.[71]

As of 28 March 2007, the PVPO had granted four plant variety protection certificates. Two of them were granted to domestic holders for the protection of hybrid rice varieties.[72] The other two PVP certificates were granted to foreign holders—namely Monsanto and Syngenta—for two hybrid corn varieties. In July 2008, the USDA Foreign Agricultural Service reported that the number of protected varieties has increased to 11 hybrid rice varieties and seven hybrid corn varieties.[73]

As regards enforcement cases, the Agricultural University of Hanoi is reported to have alleged infringement against farmers, who where cultivating a protected variety; however, the case was resolved through amicable dispute settlement. Syngenta is also reported to have complained of infringement for the import from outside the country of a protected variety; however, no case has been brought to courts so far.[74]

5.2.6   Seed certification and market regulation

The Ordinance on Plant Varieties No. 15/2004/PL-UBTVQH11 of 24 March 2004 regulates important issues relating to the management of

---

equities represent 20 per cent of the total, equities sold to labourers of the enterprise is 55 per cent, and equities sold to the outsiders amounts to 25 per cent. Information is available at: www.asianlii.org/vn/legis/laws/ctsscaseiajc807/ (accessed 10 March 2007).

[67]   See: www.monsanto.com/whoweare/Pages/vietnam.aspx (accessed 17 March 2011).

[68]   See: www2.syngenta.com/de/country/vn.html (accessed 17 March 2011).

[69]   See: www.bayer.com.vn/ (accessed 10 March 2007).

[70]   See: www.seedquest.com/id/b/bioseedgenetics.htm (accessed 17 March 2011).

[71]   GP Group of Companies, 'A Quick Chronology of the GP Group', available at: www.premjee.com/content/timeline (accessed 17 March 2011).

[72]   In both cases the applicant is a breeder working at the Agricultural University of Hanoi. Besides, the breeder has subsequently licensed one PVP certificate to a joint stock company.

[73]   B.T. Huong (2008), above note 63, at p. 6.

[74]   This information is correct as of 28 March 2007.

plant genetic resources. In particular, it provides specific rules for the conservation, evaluation, breeding, selection, release, trade and other commercial aspects of seed provision in Viet Nam.[75] Article 7 of the Ordinance establishes that the Government is responsible for the management of plant varieties and provides that MARD is the central state management authority in the field of agriculture and forest varieties.

Decision No. 52/2006/QD-BNN of 23 June 2006, promulgates the Regulation on Certification of Quality Standard Conformity of Plant Varieties and establishes a compulsory seed certification scheme for listed varieties.[76] Under the scheme the Department of Crop Production—established under MARD—is the authority with the oversight role for quality standard seed certification,[77] while plant variety quality-testing organizations are responsible for testing the quality of seed lots.[78]

5.2.7 The enforcement of patents and plant variety rights

In May 2008, Viet Nam submitted to the Office of the US Trade Representative 'a request to be designated as a beneficiary developing country under the US Generalized System of Preferences program'.[79] Such designation depends on the results of a comprehensive examination

---

[75] The management and conservation of plant genetic resources is addressed in Chapter II; Chapter III regulates: research, selection, breeding, evaluation and release of new plant varieties; selection and release of mother trees, clones, botanical gardens and forest varieties; Chapter IV regulated *sui generis* plant variety rights protection, but is now repealed by the IP Law (2005) and its implementing Decree No. 104/2006/ND-CP; Chapter V regulates the production and trade of plant varieties; and Chapter VI establishes a seed and seedling quality management framework.

[76] Article 3 provides that 'organisations and individuals involved in the production and/or trade of plant varieties subject to certification of quality standard conformity shall, before producing or importing plant varieties, have to register with one of the plant variety quality-testing organizations'.

[77] Article 12.

[78] Plant variety quality-testing organizations 'shall have the responsibility ... to test the quality of seed lots according to the provisions of Circular No. 02/2006/TT-BKHCN of January 10, 2006, of the Ministry of Science and Technology, and other provisions of this Regulation'.

[79] 'The GSP program is designed to promote economic growth in the developing world by providing preferential duty-free entry for qualifying products.' Vietnam Trade Office in Washington DC (2008), 'Understanding Vietnam and the Generalized System of Preferences Program' (10 June 2008) available at: www.us-asean.org/Vietnam/GSP/FAQ.pdf (accessed 10 November 2008).

of all trade-related laws and policies adopted by the beneficiary country, including protection and enforcement of IPRs.

In 2008, despite remarkable progress in improving domestic IP legislation, enforcement capacity and interagency coordination, Viet Nam was included in the US Special 301 'Watch List'.[80] The 'Special 301' Report notes that 'significant weaknesses remain, particularly with respect to its criminal regime, administrative regime, and its border enforcement regime'.[81]

In Viet Nam, right-holders may seek to enforce patents and plant variety rights in courts as well as through administrative remedies. As a result of the above pressures, both routes have been recently strengthened, including through criminal penalties for the most serious cases. As regards available administrative remedies, an ordinance issued by the Standing Committee of the National Assembly on 2 April 2008 has provided for a fivefold increase of the upper limit of administrative sanctions (up to VND 500 million). It has also strengthened non-pecuniary remedies such as the seizure, re-export or destruction of the infringing goods.[82]

Viet Nam has also amended Article 171 of the Criminal Code, which concerns the infringement of industrial property rights and plant variety rights. In particular, it states that those who intentionally infringe upon industrial property rights or plant variety rights on a commercial scale shall be subject to a fine ranging from VND 50–500 million or to non-custodial re-education for up to two years when the infringement causes 'serious consequences'. If the infringement is committed 'in an organized manner' or 'more than once', the infringer may be subject to a fine that ranges from VND 400 million to VND 1 billion, or can be imprisoned for a term of six months to three years.

5.2.8   Post-WTO accession IP-related technical assistance needs assessment

This section sets out the needs of Viet Nam as regards IP-related technical assistance after its accession to the WTO. It also investigates the extent of

---

[80] 'The "Special 301" Report is an annual review of the global state of intellectual property rights ... protection and enforcement, conducted by the Office of the United States Trade Representative (USTR)', which reflects the latter's 'resolve to encourage and maintain effective IPR protection and enforcement worldwide'. Office of the US Trade Representative (2008), '2008 Special 301 Report', at p. 47.

[81] Ibid.

[82] WTO TRIPs Council (2008), 'Minutes of Meeting', IP/C/M/57, WTO, Geneva (16 September 2008), at p. 3.

its capacity deficit in order to identify what might constitute appropriate IP-related technical assistance for the country focusing on the agriculture sector.

Viet Nam has received a great deal of IP-related technical assistance and various typologies of technical assistance have been deployed by providers.[83] Because of this, it might be appropriate to assess whether such technical assistance has matched the needs of Viet Nam. Therefore, this *ex-post* assessment identifies the extent to which further cooperation might be required to fulfil the remaining capacity gaps.

Various indicators can provide a useful framework to carry out a post-WTO accession IP-related technical assistance needs assessment for Viet Nam. Overall, the goal of updating the Vietnamese IP policy and legal framework was accomplished through an adequate support for coordination and development of the national IP policy framework, which lives up to international standards, as shown by documents concerning Viet Nam's accession to the WTO and UPOV.[84]

However, the training needs of policy-makers on IPR concepts, TRIPS and international IPR conventions, including obligations, flexibilities, safeguards and exceptions, and best practices from other countries, have not been completely satisfied. A recent report on 'Needs Assessment on Technical Assistance for the Deputies of the National Assembly after Vietnam's Accession to the WTO' has collected evidence in relation to all WTO-related technical assistance projects, including IP-related technical assistance.[85] The report acknowledges the positive effects of these projects on the accession negotiation process. However, it also notes that their beneficiaries were mainly government officials from implementing agencies and the related ministries. The implication of the above is that 'the group that has the greatest need for technical assistance—the

---

[83] See, for instance, L. Kilgour (2008), 'Building Intellectual Property Management Capacity in Public Research Institutions in Vietnam: Current Needs and Future Directions', *Minnesota Journal of Law, Science & Technology*, 9/1, 317–68; The EC–ASEAN Intellectual Property Rights Cooperation Programme (ECAP II), 'Activities/Events at national level—Vietnam', above note 7; and US–Vietnam Trade Council, 'Intellectual Property Rights—Technical Assistance Programs', available at: www.usvtc.org/trade/ipr/ (accessed 10 October 2008).

[84] See WTO TRIPs Council (2008), above note 82; and UPOV (2006) above note 11.

[85] Centre for Information Library and Research Services (2006), 'Needs Assessment on Technical Assistance for the Deputies of the National Assembly after Vietnam's Accession to the WTO', Hanoi, at p. 31–47. The study considers 50 WTO-related technical assistance projects, of which 11 projects specifically focus on IP-related technical assistance.

National Assembly (NA) Deputies—has largely been ignored. ... NA Deputies have not been given a comprehensive understanding of WTO-related issues and the capacity to prepare and implement the required commitments after official accession'.[86]

Besides, such assistance has not satisfied the need to develop adequate IP management policies and procedures for national universities and research institutes so far.[87] At present, national agricultural research institutes (NARIs) in Viet Nam do not have IPR policy instruments, which provide adequate guidance as to how they should manage either their own or third parties' IP assets.[88] However, some institutes have considered protecting their varieties under *sui generis* plant variety rights protection, but have often renounced these because the costs seemed to exceed the benefits, which may derive from the collection of royalties.

This is partially because farmers cultivate only small plots of land (316 square metres on average in the north and 1000 square metres in the south) and the majority of them are poor subsistence farmers.[89] In addition, the official seed market accounts only for 20 per cent of total seed trade, with the remaining 80 per cent being informally exchanged and

---

[86]   Ibid. at pp. 1–2. The importance of the involvement of NA Deputies in IP rule-making derives from the fact that they 'have supreme power over the legislative system and responsibility for the supervision of all socio-economic activities in Vietnam'.

[87]   L. Kilgour (2008) above note 83, at pp. 350–52.

[88]   Semi-structure interview, above note 45.

[89]   H. Nguyen and U. Grote (2004) above note 19, at pp. 25–6, on the land reform in Viet Nam:

The Directive No. 100 issued on 13 January 1981 allowed cooperatives to assign parcels of land to farm households based on an annual production contract. ... Most of the harvest had to be delivered to the cooperatives. While cooperatives still acted as a planning agency for households' farming activities, they no longer strictly controlled the sale of products. ... In 1988, Resolution 10 was launched giving farmers the right to use their land for 10–15 years, to fully control the production process and to hold about 40 per cent of their contracted output.

In 1993, the Land Law granted long-term land-use rights to farming households. Such land-use rights were:

20 years when the land was used for annual crops, and 50 years in the case of perennial crops. The Land Law, however, also put a ceiling on the amount of land that can be allocated to households: for annual crops, the limit is two hectares in the central and Northern provinces and three hectares in the southern provinces, and for perennials the limit on land holdings is ten hectares.

sold between farmers.[90] These characteristics make it enormously difficult to enforce PVR protection certificates. However, plant breeders in the public sector hope that improvements in the plant variety right system will increase the amount of financial resources accruing to their research programmes through the licensing of improved varieties.

This situation highlights the need for the development of an appropriate IP policy framework for public sector institutions. However, regardless of the quality of future IP-related technical assistance programmes to address this need, the structural weaknesses of Vietnamese public sector institutions are unlikely to be entirely eliminated. The key reason is that 'the intellectual property system in which [Vietnam's public research institutions] will soon find themselves immersed was not crafted in response to the needs of these institutions or the particular needs of the country they serve at its current stage of development'.[91]

The extent to which future IP capacity development activities can redress these weaknesses is to be seen in the future. Some activities, which might help to integrate crop diversity issues within the Vietnamese IP system, include: the appropriate training of Vietnamese judges and examiners on IP-related genetic resources policy issues, including aspects that regard the public interest; the development of adequate IP management policies and procedures for national agricultural universities and research institutes; and assistance with amending (and implementing) the IP Law to include an explicit mutual recognition of the breeders' and farmers' exemptions under patent law.

5.2.9 Lessons learned: privatization, equity and agriculture

Plant-related IP regimes ought to be defined on the basis of the careful assessment of relevant domestic needs in agriculture.[92] In Viet Nam the crucial contribution of farmers to national food security might be

---

[90] Interview with a senior officer of the Plant Variety Protection Office of Viet Nam, Hanoi, Viet Nam (28 March 2007).

[91] L. Kilgour (2008), above note 83.

[92] Pengelly emphasizes the need to support 'better participation in IP rule making' and argues that is necessary to broaden 'the scope of IP assistance programs to encompass a package of policy reforms and capacity building aimed at stimulating more local innovation through R&D to improve productivity and competitiveness, as well as greater use of the IP system by small and medium enterprises'. T. Pengelly (2004), above note 34, at p. 47.

curtailed, if they were not allowed to 'use their rice paddy designated for personal consumption to sell seeds'.[93] Dinh notes that:

> The informal seed sector does not exist from a legal point of view and, therefore, there is neither support nor interest in a better management of PGR by the local authorities and the extension service. ... while the formal sector is perceived as the sole opportunity to increase incomes, the informal seed sector represents the subsistence option for local communities [and] ... is by far the dominant way to exchange seeds between farmers.[94]

Therefore, the above assessment should take into account the benefits, which may reasonably be expected from the internalization of externalities that would otherwise be produced by managing PGRFA in an openly accessible manner in the context of developing countries' agricultural innovation systems.

The legislative efforts undertaken in Viet Nam have provided the country with what might be considered in the western world a 'modern' innovation system. However, such efforts have eventually resulted in excessive levels of legal restrictions on access to fundamental agricultural research inputs, including PGRFA. A key issue revolves around the question of whether they will ultimately encourage agricultural research for the benefits of the majority of Vietnamese farmers and consumers.

The implementation of the IP Law has just started. Admittedly, it is too early to provide definitive conclusions regarding the impact of strengthened patent and plant variety rights on sustainable agriculture in the country. However, a few important points can be made. On the one hand, the recognition of such rights has contributed to the creation of opportunities to forge stronger collaborations between European and Vietnamese institutions in various scientific and technological areas, including biotechnology.[95] Similarly, it might facilitate scientific cooperation between Viet Nam and other industrialized countries, such as Japan and the US.

---

[93]   (2008), 'Nation can boost rice seed crops', VietNamNet Bridge, 17 June 2008, available at: http://english.vietnamnet.vn/tech/2008/06/788998/ (accessed 10 June 2008).

[94]   V.D. Nguyen (2006), 'Summary of Elements of Farmers' Rights in the Ordinance on Plant Variety (2004) of Viet Nam', paper given at the Workshop on Exploring Legal Definitions of Farmers' Varieties in Strategies to Promote Farmers' Rights, 26–28 October 2006, at p. 2.

[95]   (2007), 'Vietnam fortifies scientific cooperation with EU', VietNamNet Bridge, 23 June 2007, available at: http://english.vietnamnet.vn/tech/2007/06/709749/ (accessed 10 June 2008).

However, the new economic climate combined with the availability of strong patent and plant variety rights can also be expected to help multinational corporations consolidate their presence in the Vietnamese seed market.[96] This entails mergers and acquisitions of strategically important domestic companies. Whether Vietnamese seed companies will also benefit from such levels of IP protection with wealth-maximizing effects for all is an open question.

Beyond the mere recognition of IPRs in agriculture, it is the response of the national agricultural research system and its *modus operandi*—in terms of decisions concerning the exploitation of these rights—that will have huge implications for the Vietnamese economy.[97] Because the domestic plant-breeding and biotechnology capacity is limited, the internalization of externalities from agricultural research is unlikely to generate remarkable incentives for the domestic public and private sectors alike and, in particular, the kind of incentives that derive from the exploitation of self-generated IP assets.[98] Instead, long-term commitments in terms of financial and human resources are required to build domestic IP management capacity at all levels.

A related problem is that the IP reform may not remedy potential supply-side market failures because of high excludability costs, namely the costs of excluding non-paying users. In Viet Nam, the average size of plots of cultivated land varies from 360 square metres per head in the north to 1000 square metres in the south.[99] Thus, the cultivated land is extremely fragmented and this can cause problems with royalty collection

---

[96] Dzung concludes that the new IP Law 'will have a wide-ranging impact', which 'shall benefit not only the United States nationals but also those from other countries who do or intend to do business and protect their intellectual property rights in Vietnam'. N.N. Dzung (2007), above note 51, at p.156.

[97] As Louwaars has recently argued, 'next to the extent of the rights themselves, it is the strategies on their use in organizations that determine whether they contribute to or oppose development goals'. N.P. Louwaars (2007), 'IPRs in Agriculture—The Law and its Use in Development', Issue Paper, South Asia Watch on Trade, Economics and Environment (SAWTEE), Kathmandu, Nepal (November 2007).

[98] As to the expected impact of IP rights on agricultural research strategies and their consequences for pro-poor agricultural research, Vietnamese agricultural scientists have growing expectations that the royalties generated from PVP and licensing will contribute to their research budget. However, so far the costs of protecting and enforcing these rights have generally exceeded the benefits derived from their exploitation. Semi-structured interview, above note 45.

[99] These variations largely depend on the fact that the Mekong Delta (*đồng bằng sông Cửu Long*) in the southwest of Viet Nam is much wider than the Red River Delta in the north.

and raise IP enforcement costs to levels not affordable by SMEs and the public sector. If patent and plant variety right restrictions are to be effective, major changes to the land ownership structure may be needed, with remarkable implications in terms of wealth-shifting effects resulting from the spread of industrial agriculture. Monoculture and associated land use changes may generate benefits for the economy from the export of cash crops; however, the resulting loss of *in-situ* crop diversity could narrow the essential food base for local people.

5.3 THE BIODIVERSITY LAW, ACCESS TO GENETIC RESOURCES AND BENEFIT SHARING

On 16 November 1994, Viet Nam became a party to the Convention on Biological Diversity. In the 'National Action Plan on Biodiversity up to 2010 and Orientations towards 2020', the Vietnamese policy framework specifically considers agricultural biodiversity and the conservation and sustainable use of PGR.[100]

In this context, the National Assembly has adopted a programme aimed at the management, conservation and development of biological resources. In 2003, the National Assembly entrusted the Government, through the MoNRE, with the formulation and submission of the draft Biodiversity Law. The Biodiversity Law was adopted on 13 November 2008 and entered into force on 1 July 2009.[101]

The elaboration of the DBL aimed at halting the loss of biodiversity through the development of a coordinated legal framework, while promoting pro-poor livelihood strategies and the participation of local communities. The heterogeneity of substantive technical areas covered by the DBL includes: ecosystems and protected areas management; the

---

[100]   With regard to the relationship between the ABS provisions of the Biodiversity Law and the Action Plan, the latter's commitment to 'increase and diversify investment capital sources for biodiversity and biosafety', including through financial instruments, 'such as taxes and fees on the exploitation and use of natural resources', may have inspired the drafters of the Biodiversity Law. (2007), 'Decision No. 79/2007/QD-TTg of 31 May 2007, Approving the National Action Plan on Biodiversity up to 2010 and Orientations towards 2020 for Implementation of the Convention on Biological Diversity and the Cartagena Protocol on Biosafety', at para. III 4.c. Further information on the state of implementation of the CBD in Viet Nam is available at: www.biodiv.org/world/map.asp?ctr=vn (accessed 20 October 2008).
[101]   'Biodiversity Law of Viet Nam', No. 20/2008/QH12 (National Assembly, Legislature XII of the Socialist Republic of Viet Nam, 4th Session, 2008).

conservation and sustainable use of species; access to genetic resources and benefit sharing; biosafety; the control of invasive alien species; and poverty alleviation.[102]

Access to genetic resources and benefit sharing has received increased attention from regulators and stakeholders, and is now an important component of the biodiversity governance framework in Viet Nam.[103] However, as agricultural biotechnology is concerned, biosafety has attracted far more attention than ABS, especially the attention of biotechnology providers.[104] This is not surprising because the regulation of biosafety touches upon remarkable economic interests and has immediate implications for the import, release and local production of genetically modified crops, while ABS only affects *future* biodiversity research and the sharing of its benefits.[105]

5.3.1 General fit of the Biodiversity Law in the Vietnamese legal system

The Biodiversity Law belongs to the first level of legislation. However, specific regulatory aspects relating to biodiversity may appear in other existing laws. For example, the Law on Environmental Protection provides for the 'conservation and rational use of natural resources'.[106] The Biodiversity Law shall be consistent with all existing laws of the same hierarchy, because the Vietnamese legal system does not normally apply

---

[102] UN Viet Nam (2008), 'First-ever Biodiversity Law to Include Pro-Poor Conservation Strategies', 16 September 2008, available at: www.un.org.vn/index.php?option=com_content&task=view&id=646&Itemid=1 (accessed 10 October 2008).

[103] Ibid. For instance, UN Viet Nam emphasises that the Biodiversity Law 'proposes benefits for those who possess traditional knowledge of biodiversity, thus encouraging them to participate in biodiversity conservation and rehabilitation.'

[104] Biosafety issues are regulated in Chapter V, Section 3 of the Biodiversity Law, titled: 'Management of Risks Caused to Biodiversity by Genetically Modified Organisms and Genetic Specimen of Genetically Modified Organisms.' However, the analysis of such provisions is outside the scope of this book.

[105] Viet Nam has not yet implemented 'restrictions on the importation of Genetically Modified (GM) products and imports huge amounts of Bt cotton, soybeans, soybean meal and corn from the United States and other countries'. However, 'production of GM crops and trade in GM seeds are still not yet allowed in Vietnam as the biotech regulations to allow these have yet to be approved'. B.T. Huong (2008), above note 63, at p. 3.

[106] 'The Law on Environmental Protection', No. 29/2005/L/CTN, National Assembly, Legislature XI of the Socialist Republic of Viet Nam, 8th Session (2005), at Chapter IV.

the principle *lex posterior derogat legi priori* and all laws remain in force for a fix period of ten years after which they may be amended or repealed. The case would be different if legal instruments of a lower ranking were inconsistent with it. In this case, the Government would have a duty to bring existing ordinances, resolutions or decrees into compliance with the Biodiversity Law.

5.3.2   The Biodiversity Law and ABS-related technical assistance

In March 2003, the Prime Minister assigned the MoNRE to coordinate the drafting of the Biodiversity Law with other relevant ministries.[107] Pursuant to its mandate, the MoNRE established a steering committee for the drafting of the Biodiversity Law.[108] During the preparation of the draft Biodiversity Law, wide consultations took place with national and international experts, non-governmental organizations and UN agencies including: the International Union for the Conservation of Nature (IUCN),[109] the UN Food and Agriculture Organization, the United Nations Development Program, the German Society for Technical Cooperation (GTZ)[110] as well as other individuals and environmental organizations.

---

[107]   (2003), 'Decision No. 35/2003/QD-TTg of March 6, 2003 Assigning Agencies to Draft, and Agencies to Coordinate in Drafting, Bills and Ordinances of the Government in the XI National Assembly's Term (2002–2007) and in 2003'.

[108]   The Steering Committee is composed by the Ministry of Agriculture and Rural Development (MARD), the Ministry of Fisheries (MOFI), the Ministry of Finance (MOF), the Ministry of Science and Technology (MOST) and the Ministry of Trade (MOT).

[109]   According to its website, IUCN 'helps the world find pragmatic solutions to our most pressing environment and development challenges. It supports scientific research, manages field projects all over the world and brings governments, non-government organizations, United Nations agencies, companies and local communities together to develop and implement policy, laws and best practice.' IUCN defines itself as 'the world's oldest and largest global environmental network—a democratic membership union with more than 1,000 government and NGO member organizations, and almost 11,000 volunteer scientists in more than 160 countries'. IUCN, 'About IUCN', available at: www.iucn.org/about/index.cfm (accessed 10 October 2008).

[110]   GTZ (Deutsche Gesellschaft für Technische Zusammenarbeit GmbH) defines itself as 'an international cooperation enterprise for sustainable development with worldwide operations. GTZ promotes complex reforms and change processes … Its corporate objective is to improve people's living conditions on a sustainable basis.' From the standpoint of its organizational structure, GTZ is a closed limited company (GmbH) in the private sector, which is owned by the German Federal Government. Further details on the profile of this organization

Since the beginning of the elaboration of the DBL in 2003, IUCN, through the Regional Environmental Law Programme for Asia and its Country Office in Viet Nam, has been the leader implementing organization to provide assistance to MoNRE. In particular, it has coordinated technical assistance efforts by various donors and implementing agencies. Besides, it has managed the most important TA projects through its continuous presence in the country.

With respect to the funding sources of biodiversity-related technical assistance, two key phases can be distinguished. The first phase was funded by GTZ from 7 January 2003 to 30 November 2006.[111] In the second phase, funding for the elaboration of the DBL was 'a major component of the UNDP/MoNRE Poverty and Environment Project, which seek to harmonize poverty reduction and environmental goals in policy and planning'.[112]

The involvement of several individuals and organizations, including national and international experts in all the subject areas covered by the DBL, appears to address some of the usual concerns about IP-related technical assistance, i.e. providers being enforcement driven as well as IP right-holders driven. On the one hand, this broad stakeholder and expert participation is entirely consonant with the heterogeneity of the technical fields regulated by this broad umbrella law. On the other, such participation has provided different perspectives and policy options for discussion. However, this may not always have guaranteed a balanced advice on all subject areas, some of which have received more attention and understanding than others due to their complexity, the availability of

---

can be found on its website: GTZ, 'Partner for the Future—Worldwide', available at: www.giz.de/en/home.html (accessed 10 October 2008).

[111]   In this phase, the IUCN Viet Nam Office received financial support from the German Federal Ministry for Economic Development Cooperation (BMZ) through GTZ to carry out the project 'Capacity Building on Access and Benefit Sharing in Viet Nam'. However, in the beginning, seed funding to start ABS-related technical assistance was provided as a minor element of a larger grant by the Global Environmental Facility/United Nations Environmental Programme to assist Viet Nam to develop the National Biosafety Framework to implement the Cartagena Protocol. This information was collected through a semi-structured interview with Patricia Moore, Head, IUCN Regional Environmental Law Programme for Asia, in Hanoi, Viet Nam (26 March 2007); and IUCN (2007), 'IUCN in Asia', at p. 6. Besides the provision of technical assistance during the drafting process, the most important contribution of IUCN was the establishment of a transparent network of scientists, government official and international experts 'working closely together in drafting and refining the ABS chapter'. CBD (2006), above note 8.

[112]   UN Viet Nam (2008), above note 102.

limited resources and relevant expertise, time constraints and an extremely crowded legislative agenda.

As a result of these activities, in December 2007, MoNRE submitted the DBL to the Ministry of Justice, who is responsible for reviewing its conformity with the Constitution and with the other relevant laws from the substantial and formal points of view. At the end of April 2008, the MoNRE, on behalf of the Government, submitted the revised DBL to the National Assembly's Science, Technology and Environment Committee. Then, the revised DBL was submitted to the Standing Committee of the National Assembly. After the latter's approval, the MoNRE submitted the draft Biodiversity Law to the National Assembly's plenary meeting, which was convened in October/November 2008.

The Biodiversity Law was passed on 13 November 2008 by the XII National Assembly at its 4th session and entered into effect on 1 July 2009.

5.3.3   The ABS provisions of the Biodiversity Law

The Biodiversity Law states as a general principle that 'Organizations and individuals that benefit from biodiversity exploitation and use shall share their benefits with concerned parties, ensuring harmony between the interests of the State, organizations and individuals.'[113] In terms of coverage, ABS provisions apply to all genetic resources including domestic and wild species, which are conserved in *in-situ* as well as in *ex-situ* conditions.[114]

The Biodiversity Law establishes that genetic resources shall be under the management of organizations and individuals appointed by the Government to administer the facilities or territories in which these resources are found or conserved, including: management boards of conservation areas; owners of biodiversity conservation facilities, laboratories and research facilities; organizations and individuals who are responsible for the management of forests and waters; and Commune People's Committees.[115]

---

[113]   Article 4.4 of the Biodiversity Law.

[114]   Ibid., Article 2 states: 'This Law applies to organizations, households and individuals in the country, overseas Vietnamese, foreign organizations and individuals carrying out activities related to the conservation and sustainable development of biodiversity in Viet Nam.' It is not clear yet whether human genetic materials will fall within their scope of application, as these materials are not expressly excluded.

[115]   Ibid. Article 55.2. While an earlier draft of Biodiversity Law, dated April 2008, gave to 'the Central Authority Agency in charge of natural resources and

Individuals and organizations that manage genetic resources within their respective areas of competence have the following rights and obligations: to survey, collect and transfer genetic resources; to supervise such activities, if they are carried out by authorized third parties; to enter into contracts and benefit-sharing agreements with such third parties; and to report to the competent state management agencies relevant information concerning the above activities.[116]

Individuals and organizations wishing to access genetic resources need to follow a series of sequential steps. In particular, they must: register for access to genetic resources; enter into a benefit-sharing agreement with the organizations and individuals responsible for the management of the genetic resources to be accessed; and apply for a licence from a competent state management agency.[117]

The Biodiversity Law provides that ABS contracts must include, *inter alia*: the purpose and plan of collecting activities; a description of the genetic resources to be accessed and their weight; the access location; the details of research activities, including their location and involved parties; and the details of the arrangement for the sharing of benefits that may arise from the use of genetic resources, including commercialization of derivative products and intellectual property rights.[118] Such contracts must be certified by the People's Committee of the commune where the activities take place and transmitted to the state agency competent to grant licences for access to genetic resources.[119]

Once the benefit-sharing agreement is concluded with the individuals or organizations that manage genetic resources, the collector or user needs to obtain a licence to access these resources. The licence contains the same elements that are listed in the benefit-sharing agreement and requires periodical reports 'on the results of research and development or production of commercial products.'[120] However, competent state management agencies may decide not to grant access to genetic resources if such resources pertain to critically endangered species or their use threatens human life, the environment, security, defence or the national

---

the environment' a supervising role to monitor and enforce compliance with the provisions of the Biodiversity Law, reference to such authority were eventually deleted.

[116] Ibid. Article 56.
[117] Ibid. Article 57. Besides, the Government is given the mandate to specify ABS procedures.
[118] Ibid. Article 58.3
[119] Ibid. Articles 58.2 and 58.4.
[120] Ibid. Article 59.3.

interest.[121] In addition, in cases of national or community interest, the 'state management agencies competent to grant licences' for access to genetic resources may exercise the power to grant such licences, even if the individuals or organizations that manage genetic resources have not given their consent.[122]

Organizations or individuals who have obtained a licence to access genetic resources must comply with the benefit-sharing agreement and submit a progress report on the state of research, development and commercialization of products derived from genetic resources.[123] Finally, the parties that are entitled by law to benefit sharing are: the state; the organizations and individuals that manage genetic resources and those who hold a licence for access to such resources.[124]

The Biodiversity Law also gives instructions concerning the establishment and management of genebanks to preserve the germplasm of protected species.[125] In addition, it provides for the survey, collection and evaluation of these materials, including the establishment of centralized database system.[126] Finally, it encourages traditional knowledge holders to register copyrights on genetic resources-related knowledge under the guidance of the Ministry of Science and Technology.[127]

5.3.4   Outstanding issues and gaps relevant for the implementation of the ABS system

This section makes an evaluation of the coverage of (and exemptions from) legal restrictions on access to genetic resources created by the Biodiversity Law and their consequences for agricultural research and crop diversity management.[128]

---

[121]   Ibid. Article 59.4.
[122]   Ibid. Article 59.5.
[123]   Ibid. Article 60.2.
[124]   Ibid. Article 61.1.
[125]   Ibid. Article 62.
[126]   Ibid. Article 63.
[127]   Ibid. Article 64.
[128]   Some of the following outstanding issues and gaps were discussed during the 'International Workshop on the Biodiversity Law', held in Hanoi, Viet Nam, on 2 November 2007. The workshop was held 'as part of the progress to develop the first Biodiversity Law for the country'. The aim of the workshop was to consult 'with international organizations on the second draft of the Law ... under the framework of the UNDP–GEF funded *Poverty and Environment* project'. V.V. Trieu (2007), 'Opening Statement by Vu Van Trieu, Country Representative,

A general concern is that the Biodiversity Law does not identify a single state management agency, which should act as the focal point for the administration of the ABS system. Thus, in the absence of clear ABS implementing guidelines, it is difficult to identify on a case-by-case basis the state management agencies, which may be competent in accordance with the type or location of the genetic resources to be accessed. It also appears that agricultural considerations have not been fully taken into account so far.

5.3.4.1   *Relationship with the ITPGRFA*

Participants at the 2007 Workshop on the Biodiversity Law agreed that the Law is consistent in spirit with the international agreements to which Viet Nam is a party. However, experts noted that the DBL would not provide sufficient scope for implementing the ITPGRFA, if Viet Nam decides to become a party thereto.

Upon MoNRE's request to provide technical assistance, the UN Food and Agriculture Organization suggested that it would be advisable to introduce an *ad hoc* exemption to regulate access to the PGRFA covered by the FAO Multilateral System (and the sharing of their benefits) in accordance with the ITPGRFA.[129] In particular, it was recommended that the ABS provisions of the Biodiversity Law should not be applied to plant genetic resources listed in Annex I of the ITPGRFA.[130]

The importance of such exemption is twofold: first, it could have provided legal space to ensure that PGRFA are managed in an openly accessible manner so as to generate higher social value and positive externalities; and, second, it could have ensured that the Biodiversity Law does not need to be amended to be consistent with any later national piece of legislation inspired by the ITPGRFA. Thus, if Viet Nam were to ratify the ITPGRFA, it should consider the possibility of allowing the use of the Standard Material Transfer Agreement for PGRFA included in Annex I, in conjunction with ordinary ABS agreements negotiated on a case-by-case basis for other types of genetic resources.

IUCN Viet Nam Country Office', International Workshop on the Biodiversity Law, Hanoi, Viet Nam (2 November 2007).
[129]   Such exemption was included in an earlier version of the DBL dated March 2007 and it was deleted during the drafting process.
[130]   C. Chiarolla (2007), 'Legal Assistance for the Development of National Legislation on Biodiversity', TCP/VIE/3101, FAO, Hanoi, Viet Nam.

5.3.4.2   *Farmers' exemptions*

Farmers' exemption could be made available to all Vietnamese farmers under the Biodiversity Law. Poor farmers should be allowed to access PGRFA for non-commercial purposes, such as subsistence farming and direct cultivation, without additional burdens. Indeed, improving access to and use of good quality seeds and other basic agricultural inputs is an essential component of rural development policies, regardless of whether particular public or private actors may be in the best position to develop, produce and deliver such inputs in each particular case.

For example, IUCN suggested exempting the exchange of seeds and other genetic resources among local people and communities for traditional, non-commercial purposes.[131] Instead, the application of ordinary ABS requirements and procedures may be appropriate in the case of activities that involve the transfer of PGRFA for purposes other than direct cultivation, breeding and consumption. As regards the guidance given by the farmers' rights provision of the ITPGRFA, the interpretation of Article 9.3 suggests that the Biodiversity Law has missed an important opportunity to recognize legally the farmers' rights to save, sell and exchange seeds according to their customary practices in Viet Nam.

5.3.4.3   *Domestic non-commercial research*

Facilitated access procedures for university students and Vietnamese scientists, who work in public or non-profit research institutions, may be necessary to encourage the development and conservation of plant genetic resources. However, the Biodiversity Law does not specify any kind of differential treatment for such domestic collection and transfer activities.

As a consequence, the competent state management agencies may have to process a huge volume of requests for the grant of licences. This is likely unnecessarily to increase the amount of financial and human resources required to manage the ABS system without generating additional benefits. Because of this, the costs of doing research could grow with a potential negative impact on domestic research capacity. As in the case of excessively strong plant-related IP rights, access to genetic

---

[131]   IUCN (2007), 'Development of the Biodiversity Law in Viet Nam—Proposed Draft Chapters', IUCN Regional Environmental Law Programme for Asia.

resources for domestic non-commercial research and basic biological research might need a more streamlined ABS procedure not to be held back by inappropriately restrictive legal requirements.[132]

In general, plant breeders and bio-industries' representatives appear to be concerned about the perceived wider scope of exemptions allowed under PVP systems—and even under some patent law systems—in comparison with the exemptions provided for in ABS laws.[133] In agriculture, these concerns derive from the increasing difficulties of agricultural research institutions both in the private and public sectors to access breeding materials.[134]

An interesting comparison may be drawn between the relevant provisions of the Biodiversity Law of Viet Nam (2008) and the exemptions provided for in the Indian Biological Diversity Act (2002) and implementing guidelines (2006). In particular, the Indian Biodiversity Act (2002) provides exemptions: for local people to freely access bio-resources; for growers, cultivators, and local/native healers to use such resources; for collaborative research with government-sponsored institutes;[135] and for value added products and normally traded commodities in order to avoid

---

[132]   In the field of IP protection, see J. Sulston and J. Stiglitz (2008), 'Science is being held back by outdated laws. The question 'who owns science?' is now crucial', The Times, 5 July 2008, available at: www.timesonline.co.uk/tol/comment/letters/article4271555.ece (accessed 10 August 2008).

[133]   D.D. Verma (2006), 'Policy on Access and Benefit Sharing in India', paper presented at the Japan-India Workshop on 'Access and Benefit Sharing of Genetic Resources and Traditional Knowledge in the context of CBD', organized by the Japanese Bioindustry Association, Tokyo, Japan (8 December 2006).

[134]   They also reflect the need to identify cases in which a simplified access procedure may benefit providers and users of PGRFA by facilitating collaborative research. However, globally only a few countries have specific ABS laws in place. Therefore, in many cases, it is the absence of such laws that makes it difficult to identify the national authorities and stakeholders, which should be involved in ABS procedures.

[135]   In particular, clause 5 of the Biological Diversity Act (2002) states that the approval of the National Biodiversity Authority, which is required under Sections 3 and 4, shall 'not to apply to collaborative research projects involving transfer or exchange of biological resources or information relating thereto between institutions, including Government sponsored institutions of India, and such institutions in other countries, if such collaborative research projects satisfy the conditions specified in subsection (3)'. Sub-section 3 provides that such 'collaborative research projects shall: (a) conform to the policy guidelines issued by the Central Government ...; and (b) be approved by the Central Government.' Government of India (2006), 'Guidelines for International Collaboration Research Projects Involving Transfer or Exchange of Biological Resources or Information', *The Gazette of India,* 8 November 2006, No.1339, New Delhi, India.

affecting trade through a system that requires specific notifications to the central government.[136]

The Government of Viet Nam, in consultation with MoNRE and other relevant ministries, could consider drafting implementing guidelines along the lines traced by the Indian legislation. Such guidelines may include facilitated access procedures for specific cases that could be identified taking into account the need to promote biodiversity research as well as the know-how and technology transfer needs of Vietnamese scientists.

5.3.4.4   Traditional knowledge protection

The Biodiversity Law specifically encourages the registration of copyrights on knowledge derived from genetic resources.[137] In general, authors are not required by law to register their creative works to enjoy the benefits of copyright protection.[138] However, such registration may help to enforce their rights.

Copyright does not cover genetic resources *per se* or the indigenous and traditional knowledge that may relate to such resources. However, copyright protection can cover the form of fixation of such knowledge, including the results from research carried out on plant genetic resources.[139]

Copyright may not always be the most appropriate form of protection for traditional and indigenous biodiversity-related knowledge, because in most cases it is orally transmitted within communities. In order to protect this knowledge, it must be fixed or recorded in some form. Thus, the subject matter of protection is the form of fixation and not knowledge *per se*.

---

[136]   D.D. Verma (2006), above note 133. In particular, clause 40 of the Biological Diversity Act (2002) states: 'Notwithstanding anything contained in this Act, the Central Government may, in consultation with the National Biodiversity Authority, by notification in the Official Gazette, declare that the provisions of this Act shall not apply to any items, including biological resources normally traded as commodities.' In 2007, consultations were undertaken with the aim of developing a list of exempted products.

[137]   Copyright is a type of intellectual property which is awarded to authors to protect their creative works that are *fixed* in a printed, video, audiotape or other recorded form. These rights are negative in nature in the sense that they prevent third parties from exploiting the protected works without the authorization of the author.

[138]   For example, if one writes a book, she does not need to register the book to have author's rights over it.

[139]   For example, a DVD that contains a graphic description of the rice genome can be copyrighted.

In conclusion, it may not be appropriate for the Biodiversity Law to prescribe copyright as the unique or primary legal tool for the protection TK. This is not only because biodiversity-related knowledge is often orally transmitted and cannot be easily copyrighted or registered. It is also because copyright cannot prevent the misappropriation of TK, if such knowledge is used in a form different from the initial form of fixation. Other *sui generis* forms of intellectual property protection may be more appropriate in these cases and they may deserve further consideration by the competent implementing authorities.[140] Besides, such authorities may consider recognizing the rights of indigenous and local communities and farmers to PIC and MAT in their national legislation in accordance with relevant international instruments, as proposed in Chapter 4.[141]

Therefore, it is important that the interpretation of the Biodiversity Law's provisions related to traditional knowledge does not preclude developments in this area. In addition, the introduction by law of an obligation to disclose the origin of genetic resources in patent and plant variety rights applications might have helped reducing concerns for biopiracy. However, such obligation has not encountered the necessary support of the drafters of the Intellectual Property Law (2005).

5.3.5 Concluding observations on PGR and the Biodiversity Law

The Biodiversity Law is consistent in spirit with the international agreements to which Viet Nam is a party and the IUCN has efficiently coordinated the delivery of biodiversity-related technical assistance by several donors and implementing agencies. A general concern is that the Biodiversity Law does not identify a single state management agency to act as the focal point for the administration of the ABS system. Without limiting the involvement of domestic stakeholders who are closely connected with such resources, a streamlined procedure to facilitate access and reduce transaction costs by identifying a single focal point for the administration of the ABS system should be recommended.

The ABS provisions of the Biodiversity Law give little recognition to the special nature of plant genetic resources for food and agriculture. In particular, they could be improved in four key areas. First, if Viet Nam

---

[140]   See, for instance, G. Dutfield (2003), 'Protecting Traditional Knowledge and Folklore: A Review of Progress in Diplomacy and Policy Formulation', Issue Paper No. 1, UNCTAD–ICTSD Project on IPRs and Sustainable Development.

[141]   See, in general, section 4.2.3 and, in particular, sub-sections 4.2.3.4 and 4.2.3.5.

decides to become a party to the ITPGRFA, an *ad hoc* exemption to regulate access to PGRFA covered by the FAO Multilateral System (and the sharing of their benefits) should be introduced, including the use of the SMTA. Second, the Biodiversity Law could have taken a proactive stand in recognition of the rights of farmers to save, sell and exchange seeds according to their customary practices in Viet Nam. The possibility to recognize legally such rights should be considered in the implementing guidelines.[142] Third, domestic non-commercial biodiversity research and, in particular, agricultural research, has not been afforded any kind of special treatment, which might be justified in the case of purely domestic collection, research and transfer activities.

Finally, the Biodiversity Law seems to prescribe copyright as the unique or primary legal tool for the protection of TK. Copyright may not always be appropriate and should not preclude the use of other effective means of TK protection either within or outside the IPR system.

5.4   LESSONS LEARNED AND CONCEPTUAL CONTRIBUTION OF THE CASE STUDY

This case study makes a fundamental conceptual contribution to the subject matter of this book, i.e. the study of international law relevant to the protection of crop diversity. In part this is because it tests the validity of the theoretical approaches, which have been adopted to identify and explain key factors that influence IP and ABS policy-making and standard-setting activities and their developmental implications in the study country. It is also because it presents concrete examples of instances where the national implementation of such norms has proven to be problematic, because of their disconnection with domestic realities both in research and farming. It provides important lessons for making the law a real instrument of intervention for crop diversity protection, sustainability and development in agriculture.

In order to make this conceptual contribution, this chapter has analysed the effectiveness and limitations of the law reform process in the

---

[142]   In addition, such rights could also be recognized mutually by the IP Law along the lines traced by the 1998 Biotechnology Directive, which recognizes the existence of a general right of farmers to replant saved seeds in accordance with Article 14 of the EC Regulation 2100/94 on the protection of plant variety rights.

area of plant genetic resource in the Viet Nam. The case study has noted that the country's efforts to join the WTO and UPOV have injected a remarkable sense of urgency in the IP law reform process. In particular, it has explained current legislative reforms as the result of tensions between IPR and ABS policies, interest group activities, and the interaction between public and private actors, including the role of technical assistance and the negotiation of free trade agreements. Challenges and opportunities for improving domestic legislation have been identified, including areas where further work may be required, such as: training and capacity development for domestic stakeholders and institutions, and enhanced implementation and/or revision of legislation with a focus on differentiation between technological fields.

This case study has also shown the extent to which Viet Nam has taken advantage of TRIPs-related flexibilities in designing the IP legal and policy framework for promoting agricultural innovation. In particular, it has identified bilateral TRIPs-plus obligation as a key factor, which restricts such flexibilities, and has highlighted the delicate balance of interests (e.g. promoting international trade, access to foreign markets, inflows of investments and technologies, etc.) that need to be considered when governments with similar socio-economic conditions decide to ratify bilateral deals that contain TRIPs-plus standards of IP protection. Therefore, the case study has built upon the analysis of the international plant IP protection framework that is described in Chapter 3 by providing deeper insights on flexibilities and constraints arising from the domestic implementation of the TRIPs Agreement, the UPOV Convention and relevant bilateral deals.

In relation to the Vietnamese IP Law, the main focus of IP-related technical assistance on strengthening IP protection standards and the administrative and enforcement capacity of implementing agencies has resulted in the suboptimal use of plant-related flexibilities. The extent to which future IP capacity development activities can redress systemic weaknesses, which derive from the fact that the IPR reform agenda was not shaped having in mind the needs of the Vietnamese agricultural sector and, in particular, its current level of technological capacity, remains to be seen. However, future activities, which might help to integrate crop diversity issues within the Vietnamese IP system are: the training of Vietnamese judges and patent examiners on genetic resource policy issues, including aspects that regard the public interest; the development of adequate IP management policies and procedures for national agricultural universities and research institutes; and assistance with amending (and implementing) the IP Law to include an explicit mutual recognition of the breeders' and farmers' exemptions under the patent law.

A key lesson learned is that the provision of adequate IP-related technical assistance to government agencies and relevant stakeholders may play a critical role in enhancing the capacity of countries to set their priorities in bilateral negotiations to ensure that the economic opportunities arising from trade liberalization are exploited, while preserving legal scope for promoting technology development and diffusion in the public interest, especially in relation to food security and the sustainable use of crop diversity.

Global institutional reforms governing the present and future allocation of wealth from crop diversity and, in particular, their implementation in the Vietnamese context have neither fully recognized the need to afford a special treatment to PGRFA, nor have strengthened the important role that informal seed systems still play in this country. Because of this, such reforms are insufficient to promote equity outcomes in terms of the way the value that is generated from the conservation and sustainable use of, and research on, crop diversity is captured and its benefits shared.

In Viet Nam, the neglected recognition of farmers' rights both under the Biodiversity Law and the IP Law, the limited recognition of farmers' and breeders' exemptions, the missed opportunity to adopt an enabling legal framework to participate in (and benefit from) the FAO Multilateral System of ABS, and the suboptimal use of TRIPs-related flexibilities are all examples of a trend towards an unbalanced model of commodification of resources and knowledge with far-reaching implications for wealth redistribution, agricultural innovation, sustainability and development. Under these conditions, innovation spillovers from agricultural research investments are more likely to be captured by the empowered groups, rather than promoting technology development and diffusion within distributed systems of innovation, such as those that characterize the agricultural sector in most developing countries.

Another key lesson learned from the case study is that the existence of high transaction costs, which might be associated with ABS procedures, as well as the generation, maintenance and exploitation of plant-related IP rights, in conjunction with obvious capacity constraints of most potential domestic users (i.e. small farmers), may limit their access to these new right systems, especially in the areas of plant-related IP and ABS.

This lack of capacity and legal entitlements to use critical productive resources poses a serious risk of increasing inequalities between disempowered groups, which are *de facto* excluded from making decisions on crop diversity issues, and economically and/or politically powerful groups, whose concentrated economic gains are expected to pay off the investments made in the transition between property regimes. In Chapter 2, this book has explained that the application of interest group theories suggests that institutional reforms, which lead to the commodification of crop diversity may not be expected to redress inequities and reduce the increasing gap between poor famers and elite minorities in the agricultural sector. Against this backdrop, the case study of Viet Nam has also shown that such theories can be useful in casting light on the limitations and systemic weaknesses of global institutional reforms that concern agricultural innovation systems.

Against the complexity and diversity of ABS issues, the Viet Nam country study has finally shown the increasing interest that has arisen around such issues. The efforts of national legislators in this regard have been remarkable and they confirm that the implementation of the benefit-sharing objective of the CBD (based on prior informed consent and mutually agreed terms) is perceived as a critical element for the development of a more equitable global regime for the exchange and use of genetic resources. However, despite such efforts, the magnitude of the capacity gap, which needs to be filled in order to integrate PGRFA-related concerns into national ABS frameworks, remains large, in particular with regard to making use of the FAO Multilateral System and the rights of indigenous and local communities and farmers.

5.5 EXAMPLE PCT INTERNATIONAL APPLICATION

PCT WORLD INTELLECTUAL PROPERTY ORGANIZATION
International Bureau

INTERNATIONAL APPLICATION PUBLISHED UNDER THE PATENT COOPERATION TREATY (PCT)

(51) International Patent Classification [7] : C12N 15/82, C07K 14/415, C12N 15/11, A01H 5/00	A2	(11) International Publication Number: **WO 00/26389** (43) International Publication Date: 11 May 2000 (11.05.00)

(21) International Application Number: PCT/EP99/08360

(22) International Filing Date: 2 November 1999 (02.11.99)

(30) Priority Data:
    1998/46973   3 November 1998 (03.11.98)   KR
    1998/50126   19 November 1998 (19.11.98)   KR

(71) Applicant *(for all designated States except AT US)*: NOVARTIS AG [CH/CH]; Schwarzwaldallee 215, CH–4058 Basel (CH).

(71) Applicant *(for AT only)*: NOVARTIS–ERFINDUNGEN VERWALTUNGSGESELLSCHAFT MBH [AT/AT]; Brunner Strasse 59, A–1230 Vienna (AT).

(72) Inventors; and
(75) Inventors/Applicants *(for US only)*: AN, Gynheung [US/KR]; Faculty Apt. 9–1803, Jigok–dong, Nam–gu, Pohang, Kyungbook 790–730 (KR). JEON, Jong–Seong [KR/KR]; HanSin Apartment 11–1303, 1095, Doksan–dong, Kumchun–gu, Seoul 153–011 (KR). CHUNG, Yong–Yoon [KR/KR]; Mido Apartment 101–109, Kangnam–ku, Daechi–dong, Seoul (KR). LEE, Sichul [KR/KR]; 1 Ri, 9 Ban, Dokye–eup, Samchok, Kangwon–do 235–900 (KR).

(74) Agent: BECKER, Konrad; Novartis AG, Corporate Intellectual Property, Patent & Trademark Department, CH–4002 Basel (CH).

(81) Designated States: AE, AL, AM, AT, AU, AZ, BA, BB, BG, BR, BY, CA, CH, CN, CR, CU, CZ, DE, DK, EE, ES, FI, GB, GD, GE, GH, GM, HR, HU, ID, IL, IN, IS, JP, KE, KG, KP, KR, KZ, LC, LK, LR, LS, LT, LU, LV, MA, MD, MG, MK, MN, MW, MX, NO, NZ, PL, PT, RO, RU, SD, SE, SG, SI, SK, SL, TJ, TM, TR, TT, TZ, UA, UG, US, UZ, VN, YU, ZA, ZW, ARIPO patent (GH, GM, KE, LS, MW, SD, SL, SZ, TZ, UG, ZW), Eurasian patent (AM, AZ, BY, KG, KZ, MD, RU, TJ, TM), European patent (AT, BE, CH, CY, DE, DK, ES, FI, FR, GB, GR, IE, IT, LU, MC, NL, PT, SE), OAPI patent (BF, BJ, CF, CG, CI, CM, GA, GN, GW, ML, MR, NE, SN, TD, TG).

Published
    Without international search report and to be republished upon receipt of that report.

(54) Title: DNA COMPRISING RICE ANTHER–SPECIFIC GENE AND TRANSGENIC PLANT TRANSFORMED THEREWITH

(57) Abstract

    This invention describes novel DNA sequences which function as promoters of anther–specific transcription of coding DNA sequences in recombinant or chimeric DNA sequences. The invention also describes recombinant or chimeric DNA sequences, which are expressed specifically in the anther of a plant. The said recombinant or chimeric DNA sequences may be used to create transgenic plants, but especially transgenic male–sterile plants.

6. Conclusions

This book sets out to test the proposition that global institutional reforms governing the present and future allocation of wealth from crop diversity are insufficient—and in some respects inappropriate—to achieve international equity in terms of the way plant genetic resources are transferred, how agricultural research is conducted, and its benefits are shared, the key reason for this being that such reforms disregard the important role of informal or farmers' seed systems.

In order to test the above proposition, this book has articulated three specific objectives, which focus on: the institutional limitations and systemic weaknesses of agricultural innovation systems in the context of the increasing commodification of crop diversity; the developmental implications of changes in the legal status of resources and knowledge that arise from such commodification; and the available options for improving the applicable legal framework with a view to making the law a real instrument to promote equity, development and sustainability in agriculture.

6.1 CROP DIVERSITY COMMODIFICATION: LIMITATIONS AND SYSTEMIC WEAKNESSES OF GLOBAL INSTITUTIONAL REFORMS

In the field of agriculture, the TRIPs Agreement leaves a remarkable degree of freedom for adjusting plant-related intellectual property legislation to domestic needs and promoting local innovation. However, the room for manoeuvre for developing countries may be quite narrow in practice. A growing number of developing countries has executed free trade and investment treaties with the US, the EU and other industrialized countries. In these treaties, they have agreed *inter alia* to provide patent protection for biotechnological inventions and to become members of UPOV.[1]

---

[1]   Besides, UPOV, which advocates its 1991 Act as the most effective *sui generis* model law for the protection of plant varieties, discriminates against aspirant new members. In fact, since 1996 onwards, developing countries that implement a *sui generis* system of PVP compliant with the 1978 UPOV Act are not entitled to join the Union.

In most cases, the industrialized countries' international IP policies have significantly limited the options for designing *sui generis* plant variety right systems that can safely be adopted by developing countries without violating bilateral deals. However, not all countries have accepted to ratify TRIPs-plus standards for the protection of agricultural innovation and biotechnology products. When free trade and investment agreements are negotiated, there is an increasing awareness among developing countries' negotiators that strong patent and plant variety rights may fail to support crop research and domestic innovation, especially if they have not yet reached the technological frontier, i.e. when they have not yet developed advanced breeding and biotechnological capacity that would allow their firms and research centres to compete with foreign innovations in domestic and international markets.

The Viet Nam case study has highlighted the delicate balance of interests (e.g. promoting international trade, access to foreign markets, inflows of investments and technologies, etc.) that needs to be considered when governments with similar socio-economic conditions decide to ratify bilateral deals that contain such TRIPs-plus standards. Against this backdrop, it is not surprising that the efforts that poor countries should make to join the WTO and please their major trade partners may eventually leave unheard important equity instances of local actors, individuals, communities and organizations, who continue to preserve crop diversity *in situ* not only for future generations but also for their own survival. Thus, the case study has shown that often legislative outcomes are influenced by the imperatives of international obligations under various forms of external pressures, while important sectoral issues may be sidelined. Under such circumstances, hidden threats to food security may still be avoided by enacting specific interface provisions between patents and plant variety rights, including the recognition of broad research and farmers' exemptions.

A key lesson learned is that the provision of adequate IP-related technical assistance to government agencies and relevant stakeholders plays a critical role in enhancing the capacity of countries to set their priorities in bilateral negotiations to ensure that emerging economic opportunities are not foregone, while preserving legal scope for technology development and diffusion in the public interest. However, the focus of most IP technical assistance providers on strengthening IP protection standards and the administrative and enforcement capacity of implementing agencies may result in the suboptimal use of plant-related flexibilities. If the IPR reform agenda is not shaped having in mind also the needs of domestic agriculture sectors and the level of technological capacity, the extent to which the resulting systemic weaknesses can be redressed through ex-post capacity-building activities is uncertain.

In 1992, the UN Convention on Biological Diversity reaffirmed the principle that national sovereignty extends to all natural resources within national borders, including genetic resources. ABS restrictions on access to genetic resources could be understood as a tool used by governments to internalize positive externalities that would otherwise be distributed in the form of benefits derived from unfettered access to such resources. However, bilateral benefit-sharing mechanisms are not appropriate for crop research, because all countries are interdependent in terms of plant genetic diversity and many breeding materials are necessary to develop a new plant variety. In order to overcome this problem, the ITPGRFA creates a Multilateral System of ABS, which does not require *ad hoc* negotiations between providers and recipients of PGRFA, and reduces transaction costs. It also makes use of a Standard Material Transfer Agreement to track individual accessions and ensures that some benefits flow back to the Multilateral System when a product based on MLS material is commercialized on the market.

This book has highlighted that there is a strong correlation between restrictions on access to PGRFA (in particular, patents, which are the strongest form of protection for plant-related inventions), and benefit sharing in the FAO Multilateral System. By contrast, because of the breeders' exemption, *sui generis* plant variety protection systems do not generate benefits that can be captured in the form of compulsory payments to the MLS. However, strong monopoly protection for intermediate products may be at odds with the ITPGRFA open access regime. Among other factors, the successful implementation of the Multilateral System will depend on whether the patenting of plant-related inventions will make it more cumbersome for poor countries to acquire and integrate new scientific and technical knowledge related to the conservation and sustainable use of PGRFA in their production systems. This highlights the need to protect the public domain status of materials included in the Multilateral System.

6.2 DEVELOPMENTAL IMPLICATIONS OF CHANGES IN THE LEGAL STATUS OF PGRFA

Interest group theories suggest the costs associated with the commodification of crop diversity are likely to be unfairly distributed with the developing world bearing a disproportionate amount of such costs, while minorities in industrialized countries appropriate most of the benefits.[2] Where formal seed markets have worked efficiently, plant intellectual property protection has accelerated technological change in terms of faster varietal turnover. However, it has also influenced the distribution of benefits from research investments and innovation spillovers. As a result, such spillovers are not available to less developed countries and the public sector to the same extent as they were in the past. Against this backdrop, the commodification of crop diversity should not be expected to promote a shift towards a fairer global food system.

Agricultural innovation is typically a cumulative process and PGRFA should be managed in an openly accessible manner, because such 'non-traditional infrastructural resources' may generate higher social value and positive externalities if they are managed as regulated commons. Innovation, and in particular agricultural innovation, crucially depends on the balance between the realms of the public domain, private property and common property more than on a single component of such balance. This is because physical access to PGRFA for the purpose of breeding new varieties is important as much as the incentives that IPRs, such as patents and plant variety rights, may create to encourage private sector agricultural research.

In Viet Nam, the neglected recognition of farmers' rights both under the Biodiversity Law and the IP Law, the limited recognition of farmers' and breeders' exemptions, the missed opportunity to adopt an enabling legal framework to participate in (and benefit from) the FAO Multilateral System of ABS, and the suboptimal use of TRIPs-related flexibilities are all examples of a trend towards an unbalanced model of commodification of resources and knowledge with far-reaching implications for wealth redistribution, agricultural innovation, sustainability and development. Under these conditions, innovation spillovers from agricultural research investments are more likely to be captured by the empowered groups, rather than promoting technology development and diffusion within distributed systems of innovation, such as those that characterize the agricultural sector in most developing countries.

Another key lesson learned from the case study that may be relevant to other developing countries (especially those that are planning to join the WTO, implement the TRIPs Agreement, the UPOV Convention, the ITPGRFA, and the access and benefit-sharing pillar of the CBD) is the following. The existence of high transaction costs, which might be

---

[2]   As regards interest group theories, see S. Banner (2002), 'Transitions between Property Regimes', *The Journal of Legal Studies,* XXXI (2), 359–71, and section 2.3.4 of this book.

associated with ABS procedures, as well as the generation, maintenance and exploitation of plant-related IP rights, in conjunction with obvious capacity constraints of most potential domestic users (i.e. small farmers), may limit their access to these new right systems, especially in the areas of plant-related IP and ABS for plant genetic resources.

Against the complexity and diversity of ABS issues, which are being discussed at the international, national and community levels, as analysed in Chapter 4 of this book, the Viet Nam case study has shown the increasing interest that has arisen around such issues. The efforts of national legislators in this regard have been remarkable and they confirm that the implementation of the benefit-sharing objective of the CBD (based on prior informed consent and mutually agreed terms) is perceived as a critical element for the development of a more equitable global regime for the exchange and use of genetic resources in general and plant genetic resources in particular.

Despite such efforts, the magnitude of the capacity gap that needs to be filled in order to integrate PGRFA-related concerns into national ABS frameworks remains large, in particular with regard to making use of, and implementing, the FAO Multilateral System and the rights of indigenous and local communities and farmers. The lack of capacity and legal entitlements to use critical productive resources poses a serious risk to increase inequalities between disempowered groups, which are *de facto* excluded from making decisions on crop diversity issues, and economically and/or politically powerful groups, whose concentrated economic gains are expected to pay off the investments made in the transition between property regimes.

6.3 AVAILABLE OPTIONS AND WAYS FORWARD

The link between the benefit-sharing provisions of the SMTA and the treatment of IPRs is important to understand the extent to which the ITPGRFA can make a contribution to international equity as regards the substance of its terms on PGRFA transfer and use. At its first meeting, the Governing Body of ITPGRFA established the level, form and manner of equitable benefit-sharing payments to be implemented through the SMTA. These payments depend on: A) the incorporation of MLS material into commercial plant varieties (i.e. PGRFA) and B) the existence of research and breeding restrictions on access to such varieties, including IPR restrictions.

This book argued that access to PGRFA can be legally restricted (to meet the requirement under letter B above) only if they incorporate non-MLS patented technologies. By contrast, it is contended that the SMTA should not allow patents to claim genetic components 'in the form received' from the Multilateral System, e.g. in the form of unmodified derivatives of MLS material and their progeny. As regards the 'incorporation requirement' (under letter A above), it should encompass the 'progeny' and 'unmodified derivatives' of the material transferred through the SMTA, with the consequent applicability of benefit-sharing obligations to the sale of such products. Besides, if the requirement under letter B above is met, the incorporation into a proprietary product of patented information (that results from research and development carried out on MLS material) may give rise to benefit sharing payments *per se*, i.e. even without the physical incorporation of the material.

Additional measures that may be taken at the international level to promote *in-situ* conservation of PGRFA and to protect traditional agricultural knowledge, innovation and practices of indigenous and local communities, and farmers' rights under the ITPGRFA, include *inter alia*: providing direct access to the Benefit-sharing Fund of the Treaty; reviewing the benefit-sharing conditions of the SMTA; and implementing access to PGRFA-related traditional knowledge under terms that recognize the right of ILCs and farmers to provide their prior informed consent and to negotiate mutually agreed terms for the use of their TK. This book also finds that voluntary contributions to the Benefit-sharing Fund do not take into account whether (and the extent to which) such contributions are additional to resources that were previously earmarked for agriculture and development projects in general. Therefore, the Governing Body should take effective measures to promote additionality of voluntary contributions to the Benefit-sharing Fund.

On the relationship between the CBD and the 'Nagoya Protocol on Access to Genetic Resources and the Fair and Equitable Sharing of Benefits Arising from their Utilization' on the one hand, and the ITPGRFA, on the other, this book stresses that the ABS Protocol appears neither to affect the rights and obligations of any party deriving from existing international agreements nor to prevent parties from developing new specialized ABS agreements. However, legal requirements that may be established under the ABS Protocol need to be mutually supportive of and coexist alongside the ITPGRFA. Besides, to the extent that such ABS requirements (applicable to PGRFA not included into the MLS) may add complexity to the definition of the ownership status of PGR, as opposed to streamlining the widest application of the ITPGRFA's commons management principles, they risk acting as a barrier to agricultural research and plant-related innovation.

6.4 CONCLUDING REMARKS

In the face of concerns regarding food security, genetic erosion, and the need to provide equitable accesses to seeds and strengthen the domestic plant-breeding sector, certain commercial interests may prevail as a consequence of economic law reforms, while others may lose from harmonization processes and the opening up of new markets for biological information and materials. The function of benefit sharing is precisely to compensate the losers from the international business regulatory game, linking economic law reforms with capacity building, information exchange and technology transfer.

In agriculture, the Standard Material Transfer Agreement under the ITPGRFA is a fundamental mechanism for benefit sharing. Other critical issues concern the treatment of derivatives, the protection of the public domain status of PGRFA within the FAO Multilateral System and the implementation of farmers' rights under Article 9. However, the balanced implementation of the ITPGRFA's commons management principles will present critical challenges for developing countries, which may have limited resources and capacity to use existing flexibilities and influence the outcomes of international negotiating processes in terms of increased transparency and equity.

As regards monetary benefit sharing, there is an urgent need to clarify who has to pay mandatory benefit-sharing and who is exempted. This should be done by keeping in mind the needs of on-farm breeding. Therfore, varieties protected in accordance with 1991 UPOV-type legislation or by widespread technical restrictions could also incur benefit-sharing payments. This solution could simplify monitoring compliance with benefit sharing and broaden the amount of resources that will be made available through the Benefit-sharing Fund. In addition, the SMTA's provision, that prohibits IPRs on PGRFA and their genetic parts or components, in the form received from the Multilateral System, also needs clarification and subsequent implementation. Therefore the Governing Body should:

- clarify the application of relevant SMTA's provisions and fence off the public domain status of materials in the Multilateral System;
- spell out the critical distinction between restrictions that may derive from the patenting of MLS materials *per se*, which would violate the SMTA, and all other patent-related restrictions that can trigger benefit sharing;
- clarify that patents that cover PGRFA products under current IP laws should be presumed to restrict access for research and breeding and to fulfil the relevant benefit-sharing requirement of the SMTA;

- clarify that 1991 UPOV-type plant variety protection impedes informal exchange and sale of seeds and it reduces opportunities for on-farm breeding, varietal improvement and selection by farmers. By doing so, UPOV 1991 also imposes restrictions on research and breeding, especially when it takes place outside the formal seed system; and
- clarify that there are already technical means in widespread use that are restricting access to PGRFA for research and breeding (e.g. CMS-Hybrids), and that such restrictions would therefore fulfil the benefit-sharing requirement of the SMTA.

A possible way to enhance transparency and the mutual supportiveness between the Nagoya Protocol and the ITPGRFA would be to amend the SMTA in order to request recipients to disclose, at plant variety protection and patent offices, that the materials for which protection is sought have been obtained from the Multilateral System, and to inform the Governing Body accordingly. The disclosure of legal access from the MLS and the related notifications should include a quote of the accessions' unique identifier numbers. Parties that endeavour to implement the FAO International Treaty and the Nagoya Protocol in a mutually supportive manner may envisage using the SMTA as an internationally-recognized certificate of compliance to be presented by resource users at all relevant checkpoints. Finally, the Governing Body should decide to make the annual payments on a product-by-product basis under Article 6.7 of the SMTA mandatory for all commercialized products that incorporate MLS material, regardless whether such 'products' are available without restrictions or not.[3]

Besides, while global institutional reforms governing the present and future allocation of wealth from crop diversity have recognized the need to afford a special treatment to PGRFA, countries have failed to strengthen the important role that informal seed systems still play in most parts of the world. Because of this, such reforms are insufficient—and in some respects inappropriate—to promote equity outcomes in terms of the way the value that is generated from the conservation and sustainable use of, and research on, crop diversity is captured and its benefits are shared.

---

[3]   See also: C. Chiarolla and S. Jungcurt (2011), 'Outstanding Issues on Access and Benefit Sharing under the Multilateral System of the International Treaty on Plant Genetic Resources for Food and Agriculture', a background study paper by the Berne Declaration and the Development Fund, available at: www.evb.ch/en/ p25019093.html.

Bibliography

ARTICLES

Altieri, A.M. and Rosset, P. (1999), 'The Reasons Why Biotechnology Will not Ensure Food Security, Protect the Environment and Reduce Poverty in the Developing World', *AgBioForum*, 2 (3–4), 155–62.

Baldock, C. and Kingsbury, O. (2000), 'Where did it come from and where is it going? The Biotechnology Directive and its Relation to the EPC', *Biotechnology Law Report*, 19 (1), 7–17.

Banner, S. (2002), 'Transitions between Property Regimes', *The Journal of Legal Studies*, XXXI (2), 359–71.

Barzel, Y. (1968), 'Optimal Timing of Innovations', *The Review of Economics and Statistics*, 50 (3), 448–55.

Bonell, M.J. (2004), 'UNIDROIT Principles 2004—The New Edition of the Principles of International Commercial Contracts adopted by the International Institute for the Unification of Private Law', *Uniform Law Review*, 2004 (1), 5–40.

Boyle, J. (2003), 'Foreword: the Opposite of Property?' *Law and Contemporary Problems*, 66 (1–2).

Boyle, J. (2003), 'The Second Enclosure Movement and the Construction of the Public Domain', *Law and Contemporary Problems*, 66 (1–2).

Brush, B.S. (2007), 'Farmers' Rights and Protection of Traditional Agricultural Knowledge', *World Development*, 35 (9), 1499–514.

Chambers, W.B. (2003), 'WSSD and an International Regime on Access and Benefit Sharing: Is a Protocol the Appropriate Legal Instrument?' *Review of European Community & International Environmental Law*, 12 (3), 310–20.

Chandler, M. (1993), 'The Biodiversity Convention: Selected Issues of Interest to the International Lawyer', *Colorado Journal of International Environmental Law and Policy*, 4, 141–76.

Chiarolla, C. (2006), 'Commodifying Agricultural Biodiversity and Development-Related Issues', *The Journal of World Intellectual Property*, 9 (1), 25–60.

Chiarolla, C. (2008), 'Plant Patenting, Benefit Sharing and the Law Applicable to the FAO Standard Material Transfer Agreement', *The Journal of World Intellectual Property*, 11 (1), 1–28.

Cook, T. (2006), 'Responding to Concerns about the Scope of the Defence from Patent Infringement for Acts Done for Experimental Purposes relating to the Subject Matter of the Invention', *Intellectual Property Quarterly*, 3, 193–222.

Cornish, W.R. (1993), 'The International Relations of Intellectual Property', *Cambridge Law Journal*, 52 (1), 46–63.

Cullet, P. (2005), 'Monsanto v Schmeiser: A Landmark Decision concerning Farmer Liability and Transgenic Contamination: Monsanto Canada Inc v Schmeiser', *Journal of Environmental Law*, 17 (1), 83–108.

Dasgupta, P. (1988), 'The Welfare Economics of Knowledge Production', *Oxford Review of Economic Policy*, 4 (4), 1–12.

Demsetz, H. (1967), 'Toward a Theory of Property Rights', *The American Economic Review*, 57 (2), 347–59.

Demsetz, H. (2002), 'Toward a Theory of Property Rights II: The Competition between Private and Collective Ownership', *The Journal of Legal Studies*, XXXI (2), 653–72.

Donnenwirth, J., Grace, J. and Smith, S. (2004), 'Intellectual Property Rights, Patents, Plant Variety Protection and Contracts: A perspective from the Private Sector', *IP Strategy Today*, No. 9.

Duffy, F.J. (2004), 'Rethinking the Prospect Theory of Patents', *University of Chicago Law Review*, 71, 439.

Dzung, N.N. (2007), 'Vietnam Patent Law—Substantive Law Provisions and Existing Uncertainties', *Chicago—Kent Journal of Intellectual Property*, 6, 138–56.

Eisenberg, R.S. (2003), 'Patent Swords and Shields', *Science Magazine*, 299, 1018–19.

Esquinas-Alcazar, J. (2005), 'Protecting crop genetic diversity for food security: political, ethical and technical challenges', *Nature*, 6 (12), 946–53.

Fowler, C., Hawtin, G., Ortiz, R., Iwanaga, M. and Engels, J. (2004), 'The Question of Derivatives. Promoting Use and Ensuring Availability of Non-Proprietary Plant Genetic Resources', *The Journal of World Intellectual Property*, 7 (5), 641–63.

Frischmann, M.B. (2005), 'An Economic Theory of Infrastructure and Commons Management', *Minnesota Law Review*, 89, 917–1030.

Graff, D.G., Cullen, E.S., Bradford, J.K., Zilberman, D. and Bennet, B.A. (2003), 'The Public-Private Structure of Intellectual Property Ownership in Agricultural Biotechnology', *Nature Biotechnology*, 21 (9).

Heller, M.A. and Eisenberg, R. (1998), 'Can Patents Deter Innovation? The Anticommons in Biomedical Research', *Science*, 280 (5364), 698–701.

Hoare, L.A. and Tarasofsky, G.R. (2007), 'Asking and Telling: Can 'Disclosure of Origin' Requirements in Patent Applications Make a Difference?', *The Journal of World Intellectual Property*, 10 (2), 149–69.

Hodges, J.T. and Daniel, A. (2005), 'Promises and Pitfalls: First Steps on the Road to the International ABS Regime', *Review of European Community & International Environmental Law*, 14 (2), 148–60.

Hopkins, M.M., Mahdi, S., Patel, P. and Thomas, M.S. (2007), 'DNA Patenting: the End of an Era?', *Nature Biotechnology*, 25 (2), 185–7.

International Life Sciences Institute (2007), 'Nutritional and Safety Assessments of Foods and Feeds Nutritionally Improved through Biotechnology: Case Studies: Executive Summary of a Task Force Report by the International Life Sciences Institute, Washington, D.C.', *Journal of Food Science*, 72 (9), R131–7.

Janis, M. (2001), 'Sustainable Agriculture, Patent Rights, and Plant Innovation', *Indiana Law Review*, Vol. 9 (91).

Jayaraman, K.S. (2008), 'Entomologists stifled by Indian bureaucracy. "Biopiracy" concerns thwart insect hunters', *Nature*, 452, 7.

Kilgour, L. (2008), 'Building Intellectual Property Management Capacity in Public Research Institutions in Vietnam: Current Needs and Future Directions', *Minnesota Journal of Law, Science & Technology*, 9 (1), 317–68.

Kitch, W.E. (1977), 'The Nature and Function of the Patent System', *Journal of Law and Economics*, XX (1), 265–90.

Koester, V. (2002), 'The Five Global Biodiversity-Related Conventions: A Stocktaking', *Review of European Community & International Environmental Law*, 11 (1), 96–103.

Kuanpoth, J. (2007), 'Patents and Access to Antiretroviral Medicines in Vietnam after World Trade Organization Accession', *The Journal of World Intellectual Property*, 10 (3–4), 201–24.

Lemley, A.M. and Frischmann, M.B. (2007), 'Spillovers', *Columbia Law Review*, 107 (1), 257–301.

Levmore, S. (2002), 'Two Stories about the Evolution of Property Rights', *The Journal of Legal Studies*, XXXI (2), 421–51.

Matthews, D. (2006), 'From the August 30, 2003 WTO Decision to the December 6, 2005 Agreement on an Amendment to TRIPS: Improving Access to Medicines in Developing Countries?', *Intellectual Property Quarterly*, 10, 91–130.

Matthews, D. and Munoz-Tellez, V. (2006), 'Bilateral Technical Assistance and TRIPS: The United States, Japan and the European Communities in Comparative Perspective', *The Journal of World Intellectual Property*, 9 (6), 629–53.

Mazzoleni, R. and Nelson, R. (1998), 'Economic Theories about the Benefit and Costs of Patents', *Journal of Economic Issues*, XXXI, 1031.

Mazzoleni, R. and Nelson, R. (1998), 'The Benefits and Costs of Strong Patent Protection: A Contribution to the Current Debate', *Research Policy*, 27 (3), 273–84.

McFetridge, D.G. and Smith, D.A. (1980), 'Patents, Prospects, and Economic Surplus: A Comment', *Journal of Law & Economics*, 23 (1), 197–203.

Merges, P.R. and Nelson, R. (1990), 'On the Complex Economics of Patent Scope', *Columbia Law Review*, 90 (4), 839–916.

Merrill, W.T. (2002), 'Introduction: the Demsetz Thesis and the Evolution of Property Rights', *The Journal of Legal Studies*, XXXI (2), 331–8.

Mgbeoji, I. (2003), 'Beyond Rhetoric: State Sovereignty, Common Concern, and the Inapplicability of the Common Heritage Concept to Plant Genetic Resources', *Leiden Journal of International Law*, 16 (04), 821–37.

Morten W.T. (2005), 'How Will a Substantive Patent Law Treaty Affect the Public Domain for Genetic Resources and Biological Material?' *The Journal of World Intellectual Property*, 8 (3), 311–44.

Van Overwalle, G. (1999), 'Patent Protection for Plants: a Comparison of American and European Approaches', *The Journal of Law and Technology* 39, 143–94.

Pavoni, R. (2000), 'Brevettabilità Genetica e Protezione della Biodiversità: la Giurisprudenza dell'Ufficio Europeo dei Brevetti', *Rivista di Diritto Internazionale* 83 (2), 463.

Patent Litigation (2006), 'Monsanto's Patent and License Agreement Again Upheld', *Biotechnology Law Report*, 25 (5), 564–7.

Pham & Associates (2003), 'Vietnam: Patenting biotechnology inventions', *Managing Intellectual Property*, Supplement—Patent Yearbook 2003.

Pretty, J.N., Noble, A.D., Bossio, D., Dixon, J., Hine, R.E., Penning de Vries, F.W.T. and Morison, J.I.L. (2006), 'Resource-Conserving Agriculture Increases Yields in Developing Countries', *Environmental Science and Technology*, 40 (4), 1114–19.

Public Sector Intellectual Property Resource for Agriculture (2003), 'Public Sector Collaboration for Agricultural IP Management', *Science*, 301, 174–5.

Raustiala, K. and Victor, D.G. (2004), 'The Regime Complex for Plant Genetic Resources', *International Organization* (Spring 2004), available at: http://papers.ssrn.com/sol3/papers.cfm?abstract_id=441463 (accessed 10 February 2009).

Rose, G. (2003), 'International Law of Sustainable Agriculture in the 21st Century: The International Treaty on Plant Genetic Resources for Food and Agriculture', *The Georgetown International Environmental Law Review*, XV (4), 583–632.

Safrin, S. (2004), 'Hyperownership in a Time of Biotechnological Promise: The International Conflict to Control the Building Blocks of Life', *American Journal of International Law* 98, 641.

Spielman, D.J. (2006), 'A Critique of Innovation Systems Perspectives on Agricultural Research in Developing Countries', *Innovation Strategy Today*, 2 (1), 41–54.

Winter, G. (1992), 'Patent Law Policy in Biotechnology', *Journal of Environmental Law*, 4 (2), 167–87.

BOOKS

Andersen, R. (2007), *Governing Agrobiodiversity: Plant Genetics and Developing Countries*, Aldershot, UK: Ashgate.

Birnie, P. and Boyle, A. (2002), *International Law and the Environment*, 2nd edn, Oxford, UK: Oxford University Press.

Brahy, N. (2008), *The Property Regime of Biodiversity and Traditional Knowledge—Institutions for Conservation and Innovation*, Brussels: Larcier.

Bronwyn, P. (2004), *Trading the Genome: Investigating the Commodification of Bio-Information*, New York: Columbia University Press.

Cabrera, M.J. and Silva, L.C. (2007), *Addressing the Problems of Access: Protecting Sources, While Giving Users Certainty*, IUCN Environmental Policy and Law Paper No. 67/1, Gland, Switzerland: IUCN.

Chang, H. (2002), *Kicking Away the Ladder: Development Strategy in Historical Perspective*, London, UK: Anthem Press.

Chisum, S.D. (1978), *Chisum on Patents*, New York: Matthew Bender.

Correa, M.C. (2000), *Intellectual Property Rights, The WTO and Developing Countries: The TRIPs Agreement and Policy Options*, London and New York: Zed Books.

(The) Crucible II Group (2001), *Seedling Solutions. Options for national laws governing control over genetic resources and biological innovations*, Vol. 2, Ottawa, ON, Canada: IDRI, IPGRI and Dag Hammarskjöld Foundation.

Cullet, P. (2005), *Intellectual Property Protection and Sustainable Development*, New Delhi, India: LexisNexis Butterworths.

Dutfield, G. (2003), *Intellectual Property Rights and the Life Science Industries: a Twentieth Century History*, Globalization and Law, Aldershot, UK: Ashgate.

Fowler, C. (1994), *Unnatural Selection. Technology, Politics and Plant Evolution*, International Studies in Global Change, Vol. 6, Yverdon, Switzerland: Gordon and Breach Science Publishers.

Helfer, R.L. (2004), *Intellectual Property Rights in Plant Varieties: International Legal Regime and Policy Options for National Governments*, Rome, Italy: FAO.

Kaul, I., Conceição, P., Goulven, K.L. and Mendoza, R.U. (eds) (2003), *Providing Global Public Goods: Managing Globalization*, New York: UNDP.

Krattiger, A., *et al.* (eds) (2006), *Intellectual Property Management in Health and Agricultural Innovation—A Handbook of Best Practices*, Oxford, UK: PIPRA & MIHR.

Leskien, D. and Flitner, M. (1997), *Intellectual Property Rights and Plant Genetic Resources: Options for a sui generis system*, Issues in Genetic Resources, No. 6, Rome, Italy: IPGRI.

McManis, C. (ed.) (2007), *Biodiversity and the Law. Intellectual Property, Biotechnology and Traditional Knowledge*, London, UK: Earthscan.

Millennium Assessment (2005), *Ecosystems and Human Well-being: Current State and Trends—Cultivated Systems*, Millennium Ecosystem Assessment, Vol. 1, Washington: Island Press.

Moore, G. and Tymowski, W. (2005), *Explanatory Guide to the International Treaty on Plant Genetic Resources for Food and Agriculture*, IUCN Environmental Policy and Law Paper No. 57, Gland, Switzerland and Cambridge, UK: IUCN.

Posey, A.D. (ed.) (1999), *Cultural and Spiritual Value of Biodiversity*, Nairobi and London: UNEP and IT Publications.

Ostrom, E. (1990), *Governing the Commons. The Evolution of Institutions for Collective Action*, Cambridge: Cambridge University Press.

Rao, N.K., Hanson, J., Dulloo, M.E., Ghosh, K., Nowell, D. and Larinde, M. (2006), *Manual of Seed Handling in Genebanks*, Handbooks for Genebanks No. 8, Rome, Italy: Bioversity International.

Sen, A. (1999), *Development as Freedom*, Oxford, UK: Oxford University Press.

Simpson, J. (ed.) (2007), *Oxford English Dictionary*, Oxford, UK: Oxford University Press.

Tansey, G. and Rajotte, T. (eds) (2007), *The Future Control of Food. A Guide to International Negotiations and Rules on Intellectual Property, Biodiversity and Food Security*, London, UK: Earthscan.

Heywood, V.H. (ed.) (1995), *Global Biodiversity Assessment*, UNEP, Cambridge, UK: Cambridge University Press.

Watal, J. (2000), *Intellectual Property Rights in the WTO and Developing Countries*, The Hague: Kluwer Law International.

World Commission on Environment and Development (1987), *Our Common Future*, Oxford, UK: Oxford University Press.

BOOK SECTIONS

Blakeney, M. (2005), 'Stimulating Agricultural Innovation', in Maskus, K.E. and Reichman, J.A. (eds), *International Public Goods and Transfer of Technology under a Globalized Intellectual Property Regime*, Cambridge, UK: Cambridge University Press.

Chiarolla, C. (2007), 'FAO International Treaty on Plant Genetic Resources and Farmers' Rights', *Protection of Plant Varieties with reference to Farmers' and Breeders' Rights*, Hyderabad, India: Institute of Chartered Financial Analysts of India.

Correa, M.C. (2002), 'Managing the Provision of Knowledge: the Design of Intellectual Property Laws', in Kaul, I. *et al.* (eds), *Providing Global Public Goods*, New York: Oxford University Press.

Damania, A.B. *et al.* (eds) (1997), 'Jack R. Harlan (1917–1998)—Plant Explorer, Archaeobotanist, Geneticist and Plant Breeder', in *The Origins of Agriculture and Crop Domestication—Proceedings of the Harlan Symposium, 10–14 May 1997*, Aleppo, Syria: IPGRI.

Dosi, G. (1988), 'The Nature of the Innovative Process', in Soete, L. (ed.), *Technical Change and Economic Theory*, London, UK: Pinter Publishers.

Fenny, D., Berkes, F., McCay, B.J. and Acheson, J.M. (1998), 'The Tragedy of the Commons: Twenty-Two Years Later', in Baden, J. and Noonan, D. (eds), *Managing the Commons*, Bloomington: Indiana University Press.

Goldie, L.F.E. (1987), 'Equity and the International Management of Transboundary Resources', in Utton, A. and Teclaff, L. (eds), *Transboundary Resource Law,* London & Boulder: Westview Press.

Halewood, M., Cherfas, J.J., Engels, J.M., Hazekamp, T., Hodgkin, T. and Robinson, J. (2007), 'Farmers, Landraces and Property Rights: Challenges to Allocating *Sui Generis* Intellectual Property Rights to Communities over their Varieties', in Biber-Klemm, S. and Cottier, T.

(eds), *Rights to Plant Genetic Resources and Traditional Knowledge—Basic Issues and Perspectives*, Wallingford, UK: CABI.

Heitz, A. (1986), 'The History of Plant Variety Protection', *The First Twenty-five Years of the International Convention for the Protection of New Varieties of Plants*, Geneva, Switzerland: UPOV, pp. 53–96.

Libecap, D.G. (2003), 'Contracting for Property Rights', in Terry Anderson, L. and McChesney, F.S. (eds), *Property Rights: Cooperation, Conflict, and Law*, Princeton, NJ: Princeton University Press, pp. 142–67.

Merges, P.R. and Nelson, R. (1992), 'Market Structure and Technical Advance: The Role of Patent Scope Decisions', in Jorde, T.M. and Teece, D.J. (eds), *Antitrust, Innovation and Competitiveness*, Oxford, UK: Oxford University Press.

Wallace, H. and Mayer, S. (2007), 'Scientific Research Agendas: Controlled and Shaped by the Scope of Patentability', in Waelde, C. and MacQueen, H. (eds), *Intellectual Property: The Many Faces of the Public Domain*, Cheltenham, UK: Edward Elgar.

PAPERS, REPORTS, REVIEWS AND BACKGROUND STUDIES

Adhikari, B. (2001), 'Literature Review on the Economics of Common Property Resources—Review of Common Pool Resource Management in Tanzania', report prepared for NRSP project R7857, University of York.

American Seed Trade Association (2004), 'Position Statement on Intellectual Property Rights for the Seed Industry'.

Andersen, R. (2005), 'The History of Farmers' Rights—A Guide to Central Documents and Literature', The Farmers' Project—Background Study 1, The Fridtjof Nansens Institute, Lysaker, Norway.

Blakeney, M. (2002), 'Access to Genetic Resources, Gene-based Invention and Agriculture', Study Paper 3b, UK Commission on Intellectual Property Rights.

Blakeney, M. (2003), 'TRIPS Agreement and Agriculture', paper prepared for the ADB Intensive Course on the WTO TRIPS Agreement, Bangkok, Thailand, 24–28 November 2003.

Bragdon, S. (2004), 'International Law of Relevance to Plant Genetic Resources: A Practical Review for Scientists and Other Professionals Working with Plant Genetic Resources', International Plant Genetic Resources Institute, Rome, Italy.

Centre for Information Library and Research Services (2006), 'Needs Assessment on Technical Assistance for the Deputies of the National Assembly after Vietnam's Accession to the WTO', Hanoi, Viet Nam, available at: http://siteresources.worldbank.org/INTVIETNAM/Data %20and%20Reference/21092035/na_needs_assessment_final_report_english. pdf (accessed 10 October 2008).

Chatham House (2006), 'Disclosure of Origin in IPR Applications: Options and Perspectives of Users and Providers of Genetic Resources', IPDEV, Work Programme 8: Final Report, available at: www.ecologic. de/download/projekte/1800–1849/1802/wp8_final_report.pdf (accessed 10 June 2007).

Chiarolla, C. (2007), 'Legal Assistance for the Development of National Legislation on Biodiversity', TCP/VIE/3101, FAO, Hanoi, Viet Nam.

Chiarolla C. and Jungcurt S. (2011), 'Outstanding Issues on Access and Benefit Sharing under the Multilateral System of the International Treaty on Plant Genetic Resources for Food and Agriculture', a background study paper by the Berne Declaration and the Development Fund, available at: www.evb.ch/en/p25019093.html.

Cohen, J. (1999), 'Managing Intellectual Property—Challenges and Responses for Agricultural Research Institutes' in 'Agricultural Biotechnology and the Poor: Proceedings from an International Conference', 21–22 October 1999.

Correa, M.C. (2004), 'Bilateral Investment Agreements: Agents of new global standards for the Protection of Intellectual Property?', GRAIN, available at: www.grain.org/briefings_files/correa-bits-august-2004.pdf (accessed 10 February 2009).

Correa, M.C. (2009), 'Trends in Intellectual Property Rights relating to Genetic Resources for Food And Agriculture', Background Study Paper No. 49, FAO, Rome, Italy.

Nguyen, V.D. (2006), 'Summary of elements of Farmers' Rights in the Ordinance on Plant Variety (2004) of Viet Nam', paper given at the Workshop on Exploring Legal Definitions of Farmers' Varieties in Strategies to Promote Farmers' Rights, organized by the Genetic Resources Policy Initiative (GRPI), Hanoi, Vietnam, 26–28 October 2006.

Dutfield, G. (2003), 'Literature Survey on Intellectual Property Rights and Sustainable Human Development', UNCTAD–ICTSD Project on IPRs and Sustainable Development, Geneva.

Dutfield, G. (2003), 'Protecting Traditional Knowledge and Folklore: A Review of Progress in Diplomacy and Policy Formulation', Issue Paper No. 1, UNCTAD–ICTSD Project on IPRs and Sustainable Development, Geneva.

Dutfield, G. (2006), 'Patents and Development: Exclusions, Industrial Application and Technical Effect', paper given at the WIPO Open Forum on the Draft Substantive Patent Law Treaty, Geneva, Switzerland,1–3 March 2006.

Dzung, V.V. (2008), 'Food crisis impacts in Viet Nam', International Federation of Agricultural Producers, a study paper prepared for the 2008 World Farmers Congress.

Fears, R. (2007), 'Genomics and Genetic Resources for Food and Agriculture', Background Study Paper No. 34, FAO, Rome, Italy, June 2007.

Gouache, J.C. (2004), 'Balancing Access and Protection: Lessons from the Past to Built the Future', paper given at the ISF International Conference, Berlin, Germany, 27–28 May 2004.

GRAIN (2007), 'Bilateral Agreements Imposing TRIPS-Plus Intellectual Property Rights on Biodiversity in Developing Countries', Girona, Spain.

Halewood, M. and Sood, R. (2006), 'Genebanks and Public Goods: Political and Legal Challenges', paper prepared for the 19th session of the Genetic Resources Policy Committee, El Batan, Mexico, 22–24 February 2006.

Halewood, M. (2007), 'Searching for a line in the sand: issues to consider concerning financial returns from recipients of Centres' PGRFA under Development', paper prepared for the 13th CGIAR Executive Council Meeting, CGIAR, Rome, Italy, 16–17 October 2007.

Henson-Apollonio, V. (2006), 'The Impacts of IPRs on MAS Research and Application in Developing Countries', paper prepared for the 19th Session of the Genetic Resources Policy Committee of the CGIAR, El Batan, Mexico, 22–24 February 2006.

Henson-Apollonio, V. (2002), 'Patent protection for plant Material', paper given at the WIPO–UPOV Symposium on the Co-existence of Patents and Plant Breeders' Rights in the Promotion of Biotechnological Developments, Geneva, Switzerland, 25 October 2002.

Herdt, R.W. (1999), 'Enclosing the Plant Genetic Commons', paper given at the China Centre for Economic Research, 24 May 1999.

Huong, B.T. (2008), 'Vietnam Biotechnology Update 2008', USDA Foreign Agricultural Service—Global Agriculture Information Network Report (11 July 2008).

IUCN (2006), 'Access and Benefit Sharing—Agenda Item No. 8 of the 8th meeting of the Conference of the Parties to the Convention on Biological Diversity', IUCN Position Paper for CBD COP 8, Curitiba, Brazil, 20–31 March 2006.

IUCN (2007), 'Development of the Biodiversity Law in Viet Nam— Proposed Draft Chapters', IUCN Regional Environmental Law Programme for Asia.

Jördens, R. (2002), 'Legal and Technological Development Leading to the Symposium: UPOV's Perspective', paper given at the WIPO-UPOV Symposium on the Co-existence of Patents and Plant Breeders' Rights in the Promotion of Biotechnological Developments, Geneva, Switzerland, 25 October 2002.

Laird, S. and Wynberg, R. (2008), 'Access and Benefit-Sharing in practice: Trends in Partnerships Across Sectors', Technical Series No. 38, CBD Secretariat, Montreal, Canada, available at: www.cbd.int/doc/publications/cbd-ts-38-en.pdf (accessed 10 December 2008).

Lettington, R.J.L. (2003), 'Small-scale Agriculture and the Nutritional Safeguard under Article 8(1) of the Uruguay Round Agreement on Trade-Related Aspects of Intellectual Property Rights: Case Studies from Kenya and Peru', UNCTAD–ICTSD Project on IPRs and Sustainable Development, Geneva, Switzerland (November 2003).

Lobe, K. (2007), 'A Green Revolution for Africa: Hope for Hungry Farmers?', Canadian Foodgrains Bank Working Paper, available at: www.foodgrainsbank.ca/uploads/A%20Green%20Revolution%20for%20Africa%20-%20Mar%202007%20-%20FINAL.pdf (accessed 10 February 2009).

Louwaars, N.P., Tripp, R., Eaton, D., Henson-Apollonio, V., Hu, R., Mendoza, M., Muhhuku, F., Pal, S. and Wekundah, J. (2005), 'Impacts of Strengthened Intellectual Property Rights Regimes on the Plant Breeding Industry in Developing Countries', World Bank.

Louwaars, N.P. (2007), 'Seeds of Confusion: The Impact of Policies on Seed Systems' (Wageningen University).

Louwaars, N.P. (2007), 'IPRs in Agriculture—The Law and its Use in Development', Issue Paper, South Asia Watch on Trade, Economics and Environment (SAWTEE), Kathmandu, Nepal, November 2007.

McManis, C.R. (2002), 'Are There TRIPs-Compliant Measures for a Balanced Co-existence of Patents and Plant Breeders' Rights? Some Lessons from the U.S. Experience to Date', paper given at the WIPO-UPOV Symposium on the Co-existence of Patents and Plant Breeders' Rights in the Promotion of Biotechnological Developments, UPOV, Geneva, Switzerland, 25 October 2002.

Michiels, A. and Koo, B. (2008), 'Publish or Patent? Knowledge Dissemination in Agricultural Biotechnology', Discussion Paper No. 00795, IFPRI, Environment and Production Technology Division, available at: www.ifpri.org/pubs/dp/IFPRIDP00795.pdf (accessed 10 February 2009).

Moore, G. and Moore, S. (2005), 'Methods of Expressing Acceptance of the Terms and Conditions of MTAs: Shrink-Wrap and Click-Wrap Agreements', Background Study Paper No. 26, FAO, Rome, Italy.

Moufang, R. (2003), 'The Interface between Patents and Plant Variety Rights in Europe', paper given at WIPO–UPOV Symposium on Intellectual Property Rights in Plant Biotechnology, Geneva, Switzerland, 24 October 2003.

Murphy, S. and Santarius, T. (2007), 'The World Bank's WDR 2008: Agriculture for Development—Response from a Slow Trade—Sound Farming Perspective', Discussion Paper No. 10, November 2007.

Musungu, S. and Dutfield, G. (2003), 'Multilateral Agreements and TRIPs-plus World: The World Intellectual Property Organization (WIPO)', TRIPs Issue Paper No. 3, Quaker United Nations Office and Quaker International Affairs Programme.

Ngongi, N. (2008), 'Policy Implications of High Food Prices for Africa', Responding to the Global Food Crisis: Three Perspectives, IFPRI.

Nguyen, H. and Grote, U. (2004), 'Agricultural Policies in Vietnam, Producer Support Estimates, 1986–2002', Discussion Paper No. 79, IFPRI, available at: www.ifpri.org/sites/default/files/publications/mtidp79.pdf (accessed 17 March 2011).

Nguyen, T.V. (2000), 'Agricultural Biotechnology in Vietnam', paper given at the Regional Conference on Agricultural Biotechnology organized by SEAMEO—SEARCA Biotechnology Information Center, Bangkok, Thailand, 29–30 June 2000.

Nuffield Council on Bioethics (1999), 'Genetically Modified Crops: The Ethical and Social Issues', available at: www.nuffieldbioethics.org/gm-crops (accessed 17 March 2011).

Office of the United States Trade Representative (2008), '2008 Special 301 Report', available at: www.ustr.gov/about-us/press-office/reports-and-publications/archives/2008/2008-special-301-report (accessed 17 March 2011).

Oldham, P. (2004), 'Global Status and Trends in Intellectual Property Claims: Genomic, Proteomics and Biotechnology', ESRC Centre for Economic and Social Aspects of Genomics (CESAGen), Cardiff.

Organisation for Economic Co-operation and Development (2007), 'OECD Science, Technology and Industry Scoreboard 2007— Innovation and Performance in the Global Economy'.

Pengelly, T. (2004), 'Technical Assistance for the Formulation and Implementation of Intellectual Property Policy in Developing Countries and Transition Economies', ICTSD.

Pengelly, T. and Leesti, M. (2002), 'Institutional Issues for Developing Countries in Intellectual Property Policymaking, Administration &

Enforcement', Study Paper 9, UK Commission on Intellectual Property Rights, London, available at: www.iprcommission.org/papers/pdfs/study_papers/sp9_pengelly_study.pdf (accessed 10 November 2008).

Pérez-Casas, C. (2000), 'HIV/AIDS Medicines Pricing Report. Setting Objectives: Is There a Political Will?' Campaign for Access to Essential Medicines and Medecins Sans Frontieres, available at: www.msfaccess.org/fileadmin/user_upload/key-publication/Durban%20report%20update%20dec%202000.pdf (accessed 10 January 2009).

Persley, G.D. (1999), 'Agricultural Biotechnology and the Poor: Promethean Science', in 'Agricultural Biotechnology and the Poor: Proceedings from an International Conference', 21–22 October 1999.

Pimbert, M. (1999), 'Agricultural Biodiversity: Conference Background Paper No. 1', prepared for the FAO/Netherlands Conference on the Multifunctional Character of Agriculture and Land, Maastricht, The Netherlands (12–17 September 1999).

Queen Mary Intellectual Property Research Institute, CEAS Consultants (Wye) Ltd Centre for European Agricultural Studies and Tansey G. (2000), 'Study on the Relationship between the Agreement on TRIPs and Biodiversity Related Issues', Final Report, DG TRADE European Commission, London, UK, available at: http://trade.ec.europa.eu/doclib/docs/2003/september/tradoc_111143.pdf (accessed 10 April 2005).

Rangnekar, D. (2000), 'Plant Breeding, Biodiversity Loss and Intellectual Property Rights', Kingston University, Economics Discussion Papers—No. 00/5.

Rangnekar, D. (2006), 'Assessing the Economic Implications of Different Models for Implementing the Requirement to Protect Plant Varieties: A Case Study of India', produced for the European Commission under its 6th Framework Programme for Research as part of the project 'Impacts of the IPR Rules on Sustainable Development (IPDEV).'

Rubenstein, K.D., Heinsey, P., Shoemaker, R., Sullivan, J. and Frisvold, G. (2005), 'Crop Genetic Resources: An Economic Appraisal', Economic Information Bulletin No. 2, United States Department of Agriculture (May 2005).

Runnalls, D. (2008), 'Why Aren't We There Yet? Twenty Years of Sustainable Development', 2007–2008 IISD Annual Report—Sustaining Excellence, Winnipeg, Manitoba.

Sagar, R. (2006), 'Identifying Models of Best Practices in the Provision of Technical Assistance to Facilitate the Implementation of the TRIPS Agreement', produced for the European Commission under its 6th Framework Programme for Research as part of the project 'Impacts of

the IPR Rules on Sustainable Development (IPDEV)', available at: www.
ecologic.de/download/projekte/1800–1849/1802/wp4_final_report.pdf
(accessed 10 July 2007).

Sarnoff, J.D. and Correa, M.C. (2006), 'Analysis of Options for Implementing Disclosure of Origin Requirements in Intellectual Property Applications', UNCTAD/DITC/TED/2004/14, United Nations Conference on
Trade and Development, New York, US, available at: www.unctad.org/
en/docs/ditcted200514_en.pdf (accessed 10 July 2007).

Siegele, L. (2008), 'How Many Roads? Negotiating an International
Regime on Access and Benefit Sharing', paper given at SOAS LEDC/
FIELD Lecture Series, IALS, London, 31 January 2008.

South Centre (2005), 'Intellectual Property in Investment Treaties: the
TRIPs-plus Implications for Developing Countries', South Centre
Analytical Note.

Stads, G.J. and Viet-Hai, N. (2006), 'Vietnam—Agricultural Science and
Technology Indicators', ASTI Country Brief No. 33, International
Food Policy Research Institute.

Stannard, C. (2006), 'Presentation by the Food and Agriculture
Organization of the United Nations (FAO) on the International Treaty
on Plant Genetic Resources for Food and Agriculture', C/40/17, UPOV
Council, Fortieth Ordinary Session, Geneva (19 October 2006).

Straus, J. (2002), 'Measures Necessary for the Balanced Co-existence of
Patents and Plant Breeders' Rights—A Predominantly European view',
paper given at WIPO–UPOV Symposium on the Co-existence of Patents and Plant Breeders' Rights in the Promotion of Biotechnological
Developments, Geneva, Switzerland, 25 October 2002.

Taylor, M.R. and Cayford, J. (2003), 'American Patent Policy,
Biotechnology and African Agriculture: The Case for Policy Changes',
RFF Report (November 2003).

Thornström, C.G. (2005), 'Public Research in the Context of Proprietary
Science—The Case of the Consultative Group on International
Agricultural Research', paper given at the Workshop on the
Globalisation of Agricultural Biotechnology: Multi-Disciplinary
Views from the South, 11–13 March 2005.

Toenniessen, G. and Delmer, D. (2005), 'The Role of Intermediaries in
Maintaining the Public Sector's Essential Role in Crop Varietal
Improvement', report prepared and submitted at the request of the
Science Council of the Consultative Group on International
Agricultural Research, The Rockefeller Foundation, New York, US.

Trieu, V.V. (2007), 'Opening Statement by Vu Van Trieu, Country Representative, IUCN Viet Nam Country Office', International Workshop on the Biodiversity Law, Hanoi, Viet Nam (2 November 2007).

UK Commission on Intellectual Property Rights (2002), 'Integrating Intellectual Property Rights and Development Policy', London, UK (September 2002).

UNCTAD (2008), 'Economic Development in Africa 2008—Export Performance Following Trade Liberalization: Some Patterns and Policy Perspectives', UN, New York and Geneva.

UNESCAP, 'Agricultural Background—Socialist Republic of Viet Nam', United Nations Economic and Social Commission for Asia and the Pacific, available at: www.unapcaem.org/ppt/vn-01.htm#bg (accessed 10 June 2008).

UNU-IAS (2003), 'User Measures: Options for Developing Measures in User Countries to implement the Access and Benefit Sharing of the Convention on Biological Diversity', UNU–IAS (March 2003).

Verma, D.D. (2006), 'Policy on Access and Benefit Sharing in India', paper presented at the Japan-India Workshop on 'Access and Benefit Sharing of Genetic Resources and Traditional Knowledge in the context of CBD', organized by the Japanese Bioindustry Association, Tokyo Japan (8 December 2006).

Visser, B., Pistorius, R., Van-Raalte, R., Eaton, D. and Louwaars, P.N. (2005), 'Options for Non-Monetary Benefit-Sharing—An Inventory', Background Study No. Paper 30, FAO, Rome, Italy (October 2005).

Vivas-Eugui, D. (2003), 'Regional and Bilateral Agreements and a TRIPs-plus world: the Free Trade Area of Americas (FTAA)', TRIPs Issue Papers No. 4, QUNO, QIAP and ICTSD.

World Bank (2007), 'World Development Report 2008: Agriculture for Development', available at: http://econ.worldbank.org/WBSITE/EXTERNAL/EXTDEC/EXTRESEARCH/EXTWDRS/EXTWDR2008/0,,contentMDK:21410054~menuPK:3149676~pagePK:641676 89~piPK:64167673~theSitePK:2795143,00.html (accessed 10 December 2008).

World Bank (2007), 'Country Report—Vietnam: Laying the Foundations for Steady Growth', IDA at Work.

ELECTRONIC SOURCES AND WEBSITES

'EU-ASEAN News and Analysis', Bilateral.org, available at: www.bilaterals.org/spip.php?rubrique151 (accessed 10 October 2008).

'Intellectual Property Ownership and Cross License Agreement', Find Law for Legal Professionals, available at: http://contracts.corporate.findlaw. com/agreements/genuity/gte.ip.html (accessed 1 October 2009).

'Nation can boost rice seed crops', VietNamNet Bridge (17 June 2008), available at: http://english.vietnamnet.vn/tech/2008/06/788998/ (accessed 10 June 2008).

'The Farmers' Rights Project', The Fridtjof Nansen Institute, available at: www.farmersrights.org/ (accessed 10 April 2009).

'The "system of innovation" approach and its relevance to developing countries', SciDevNet (1 April 2005) available at: www.scidev.net/en/ policy-briefs/the-system-of-innovation-approach-and-its-relevanc.html (accessed October 2006).

'Vietnam fortifies scientific cooperation with EU', VietNamNet Bridge (23 June 2007), available at: http://english.vietnamnet.vn/tech/2007/ 06/709749/ (accessed 10 June 2008).

Abbott, F.M. (2008), 'Post-mortem for the Geneva Mini-Ministerial: Where does TRIPS go from here?', Information Note No. 7, ICTSD, Geneva (August 2008), available at: http://ictsd.net/i/publications/ 16949/?view=document (accessed 10 November 2008).

AgBiotech Vietnam, available at: www.agbiotech.com.vn/en/ (accessed 10 May 2008).

Andersen, R. (2005), 'Norway say "no" to UPOV 1991', Grain (8 December 2005) available at: www.grain.org/bio-ipr/?id=458 (accessed 10 November 2008).

Asian Legal Information Institute, available at: www.asianlii.org/ (accessed 10 March 2007).

Barba, A. (2008), ' "Biopiracy" thwarted as US revokes bean patent', Science and Development Network, 13 May 2008, available at: www. scidev.net/en/news/-biopiracy-thwarted-as-us-revokes-bean-patent.html (accessed 23 May 2008).

Bayer, available at: www.bayer.com.vn/ (accessed 10 March 2007).

Berlan, J.P. and Lewontin, R.C. (1998), 'Cashing in on Life—Operation Terminator', Le Monde Diplomatique, available at: http:// mondediplo.com/1998/12/02gen (accessed 10 January 2008).

BIOS-CAMBIA (2008), 'Rice Genome Landscape', Patent Lens, available at: www.patentlens.net/daisy/RiceGenome/3648.html (accessed 10 November 2008).

BIOS-CAMBIA Initiative (The), 'Biological Innovation for Open Society', available at: www.bios.net/daisy/bios/bios/bios-initiative.html (accessed 10 November 2008).

Bioseed Genetics International Inc., available at: www.seedquest.com/id/ b/bioseedgenetics.htm (accessed 17 March 2011).

Boyle, J. (2003), 'Enclosing the Genome: What the Squabbles over Genetic Patents Could Teach Us', Advances in Genetics, available at: www.law.duke.edu/boylesite/low/genome.pdf (accessed 10 November 2006).

Brookes, A. (2007), 'Corn's key role as food and fuel', BBC News, available at: http://news.bbc.co.uk/2/hi/americas/7149079.stm (accessed 17 December 2007).

Buckman, R. (2007), 'Patent Firm Lays Global Plans', The Wall Street Journal, 12 November 2007, available at: http://online.wsj.com/article/SB119482858758489569.html (accessed 10 February 2009).

Center for International Environmental Law, available at: www.ciel.org (accessed 10 February 2008).

Delegation of the European Commission to Malaysia, 'The Trans-Regional EU-ASEAN Trade Initiative', updated: 13 June 2006, available at: www.delmys.ec.europa.eu/en/special_features/The%20Trans-Regional%20EU-ASEAN%20Trade%20Initiative.htm (accessed 9 October 2008).

Dutfield, G. (2005), 'The US and Europe Are "Intellectual Property Fundamentalists"', Science and Development Network, available at: www.scidev.net/en/science-communication/opinions/the-us-and-europe-are-intellectual-property-funda.html (accessed 10 February 2009).

French Embassy in Viet Nam, 'Country Fact File for Vietnam', available at: www.ambafrance-vn.org/IMG/doc/CountryFactFile_-_CFF2004V.doc (accessed 10 November 2008).

GP Group of Companies, 'A Quick Chronology of the GP Group', available at: www.premjee.com/content/timeline (accessed 17 March 2011).

GTZ, 'Partner for the Future—Worldwide', available at: www.giz.de/en/home.html (accessed 10 October 2008).

Institute for Global Justice (2008), 'ASEAN–EU FTA will bring disaster and sovereignty losing', Bilaterals.org, 19 March 2008, available at: www.bilaterals.org/spip.php?article11687 (accessed 10 October 2008).

IUCN (2008), 'Leveraging legal mechanisms to safeguard biodiversity in Viet Nam', 7 January 2008, available at: www.iucn.org/about/union/secretariat/offices/asia/asia_where_work/vietnam/news/?uNewsID=431 (accessed 17 March 2011).

IUCN, 'About IUCN', available at: www.iucn.org/about/index.cfm (accessed 10 October 2008).

Jensen, K. (2008), 'Wrap-up of PIPRA's workshop in Vietnam', 2 January 2008, available at: http://blog.pipra.org/search/label/vietnam (accessed 10 May 2008).

Logan, M. (2007), 'Agro-biodiversity in Nepal: Wise Insurance', IDRC News, No. 17, available at: www.idrc.ca/en/ev-110870-201-1-DO_ TOPIC.html (accessed 10 February 2008).

Luu, A. (2006), 'Vietnam Legal Research', GlobaLex, available at: www.nyulawglobal.org/globalex/Vietnam.htm#_edn9 (accessed 10 April 2007).

Mara, K. (2008), 'Push for TRIPs Changes Reaches Highest Level at WTO as Meetings Intensify', Intellectual Property Watch, 21 November 2008, available at: www.ip-watch.org/weblog/index. php?p=1329 (accessed 27 November 2008).

Max Planck Society (2005), 'Patent Dispute Resolved', Press Release, 4 February 2005, available at: www.mpg.de/english/illustrations Documentation/documentation/pressReleases/2005/pressRelease2005 0203/genPDF.pdf (accessed 10 November 2008).

Monsanto (2008), 'Monsanto Sees Record Sales in Fiscal Year 2008; Growth Serves as Strong Base for 2009', News Releases, 8 October 2008, available at: http://monsanto.mediaroom.com/index.php?s= 43&item=650 (accessed 10 November 2008).

Monsanto Viet Nam Representative Office, available at: www. monsanto.com/whoweare/Pages/vietnam.aspx (accessed 17 March 2011).

Padma, T.V. (2008), 'Can crops be climate-proofed?', *Science and Development Network*, available at: www.scidev.net/gateways/ index.cfm?fuseaction=readitem&rgwid=3&item=Features&itemid= 671&language=1 (accessed 10 January 2008).

Plant Variety Protection office of Viet Nam (PVPO), available at: http:// pvpo.mard.gov.vn/english.asp?m=tn&ClassID=101 (accessed 10 January 2009).

Syngenta, available at: www2.syngenta.com/de/country/vn.html (accessed 17 March 2011).

South Centre, available at: www.southcentre.org (accessed 10 December 2006).

Sulston, J. and Stiglitz, J. (2008), 'Science is being held back by outdated laws. The question 'who owns science?' is now crucial', The Times, 5 July 2008, available at: www.timesonline.co.uk/tol/comment/letters/ article4271555.ece (accessed 10 August 2008).

Tengku, T. N.S.A. (2008), 'Flexible approach to drive EU–Asean FTA negotiations', Bilaterals.org, 9 May 2008, available at: www. bilaterals.org/spip.php?article12075 (accessed 14 March 2011).

Thornström, C.G. (2005), 'Producing International Public Goods in a Proprietary Science World—the CGIAR Contribution', Bridges

Monthly, 9 (1), available at: http://ictsd.net/downloads/bridges/bridges 9–1.pdf (accessed 10 June 2006).

United States Trade Representative (2007), 'Statement by U.S. Trade Representative Susan C. Schwab on Vietnam Becoming WTO Member', available at: www.ustr.gov/about-us/press-office/press-releases/archives/2007/january/statement-us-trade-representative-susan–0 (accessed 10 February 2009).

US–Vietnam Trade Council, 'Intellectual Property Rights—Technical Assistance Programs', available at: www.usvtc.org/trade/ipr/ (accessed 10 October 2008).

Vietnam Trade Office in Washington DC (2008), 'Understanding Vietnam and the Generalized System of Preferences Program', 10 June 2008, available at: www.us-asean.org/Vietnam/GSP/FAQ.pdf (accessed 10 November 2008).

Wilbanks, J.F.B. and Jefferson, R. (2007), 'Could the key to feeding the world be locked up in a company fridge somewhere?', Alfred Deakin Innovation Lecture, 29 December 2007, available at: www.abc.net.au/rn/scienceshow/stories/2007/2122486.htm (accessed 10 January 2008).

DOCUMENTS OF SELECTED INTERNATIONAL ORGANIZATIONS

Consultative Group on International Agricultural Research

CGIAR (2002), 'Revised 2003–2004 Plan of Work for CAS—Turning the Corner', CGIAR Central Advisory Service (CAS) on Intellectual Property.

CGIAR (2007), 'Submission by the International Agriculture Research Centres of the Consultative Group on International Agriculture Research to the Group of Technical Experts on an Internationally Recognized Certificate of Origin/Source/Legal Provenance (Addendum)', Lima, Peru (22–25 January 2007) UNEP/CBD/GTE-ABS/1/3/ADD2.

GRPC (2009), 'Minutes of the Genetic Resources Policy Committee (GRPC)', 25th Session, Penang (17–19 March 2009), Appendix 4.

SGRP (2003), *Booklet of the CGIAR Centre Policy Instruments, Guidelines and Statements on Genetic Resources, Biotechnology and Intellectual Property Rights*, Version II, Produced by the System-wide Genetic Resources Programme with the CGIAR Genetic Resources Policy Committee, Version II (Rome, Italy: IPGRI).

SGRP (2007), 'A *de facto* Certificate of Source: the Standard Material Transfer Agreement under the International Treaty', System-wide Genetic Resources Programme, Rome, Italy.

Convention on Biological Diversity of the United Nations

CBD, *Joint Web Site of the Biodiversity Related Conventions*, available at: www.cbd.int/cooperation/joint.shtml (accessed 10 April 2008).

CBD (2006), 'Capacity Building on Access and Benefit-Sharing (ABS) in Vietnam', source: CBD Database on Capacity Building Projects; Lead Organisation: IUCN Country Office, Hanoi, Viet Nam, available at: www.cbd.int/abs/project.shtml?id=30939 (accessed 10 May 2008).

CBD (2007), 'Report of the Meeting of the Group of Technical Experts on an Internationally Recognized Certificate of Origin/Source/Legal Provenance', UNEP/CBD/WG-ABS/5/7, Lima, Peru (January 2007), available at: www.cbd.int/doc/meetings/abs/abswg-06/official/abswg-06-abswg-05–07-en.doc (accessed 10 February 2007).

CBD (2008), 'COP Decision IX/27 on Access and Benefit Sharing', Bonn, Germany (30 May 2008).

CBD (2009), 'Submission by NATURAL JUSTICE—Information and views in preparation for the meeting of the Expert Group on traditional knowledge associated with genetic resources', Answers to the questions posed to the Expert Group on TK associated with GR as specified in COP decision IX/12, Hyderabad, India (16–19 June 2009), available at: www.cbd.int/abs/submissions/absgtle-03-natural-justice-en.pdf.

CBD (2009), 'Submission by the International Institute for Environment and Development (IIED) *et al.*—Information and views in preparation for the meeting of the Expert Group on traditional knowledge associated with genetic resources', Answers to the questions posed to the Expert Group on TK associated with GR as specified in COP decision IX/12, Hyderabad, India (16–19 June 2009), available at: www.cbd.int/abs/submissions/absgtle-03-iied-en.pdf.

European Union

EC–ASEAN Intellectual Property Rights Cooperation Programme (ECAP II), 'Activities/Events at national level—Vietnam', available at: www.ecap-project.org/archive/index.php?id=135 (accessed 14 March 2011).

European Commission, *VAT Rates Applied in the Member States of the European Community*, DOC/1829/2006 (1 September 2006), available at: www.nationaltextile.org/VAT/appendix_b.pdf.

European Parliament (2008), 'European Parliament resolution of 8 May 2008 on Trade and Economic Relations with the Association of East Asian Nations (ASEAN)', A6–0151/2008 / P6_TA-PROV(2008)0195, Brussels (8 May 2008), available at: www.europarl.europa.eu/oeil/DownloadSP.do?id=14894&num_rep=7338&language=en (accessed 10 February 2009).

Food and Agriculture Organization of the United Nations

FAO, 'Plant Genetic Resources and Food Security', available at: www.fao.org/FOCUS/E/96/06/06-e.htm (accessed 10 April 2008).

FAO, 'About the Commission on Genetic Resources for Food and Agriculture', available at: www.fao.org/nr/cgrfa/cgrfa-about/cgrfa-history/en/ (accessed 7 March 2011).

FAO, 'Global System on Plant Genetic Resources', available at: www.fao.org/FOCUS/E/96/06/06-e.htm (accessed 17 March 2011).

FAO (1996), 'Rome Declaration on World Food Security', World Food Summit, FAO, Rome, Italy (13–17 November 1996), available at: www.fao.org/docrep/003/w3613e/w3613e00.htm (accessed 10 July 2008).

FAO (1998), *The State of the World's Plant Genetic Resources for Food and Agriculture*. Rome, Italy: FAO.

FAO (1999), 'Progress Report on the International Network of Ex Situ Collections under the Auspices of FAO', Eighth Regular Session of the CGRFA, Annex 2, CGRFA-8/99/7, Rome, Italy (19–23 April 1999).

FAO (2005), 'African Proposal', Working Group on the Drafting of the Standards Material Transfer Agreement, CGRFA\IC\CG-SMTA-1, Hammamet, Tunisia (21 July 2005).

FAO (2006), 'High and Volatile Food Prices in the Months to Come', FAO Newsroom, 8 June 2006, Rome, Italy, available at: www.fao.org/newsroom/en/news/2006/1000319/index.html (accessed 10 May 2008).

FAO (2006), 'Third Party Beneficiary, including in the Context of Arbitration', Information Document prepared by the FAO Legal Office, CGRFA/IC/CG-SMTA-2/06/Inf.4, Alnarp, Sweden (24–28 April 2006).

FAO (2007), 'Consideration of the Material Transfer Agreement to Be Used by the International Agricultural Research Centers of the Consultative Group on International Agricultural Research and other Relevant International Institutions for Plant Genetic Resources for

Food and Agriculture not Included in Annex 1 of the Treaty',
IT/GB-2/07/13 Rev 1, Rome, Italy (29 October–2 November 2007).

FAO (2007), 'Experience of the Centres of the Consultative Group on
International Agricultural Research (CGIAR) with the
Implementation of the Agreements with the Governing Body, with
particular reference to the Standard Material Transfer Agreement',
Second Session of the Governing Body, IT/GB-2/07/Inf. 11, Rome,
Italy (29 October–2 November 2007).

FAO (2007), 'Updated Information Provided by the International Center
for Tropical Agriculture (CIAT), regarding its Request for a Re-
Examination of U.S. Patent No. 5,894,079', Eleventh Regular Session
of the CGRFA, CGRFA-11/07/Inf.10, Rome, Italy (11–15 June 2007).

FAO (2007), 'Crop Prospects and Food Situation', Issue No. 6, FAO,
Rome, Italy (December 2007).

FAO (2007), 'Food Outlook—Global Market Analysis', Rome, Italy
(November 2007), available at: www.fao.org/docrep/010/ah876e/
ah876e00.htm (accessed 10 June 2008).

FAO (2008), 'Soaring food prices: the need for international action',
High-Level Conference on World Food Security: the Challenges of
Climate Change and Bioenergy, HLC/08/INF/1-Abstract, Rome, Italy
(3–5 June 2008).

FAO (2008), 'Summary Document of the FAO E-mail Conference:
"Coping with Water Scarcity in Developing Countries: What Role for
Agricultural Biotechnologies?" ' Electronic Forum on Biotechnology
for Food and Agriculture, available at: www.fao.org/biotech/conf14.
htm (accessed 10 January 2008).

FAO (2009), 'Report of the Third Session of the Governing Body of the
International Treaty on Plant Genetic Resources for Food and
Agriculture', GB-3/09/Report, Tunis, Tunisia (1–5 June 2009).

Union for the Protection of New Varieties of Plants

UPOV (2003), 'Annual Report of the Secretary-General for 2002', C/37/2,
Thirty-Seventh Ordinary Session of the UPOV Council, Geneva
(23 October 2003).

UPOV (2006), 'Viet Nam Accedes to the UPOV Convention', UPOV
Press Release No. 70, Geneva (24 November 2006).

UPOV (2006), 'Examination of the Conformity of the Intellectual
Property Law of Viet Nam with the 1991 Act of the UPOV
Convention', C(Extr.)/23/2, Twenty-Third Extraordinary Session of the
UPOV Council, Geneva (7 April 2006).

United Nations

UN, 'The Secretary-General's High-Level Task Force on the Global Food Security Crisis', available at: www.un.org/issues/food/taskforce/ (accessed 10 June 2008).

UN (1972), Declaration on the Human Environment, Principle 21, A/CONF.48/14/Rev. 1, Report of the United Nations Conference on the Human Environment, adopted in UNGA Resolution 2997 (XXVII) of 1972.

UN (1992), 'Declaration on Environment and Development', A/CONF. 151/26/Rev. 1, Report of the UN Conference on Environment and Development.

UN (2002), 'Johannesburg Declaration on Sustainable Development', A/CONF.199/20, Report of the World Summit on Sustainable Development, Johannesburg, South Africa, 26 August–4 September 2002.

UN (2004), 'Report by the Special Rapporteur on the Right to Food, submitted in accordance with Commission on Human Rights Resolution 2003/25', E/CN.4/2004/10.

UN (2007), 'Report of the Special Rapporteur on the Right to Food', by Jean Ziegler, A/62/289 (22 August 2007).

UN (2008), 'The Millennium Development Goals Report', available at: www.un.org/millenniumgoals/pdf/The%20Millennium%20Development%20Goals%20Report%202008.pdf (accessed 10 September 2008).

UN (2008), 'Millennium Development Goal 8—Delivering on the Global Partnership for Achieving the Millennium Development Goals', MDG Gap Task Force, available at: www.un.org/en/development/desa/policy/mdg_gap/mdg_gap_archive/mdg8report2009_enw.pdf (accessed 17 March 2011).

UN News Service (2008), 'Global Food Crisis 'Silent Tsunami' threatening over 100 Million People, warns UN', 22 April 2008, available at: www.un.org/apps/news/story.asp?NewsID=26412&Cr=food&Cr1=price (accessed 10 May 2008).

UN News Service (2008), 'Task Force on Global Food Crisis to Move at "Full Speed"', 5 May 2008, available at: www.un.org/apps/news/story.asp?NewsID=26562&Cr=food&Cr1=crisis (accessed 10 May 2008).

UN Viet Nam (2008), 'First-ever Biodiversity Law to Include Pro-Poor Conservation Strategies', 16 September 2008, available at: www.un.org.vn/index.php?option=com_content&task=view&id=646&Itemid=1 (accessed 10 October 2008).

World Intellectual Property Organization

WIPO (2000), 'Matters Concerning Intellectual Property and Genetic Resources, Traditional Knowledge and Folklore', WIPO General Assembly, Twenty-Sixth (12th Extraordinary) Session, Geneva, 25 September–3 October 2000, WO/GA/26/6.

WIPO (2004), 'Preliminary Report on Work towards the Assessment of Patent Data Relevant to Availability and Use of Material from the International Network of *Ex-Situ* Collections under the Auspices of FAO and the International Treaty on Plant Genetic Resources for Food and Agriculture', prepared by WIPO, CGRFA/MIC-2/04/Inf.5.

WIPO (2006), 'Progress Report on Work towards the Assessment of Patent Data Relevant to Agricultural Biotechnology and the Availability and Use of Material from the International Network of *Ex-Situ* Collections under the Auspices of FAO and the International Treaty on Plant Genetic Resources for Food and Agriculture: a Draft Patent Landscape Surrounding Gene Promoters relevant to Rice', prepared by WIPO, IT/GB-1/06/Inf.17.

WIPO (2007), 'The 45 Adopted Recommendations under the WIPO Development Agenda', Geneva, Switzerland, available at: www.wipo.int/ip-development/en/agenda/recommendations.html#a (accessed 10 November 2008).

World Trade Organization

WTO, 'Doha Development Agenda—Trade Capacity Building Database', available at: http://tcbdb.wto.org/advanced_search_results.aspx (accessed 10 October 2008).

WTO (2001), 'Doha Declaration on the TRIPs Agreement and Public Health', WT/MIN(01)/DEC/2, WTO, Doha (14 November 2001).

WTO (2003), 'Implementation of Paragraph 6 of the Doha Declaration on the TRIPs Agreement and Public Health—Decision of 30 August 2003', WT/L/540, WTO, Geneva, available at: www.wto.org/english/tratop_e/trips_e/implem_para6_e.htm (accessed 10 January 2009).

WTO (2005), 'Poorest Countries Given More Time to Apply Intellectual Property Rules', Press Release No. 424, 29 November 2005, available at: www.wto.org/english/news_e/pres05_e/pr424_e.htm (accessed 10 February 2009).

WTO TRIPs Council (2002), 'Extension of the Transition Period under Article 66.1 of the TRIPS Agreement for Least-Developed Country Members for Certain Obligations with Respect to Pharmaceutical Products', IP/C/25, Geneva (1 July 2002).

WTO TRIPs Council (2002), 'Review of the Provisions of Article 27.3(b)', IP/C/W/369 (8 August 2002).

WTO TRIPs Council (2005), 'Extension of the Transition Period under Article 66.1 for Least-Developed Country Members', IP/C/40, Geneva (30 November 2005).

WTO TRIPs Council (2006), 'Doha Work Programme—The Outstanding Implementation Issue on the Relationship between the TRIPs Agreement and the Convention on Biological Diversity', Communication from Brazil, India and others, WT/GC/W/564/Rev.2—TN/C/W/41/Rev.2—IP/C/W/474, Geneva (5 July 2006).

WTO TRIPS Council (2008), 'Responses from Viet Nam to the Questions Posed by Canada and Additional Questions Posed by the United States', IP/C/W/514/Add.1, Geneva (23 October 2008).

WTO TRIPS Council (2008), 'Minutes of Meeting', IP/C/M/57, Geneva (16 September 2008).

Index